Mike Holt's Illustrated Guide to

Essential Rules of the
NATIONAL
ELECTRICAL CODE®

What you need to know for Safe Electrical Installations

Based on the 2011 NEC®

MIKE HOLT ENTERPRISES, INC.

Since 1974
www.MikeHolt.com

Mike Holt Enterprises, Inc.
888.NEC.CODE (632.2633) • www.MikeHolt.com • Info@MikeHolt.com

NOTICE TO THE READER

Mike Holt's Illustrated Guide to Essential Rules of the National Electrical Code, Based on the 2011 NEC

First Printing: July 2011

Technical Illustrator: Mike Culbreath
Cover Design: Madalina Iordache-Levay
Layout Design and Typesetting: Cathleen Kwas

COPYRIGHT © 2011 Charles Michael Holt
ISBN 978-1-932685-56-5

For more information, call 888.NEC.CODE (632.2633), or e-mail Info@MikeHolt.com.

This logo is a registered trademark of Mike Holt Enterprises, Inc.

If you are an instructor and would like to request an examination copy of this or other Mike Holt Publications:

Call: 888.NEC.CODE (632.2633) • Fax: 352.360.0983

E-mail: Info@MikeHolt.com • Visit: www.MikeHolt.com

You can download a sample PDF of all our publications by visiting www.MikeHolt.com

I dedicate this book to the
Lord Jesus Christ,
my mentor and teacher.
Proverbs 16:3

One Team

To Our Instructors and Students:

We're committed to providing you the finest product with the fewest errors, but we're realistic and know that there'll be errors found and reported after the printing of this book. The last thing we want is for you to have problems finding, communicating, or accessing this information. It's unacceptable to us for there to be even one error in our textbooks or answer keys. For this reason, we're asking you to work together with us as One Team.

Students: Please report any errors you may find to your instructor.

Instructors: Please communicate these errors to us by sending an e-mail to corrections@mikeholt.com.

Our Commitment:

We'll continue to list all of the corrections that come through for all of our textbooks and answer keys on our Website. The most up-to-date answer keys will always be available to instructors to download from our instructor Website. We don't want you to have problems finding this updated information, so we're outlining where to go for all of this below:

To view textbook and answer key corrections: Students and instructors go to our Website, www.MikeHolt.com, click on "Books" in the sidebar of links, and then click on "Corrections."

To download the most up-to-date answer keys: Instructors go to our Website, www.MikeHolt.com, click on "Instructors" in the sidebar of links and then click on "Answer Keys." On this page you'll find instructions for accessing and downloading these answer keys.

If you're not registered as an instructor you'll need to register. Your registration will be sent to our educational director who in turn will review and approve your registration. In your approval e-mail will be the login and password so you can have access to all of the answer keys. If you have a situation that needs immediate attention, please contact the office directly at 888.NEC.CODE (632.2633).

Call 888.NEC.CODE (632.2633) or visit us online at www.MikeHolt.com

Table of Contents

Introduction

Mike Holt's Illustrated Guide to Essential Rules of the National Electrical Code, Based on the 2011 NEC

This book is extracted from *Mike Holt's Illustrated Guide to Understanding the National Electrical Code, Volume 1*, based on the 2011 *NEC*, for the purpose of creating a publication that specifically addresses safe electrical installations. Anyone who has any connection with electrical safety (inspectors, contractors, engineers, electricians or tradesmen) should have this book.

Every day people are shocked, injured and in rare cases electrocuted due to electrical installations that do not adhere to the *National Electrical Code*. Nowhere is this more evident than in the deaths of US service personnel serving in Iraq and Afghanistan who were shocked at military bases due to installations not compliant with the *Code*. These deaths were preventable with proper training, and this book was written in an effort to help prevent further deaths and injuries by bringing together the most Essential *NEC* Rules that specifically address safe installations as they relate to electric shock and fire.

The writing style of this textbook, and in all of Mike Holt's products, is meant to be informative, practical, useful, informal, easy to read, and applicable for today's electrical professional. Also, just like all of Mike Holt's textbooks, it contains hundreds of full-color illustrations to help you see the safety requirements of the *NEC* in practical use, as they apply to today's electrical installations.

This illustrated textbook contains advice, cautions about possible conflicts or confusing *Code* requirements, tips on proper electrical installations, and warnings of dangers related to improper electrical installations. In spite of this effort, some rules are unclear or need additional editorial improvement.

This textbook can't eliminate confusing, conflicting, or controversial *Code* requirements, but it does try to put these requirements into sharper focus to help you understand their intended purpose. Sometimes a requirement is so confusing nobody really understands its actual application. When this occurs, this textbook will point the situation out in an up-front and straightforward manner.

The *NEC* is updated every three years to accommodate new electrical products and materials, changing technologies, and improved installation techniques, along with editorial improvements. While the uniform adoption of each new edition of the *Code* is the best approach for all involved in the electrical industry, many inspection jurisdictions modify the *NEC* when it's adopted. In addition, the *Code* allows the authority having jurisdiction, also known as the "AHJ," typically the electrical inspector, the authority to waive *NEC* requirements or permit alternative wiring methods contrary to the *Code* requirements when assured the completed electrical installation is equivalent in establishing and maintaining effective safety [90.4].

Keeping up with the *NEC* should be the goal of all those who are involved in the safety of electrical installations. This includes electrical installers, contractors, owners, inspectors, engineers, instructors, and others concerned with electrical installations.

To understand the entire *National Electrical Code* you need to study Mike's comprehensive textbooks: *Understanding the NEC, Volume 1 and Volume 2*.

Volume 1 covers general installation requirements, branch circuits, feeders, services and overcurrent protection, grounding versus bonding, conductors, cables and raceways, boxes, panels, motors and transformers, and more, in Articles 90 through 480 (*NEC* Chapters 1 through 4).

Volume 2 covers requirements for wiring in special occupancies, special equipment, under special conditions, as well as communications systems requirements in Articles 500 through 820 (*NEC* Chapters 5-8).

For more information about these titles, visit www.MikeHolt.com/NEC.

About the 2011 *NEC*

The actual process of changing the *Code* takes about two years, and it involves thousands of individuals making an effort to have the *NEC* as current and accurate as possible. Let's review how this process works:

Step 1. Proposals—November, 2008. Anybody can submit a proposal to change the *Code* before the proposal closing date. Over 5,000 proposals were submitted to modify the 2011 *NEC*. Of these proposals, over 300 rules were revised that significantly effect the electrical industry. Some changes were editorial revisions, while others were more significant, such as new articles, sections, exceptions, and Informational Notes.

Step 2. *Code*-Making Panel(s) Review Proposals—January, 2009. All *Code* proposals were reviewed by *Code*-Making Panels. There were 19 panels in the 2011 *Code* process who voted to accept, reject, or modify them.

Step 3. Report on Proposals (ROP)—July, 2009. The voting of the *Code*-Making Panels on the proposals was published for public review in a document called the "Report on Proposals," frequently referred to as the "ROP."

Step 4. Public Comments—October, 2009. Once the ROP was available, public comments were submitted asking the *Code*-Making Panel members to revise their earlier actions on change proposals, based on new information. The closing date for "Comments" was October, 2009.

Step 5. Comments Reviewed by *Code* Panels—December, 2009. The *Code*-Making Panels met again to review, discuss, and vote on public comments.

Step 6. Report on Comments (ROC)—April, 2010. The voting on the "Comments" was published for public review in a document called the "Report on Comments," frequently referred to as the "ROC."

Step 7. Electrical Section—June, 2010. The NFPA Electrical Section discussed and reviewed the work of the *Code*-Making Panels. The Electrical Section developed recommendations on last-minute motions to revise the proposed *NEC* draft that would be presented at the NFPA annual meeting.

Step 8. NFPA Annual Meeting—June, 2010. The 2011 *NEC* was voted by the NFPA members to approve the action of the *Code*-Making Panels at the annual meeting, after a number of motions (often called "floor actions") were voted on.

Step 9. Standards Council Review Appeals and Approves the 2011 *NEC*—July, 2010. The NFPA Standards Council reviewed the record of the *Code*-making process and approved publication of the 2011 *NEC*.

Step 10. 2011 *NEC* Published—September, 2010. The 2011 *National Electrical Code* was published, following the NFPA Board of Directors review of appeals.

Author's Comment: Proposals and comments can be submitted online at the NFPA Website (www.nfpa.org). From the homepage, click on "Codes and Standards" at the top of the page, then from the Codes and Standards page click on "Proposals and Comments" in the box on the right-hand side of the page. The deadline for proposals to create the 2014 *National Electrical Code* is November 5, 2011. If you would like to see something changed in the *Code*, you're encouraged to participate in the process.

The Scope of this Textbook

This textbook covers the general installation requirements that Mike considers to be of critical importance in Articles 90 through 480 (*NEC* Chapters 1 through 4). This textbook is written with these stipulations:

- **Power Systems and Voltage.** All power-supply systems are assumed to be solidly grounded ac such as: 120V single-phase, 120/240V single-phase, 120/208V three-phase, 120/240V three-phase, or 277/480V three-phase, unless identified otherwise.

- **Electrical Calculations.** Unless the question or example specifies three-phase, the questions and examples are based on a single-phase power supply.

- **Rounding.** All calculations are rounded to the nearest ampere in accordance with 220.5(B).

- **Conductor Material.** All conductors are considered copper, unless aluminum is identified or specified.

- **Conductor Sizing.** All conductors are sized based on a THHN copper conductor terminating on a 75°C terminal in accordance with 110.14(C)(1), unless the question or example identifies otherwise.

- **Overcurrent Device.** The term "overcurrent device" in this textbook refers to a molded case circuit breaker, unless identified otherwise. If a fuse is identified in the text, it's to be of the single-element type, also known as a "one-time fuse," unless identified otherwise.

Mike Holt's Understanding the National Electrical Code, Volume 1 (Based on the 2011 *NEC*) Textbook with DVDs Articles 90–480

This library covers general installation requirements, branch circuits, feeders, services and overcurrent protection, grounding versus bonding, conductors, cables and raceways, boxes, panels, motors and transformers, and more, in Articles 90 through 480 (*NEC* Chapters 1 through 4). This program includes:

- *Understanding the National Electrical Code, Volume 1* textbook
- General Requirements (2) DVDs
- Grounding vs. Bonding (2) DVDs
- Wiring Methods (2) DVDs
- Equipment for General Use DVD

Mike Holt's Understanding the National Electrical Code, Volume 2 (Based on the 2011 *NEC*) Textbook with DVDs Articles 500–820

Volume 2 covers requirements for wiring in special occupancies, special equipment, under special conditions, as well as communications systems requirements in Articles 500 through 820 (*NEC* Chapters 5-8). This program includes:

- *Understanding the National Electrical Code, Volume 2* textbook
- Special Occupancies DVD
- Special Equipment DVD
- Limited Energy & Communication Systems DVD

Mike Holt's Detailed *NEC* Library

If you want to really understand the 2011 *National Electrical Code*, then Mike Holt's Detailed Code Library is the perfect study program for you. This Library covers general installation requirements, branch circuits, feeders, services and overcurrent protection, grounding and bonding, conductors, cables and raceways, boxes, panels, motors, transformers, and much more. Summary questions are included in all books to help you test your knowledge.

This program includes 3 textbooks and 10 DVDs:

- *Understanding the National Electrical Code, Volume 1* textbook
- *Understanding the National Electrical Code, Volume 2* textbook
- *NEC Exam Practice Questions* book
- General Requirements Part 1 DVD and Part 2 DVD
- Grounding vs. Bonding Part 1 DVD and Part 2 DVD
- Wiring Methods Part 1 DVD and Part 2 DVD
- Equipment for General Use DVD
- Special Occupancies DVD
- Special Equipment DVD
- Limited Energy and Communication Systems DVD

Order any of these *NEC* products by calling 888.NEC.CODE (632.2633) or visiting www.MikeHolt.com/NEC.

What is the QR code above? See page xi.

About This Textbook

This textbook is to be used along with the *NEC*, not as a replacement for it, so be sure to have a copy of the 2011 *National Electrical Code* handy. Compare what Mike is explaining in this book to what the *Code* book says, and discuss with others any topics that you find difficult to understand.

You'll notice that in this book, a great deal of the *NEC* wording has been paraphrased, and some of the article and section titles appear different from the wording in the actual *Code*. Mike believes doing so makes it easier to understand the content of the rule, so keep this in mind when comparing this textbook against the actual *NEC*.

We hope that as you read through this textbook, you'll allow sufficient time to review the text along with the outstanding graphics and examples, which are invaluable to your understanding.

Textbook Format

Mike has selected 75 Rules from the 2011 *NEC* which he considers essential, and they are listed in this book in *Code* order and not in order of importance. These Essential Rules relate directly to safety (preventing electric shock and fire); compliance with these Rules, should ensure a safe electrical installation.

Important Features for the 2011 Edition of This Textbook

In order to better meet the needs of our customers, we have improved the layout of our textbooks with some new feaures, in addition to the features from the 2008 editions which were so successful. These features include:

- Graphics that contain a 2011 *Code* change will have a green border with a green 2011 CC icon next to the heading.

- Any *NEC* changes will be in green underlined text in all graphics. If you see a green bordered graphic with no green underlined text, it most likely indicates that the *Code* change is the removal of some text. Graphics without a color border support the concept being discussed, but nothing in the graphic was affected by a change for 2011.

- Special Sections which contain additional information to better help you understand a concept are identified with a light gray background and colored frame.

- Examples or practical application questions with their answer and solution have a light yellow background.

- Essential Rules which you need to know for safe electrical installations.

- Any 2011 *Code* change is denoted by <u>underlined text and in the corresponding chapter color</u>. For example, in Article 450 the change text will be <u>green and underlined.</u>

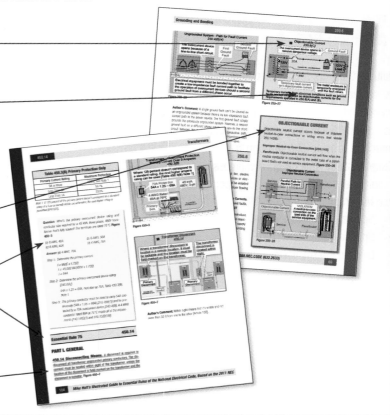

Cross-References and Author's Comments

Cross References. This textbook contains several *NEC* cross-references to other related *Code* requirements to help you develop a better understanding of how the *NEC* rules relate to one another. These cross-references are indicated by *Code* section numbers in brackets, an example of which is "[90.4]."

Author's Comments. "Author's Comments," written by Mike, are intended to help you understand the *NEC* material, and to bring to your attention things of which you should be aware.

Difficult Concepts

As you progress through this textbook, you might find that you don't understand every explanation, example, calculation, or comment. Don't become frustrated, and don't get down on yourself. Remember, this is the *National Electrical Code* and sometimes the best attempt to explain a concept isn't enough to make it perfectly clear. If you're still confused, visit www.MikeHolt.com, and post your question on the *Code* Forum for help.

Different Interpretations

Some electricians, contractors, instructors, inspectors, engineers, and others enjoy the challenge of discussing the *NEC* requirements, hopefully in a positive and productive manner. This give-and-take is important to the process of better understanding the *Code* requirements and application. However, if you're going to get into an *NEC* discussion, please don't spout out what you think without having the actual *Code* book in your hand. The professional way of discussing an *NEC* requirement is by referring to a specific section, rather than talking in vague generalities.

QR Codes

QR Code

What is this? It is a QR Code and gives you the ability to use your smartphone to take a photo (using a barcode reader app) and be directed to a Website. For example, the QR Code to the left when captured will direct your smartphone to the Mike Holt Enterprises Website. We have included these in various places in our book to make it easier for you to go directly to the Website page referenced. In order to use a QR code, you will need an app for your phone that allows your phone to read this barcode. Your phone may already have the ability to scan this barcode, but if not visit the Website www.mobile-barcodes.com/qr-code-software for more information.

Textbook Errors and Corrections

Humans develop the text, graphics, and layout of this textbook, and since currently none of us are perfect, there may be a few errors. This can occur because the *NEC* is dramatically changed each *Code* cycle; new articles are added, some are deleted, some are relocated, and many are renumbered. We take great care in researching the *NEC* requirements to ensure this textbook is correct. If you believe there's an error of any kind in this textbook (typographical, grammatical, technical, or anything else), no matter how insignificant, please let us know.

Any errors found after printing are listed on our Website, so if you find an error, first check to see if it's already been corrected. Go to www.MikeHolt.com, click on the "Books" link, and then the "Corrections" link (www.MikeHolt.com/bookcorrections.htm).

If you don't find the error listed on the Website, contact us by sending an E-mail to Corrections@MikeHolt.com. Be sure to include the book title, page number, and any other pertinent information.

You Tube

Visit the Mike Holt channel on YouTube to see video clips that accompany this and our other 2011 books (www.youtube.com/MikeHoltNEC).

How to Use the
National Electrical Code

The *National Electrical Code* is written for persons who understand electrical terms, theory, safety procedures, and electrical trade practices. These individuals include electricians, electrical contractors, electrical inspectors, electrical engineers, designers, and other qualified persons. The *Code* isn't written to serve as an instructive or teaching manual for untrained individuals [90.1(C)].

Learning to use the *NEC* is like learning to play the game of chess; it's a great game if you enjoy mental warfare. When learning to play chess, you must first learn the names of the game pieces, how the pieces are placed on the board, and how each piece moves.

Once you understand the fundamentals, you're ready to start playing the game. Unfortunately, at this point all you can do is make crude moves, because you really don't understand how all the information works together. To play chess well, you'll need to learn how to use your knowledge by working on subtle strategies before you can work your way up to the more intriguing and complicated moves.

Not a Game

Electrical work isn't a game, and it must be taken very seriously. Learning the basics of electricity, important terms and concepts, as well as the basic layout of the *NEC* gives you just enough knowledge to be dangerous. There are thousands of specific and unique applications of electrical installations, and the *Code* doesn't cover every one of them. To safely apply the *NEC*, you must understand the purpose of a rule and how it affects the safety aspects of the installation.

NEC Terms and Concepts

The *NEC* contains many technical terms, so it's crucial for *Code* users to understand their meanings and their applications. If you don't understand a term used in a *Code* rule, it will be impossible to properly apply the *NEC* requirement. Be sure you understand that Article 100 defines the terms that apply to two or more *Code* articles. For example, the term "Dwelling Unit" is found in many articles; if you don't know what a dwelling unit is, how can you apply the requirements for it?

In addition, many articles have terms unique for that specific article and definitions of those terms are only applicable for that given article. For example, Section 250.2 contains the definitions of terms that only apply to Article 250—Grounding and Bonding.

Small Words, Grammar, and Punctuation

It's not only the technical words that require close attention, because even the simplest of words can make a big difference to the application of a rule. The word "or" can imply alternate choices for equipment wiring methods, while "and" can mean an additional requirement. Let's not forget about grammar and punctuation. The location of a comma can dramatically change the requirement of a rule.

Slang Terms or Technical Jargon

Electricians, engineers, and other trade-related professionals use slang terms or technical jargon that isn't shared by all. This makes it very difficult to communicate because not everybody understands the intent or application of those slang terms. So where possible, be sure you use the proper word, and don't use a word if you don't understand its definition and application. For example, lots of electricians use the term "pigtail" when describing the short conductor for the connection of a receptacle, switch, luminaire, or equipment. Although they may understand it, not everyone does.

NEC Style and Layout

Before we get into the details of the *NEC*, we need to take a few moments to understand its style and layout. Understanding the structure and writing style of the *Code* is very important before it can be used and applied effectively. The *National Electrical Code* is organized into ten major components.

1. Table of Contents
2. Article 90 (Introduction to the *Code*)
3. Chapters 1 through 9 (major categories)
4. Articles 90 through 840 (individual subjects)
5. Parts (divisions of an article)
6. Sections and Tables (*Code* requirements)

7. Exceptions (*Code* permissions)

8. Informational Notes (explanatory material)

9. Annexes (information)

10. Index

1. Table of Contents. The Table of Contents displays the layout of the chapters, articles, and parts as well as the page numbers. It's an excellent resource and should be referred to periodically to observe the interrelationship of the various *NEC* components. When attempting to locate the rules for a particular situation, knowledgeable *Code* users often go first to the Table of Contents to quickly find the specific *NEC* Part that applies.

2. Introduction. The *NEC* begins with Article 90, the introduction to the *Code*. It contains the purpose of the *NEC*, what's covered and what isn't covered along with how the *Code* is arranged. It also gives information on enforcement and how mandatory and permissive rules are written as well as how explanatory material is included. Article 90 also includes information on formal interpretations, examination of equipment for safety, wiring planning, and information about formatting units of measurement.

3. Chapters. There are nine chapters, each of which is divided into articles. The articles fall into one of four groupings: General Requirements (Chapters 1 through 4), Specific Requirements (Chapters 5 through 7), Communications Systems (Chapter 8), and Tables (Chapter 9).

Chapter 1 General

Chapter 2 Wiring and Protection

Chapter 3 Wiring Methods and Materials

Chapter 4 Equipment for General Use

Chapter 5 Special Occupancies

Chapter 6 Special Equipment

Chapter 7 Special Conditions

Chapter 8 Communications Systems (Telephone, Data, Satellite, Cable TV and Broadband)

Chapter 9 Tables–Conductor and Raceway Specifications

4. Articles. The *NEC* contains approximately 140 articles, each of which covers a specific subject. For example:

Article 110 General Requirements

Article 250 Grounding and Bonding

Article 300 Wiring Methods

Article 430 Motors and Motor Controllers

Article 500 Hazardous (Classified) Locations

Article 680 Swimming Pools, Fountains, and Similar Installations

Article 725 Remote-Control, Signaling, and Power-Limited Circuits

Article 800 Communications Circuits

5. Parts. Larger articles are subdivided into parts.

Because the parts of a *Code* article aren't included in the section numbers, we have a tendency to forget what "part" the *NEC* rule is relating to. For example, Table 110.34(A) contains working space clearances for electrical equipment. If we aren't careful, we might think this table applies to all electrical installations, but Table 110.34(A) is located in Part III, which only contains requirements for "Over 600 Volts, Nominal installations." The rules for working clearances for electrical equipment for systems 600V, nominal, or less are contained in Table 110.26(A)(1), which is located in Part II—600 Volts, Nominal, or Less.

6. Sections and Tables.

Sections. Each *NEC* rule is called a "*Code* Section." A *Code* section may be broken down into subsections by letters in parentheses (A), (B), and so on. Numbers in parentheses (1), (2), and so forth, may further break down a subsection, and lowercase letters (a), (b), and so on, further break the rule down to the third level. For example, the rule requiring all receptacles in a dwelling unit bathroom to be GFCI protected is contained in Section 210.8(A)(1). Section 210.8(A)(1) is located in Chapter 2, Article 210, Section 8, Subsection (A), Sub-subsection (1).

Many in the industry incorrectly use the term "Article" when referring to a *Code* section. For example, they say "Article 210.8," when they should say "Section 210.8." Section numbers in this book are shown without the word "Section," unless they begin a sentence. For example, Section 210.8(A) is shown as simply 210.8(A).

Tables. Many *Code* requirements are contained within tables, which are lists of *NEC* requirements placed in a systematic arrangement. The titles of the tables are extremely important; you must read them carefully in order to understand the contents, applications, limitations, and so forth, of each table in the *Code*. Many times notes are provided in or below a table; be sure to read them as well since they're also part of the requirement. For example, Note 1 for Table 300.5 explains how to measure the cover when burying cables and raceways, and Note 5 explains what to do if solid rock is encountered.

7. Exceptions. Exceptions are *Code* requirements or permissions that provide an alternative method to a specific requirement. There are two types of exceptions—mandatory and permissive. When a rule has several exceptions, those exceptions with mandatory requirements are listed before the permissive exceptions.

Mandatory Exceptions. A mandatory exception uses the words "shall" or "shall not." The word "shall" in an exception means that if you're using the exception, you're required to do it in a particular way. The phrase "shall not" means it isn't permitted.

Permissive Exceptions. A permissive exception uses words such as "shall be permitted," which means it's acceptable (but not mandatory) to do it in this way.

8. Informational Notes. An Informational Note contains explanatory material intended to clarify a rule or give assistance, but it isn't a *Code* requirement.

9. Annexes. Annexes aren't a part of the *NEC* requirements, and are included in the *Code* for informational purposes only.

> Annex A. Product Safety Standards
> Annex B. Application Information for Ampacity Calculation
> Annex C. Raceway Fill Tables for Conductors and Fixture Wires of the Same Size
> Annex D. Examples
> Annex E. Types of Construction
> Annex F. Critical Operations Power Systems (COPS)
> Annex G. Supervisory Control and Data Acquisition (SCADA)
> Annex H. Administration and Enforcement
> Annex I. Recommended Tightening Torques

10. Index. The Index at the back of the *NEC* is helpful in locating a specific rule.

Changes to the *NEC* since the previous edition(s), are identified by shading, but rules that have been relocated aren't identified as a change. A bullet symbol "•" is located on the margin to indicate the location of a rule that was deleted from a previous edition. New articles contain a vertical line in the margin of the page.

How to Locate a Specific Requirement

How to go about finding what you're looking for in the *Code* depends, to some degree, on your experience with the *NEC*. *Code* experts typically know the requirements so well they just go to the correct rule without any outside assistance. The Table of Contents might be the only thing very experienced *NEC* users need to locate the requirement they're looking for. On the other hand, average *Code* users should use all of the tools at their disposal, including the Table of Contents and the Index.

Table of Contents. Let's work out a simple example: What *NEC* rule specifies the maximum number of disconnects permitted for a service? If you're an experienced *Code* user, you'll know Article 230 applies to "Services," and because this article is so large, it's divided up into multiple parts (actually eight parts). With this knowledge, you

can quickly go to the Table of Contents and see it lists the Service Equipment Disconnecting Means requirements in Part VI.

> **Author's Comment:** The number 70 precedes all page numbers because the *NEC* is NFPA Standard Number 70.

Index. If you use the Index, which lists subjects in alphabetical order, to look up the term "service disconnect," you'll see there's no listing. If you try "disconnecting means," then "services," you'll find that the Index specifies that the rule is located in Article 230, Part VI. Because the *NEC* doesn't give a page number in the Index, you'll need to use the Table of Contents to find the page number, or flip through the *Code* to Article 230, then continue to flip through pages until you find Part VI.

Many people complain that the *NEC* only confuses them by taking them in circles. As you gain experience in using the *Code* and deepen your understanding of words, terms, principles, and practices, you'll find the *NEC* much easier to understand and use than you originally thought.

Customizing Your *Code* Book

One way to increase your comfort level with the *Code* is to customize it to meet your needs. You can do this by highlighting and underlining important *NEC* requirements, and by attaching tabs to important pages. Be aware that if you're using your *Code* book to take an exam, some exam centers don't allow markings of any type.

Highlighting. As you read through this textbook, be sure you highlight those requirements in the *Code* that are the most important or relevant to you. Use yellow for general interest and orange for important requirements you want to find quickly. Be sure to highlight terms in the Index and the Table of Contents as you use them.

Underlining. Underline or circle key words and phrases in the *NEC* with a red pen (not a lead pencil) and use a 6-inch ruler to keep lines straight and neat. This is a very handy way to make important requirements stand out. A small 6-inch ruler also comes in handy for locating specific information in the many *Code* tables.

Tabbing the *NEC*. By placing tabs on *Code* articles, sections, and tables, it will make it easier for you to use the *NEC*. However, too many tabs will defeat the purpose. You can order a set of *Code* tabs designed by Mike Holt online at www.MikeHolt.com, or by calling 1.888.NEC.CODE (632.2633).

About the Author

Mike Holt

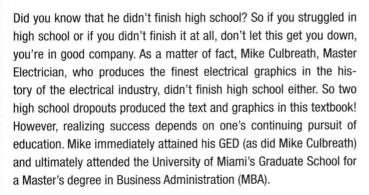

Mike Holt worked his way up through the electrical trade from an apprentice electrician to become one of the most recognized experts in the world as it relates to electrical power installations. He has worked as a journeyman electrician, master electrician, and electrical contractor. Mike's experience in the real world gives him a unique understanding of how the *NEC* relates to electrical installations from a practical standpoint. You'll find his writing style to be direct, nontechnical, and practical.

Did you know that he didn't finish high school? So if you struggled in high school or if you didn't finish it at all, don't let this get you down, you're in good company. As a matter of fact, Mike Culbreath, Master Electrician, who produces the finest electrical graphics in the history of the electrical industry, didn't finish high school either. So two high school dropouts produced the text and graphics in this textbook! However, realizing success depends on one's continuing pursuit of education. Mike immediately attained his GED (as did Mike Culbreath) and ultimately attended the University of Miami's Graduate School for a Master's degree in Business Administration (MBA).

Mike Holt resides in Central Florida, is the father of seven children, and has many outside interests and activities. He's a six-time National Barefoot Water-Ski Champion (1988, 1999, 2005, 2006, 2007, and 2008), has set many national records, has competed in three World Championships (2006, 2008, and 2010) and continues to train and work out year-round so that he can qualify to ski in the 2012 World Barefoot Championships at the age of 61!

What sets him apart from some, is his commitment to living a balanced lifestyle; placing God first, family, career, then self.

Mike Holt—Special Acknowledgments

First, I want to thank God for my godly wife who's always by my side and my children, Belynda, Melissa, Autumn, Steven, Michael, Meghan, and Brittney.

A special thank you must be sent to the staff at the National Fire Protection Association (NFPA), publishers of the *NEC*—in particular Jeff Sargent for his assistance in answering my many *Code* questions over the years. Jeff, you're a "first class" guy, and I admire your dedication and commitment to helping others understand the *NEC*. Other former NFPA staff members I would like to thank include John Caloggero, Joe Ross, and Dick Murray for their help in the past.

A personal thank you goes to Sarina, my long-time friend and office manager. It's been wonderful working side-by-side with you for over 25 years nurturing this company's growth from its small beginnings.

About the Graphic Illustrator

Mike Culbreath

Mike Culbreath devoted his career to the electrical industry and worked his way up from an apprentice electrician to master electrician. While working as a journeyman electrician, he suffered a serious on-the-job knee injury. With a keen interest in continuing education for electricians, he completed courses at Mike Holt Enterprises, Inc. and then passed the exam to receive his Master Electrician's license. In 1986, after attending classes at Mike Holt Enterprises, Inc., he joined the staff to update material and later studied computer graphics and began illustrating Mike Holt's textbooks and magazine articles. He's worked with the company for almost 25 years and, as Mike Holt has proudly acknowledged, has helped to transform his words and visions into lifelike graphics.

Special Acknowledgments

I want to thank my wonderful children, Dawn and Mac, who have had to put up with me during the *Code* revision seasons.

I would like to thank Steve Arne, our amazing technical editorial director, Eric Stromberg, an electrical engineer and super geek (and I mean that in the most complimentary manner, this guy is brilliant), and Ryan Jackson, an outstanding and very knowledgeable code guy, for helping me keep our graphics as technically correct as possible.

I also want to give a special thank you to Cathleen Kwas for making me look good with her outstanding layout design and typesetting skills. I would also like to acknowledge Belynda Holt Pinto, our Chief Operations Officer and the rest of the outstanding staff at Mike Holt Enterprises, for all the hard work they do to help produce and distribute these outstanding products.

And last but not least, I need to give a special thank you to Mike Holt for not firing me about 25 years ago when I "borrowed" one of his computers and took it home to begin the process of learning how to do computer illustrations. He gave me the opportunity and time needed to develop my computer graphic skills. He's been an amazing friend and mentor since I met him as a student many years ago. Thanks for believing in me and allowing me to be part of the Mike Holt Enterprises family.

Mike Holt
Enterprises Team

Editorial Team

I want to thank **Toni Culbreath** and **Barbara Parks** who worked tirelessly to proofread and edit the final stages of this publication. Their attention to detail and dedication to this project is greatly appreciated.

Production Team

I want to thank **Cathleen Kwas** who did the layout and production of this book. Her desire to create the best possible product for our customers is greatly appreciated.

Technical Editorial Director

Steve Arne
Technical Training Consultant
Arne Electro Tech
Rapid City, South Dakota
www.ElectricalMaster.com

Steve Arne has worked in various positions in the electrical industry since 1974 including electrician, electrical contractor, full-time instructor, and department chair in technical post-secondary education. Steve has developed and taught curriculum for many electrical training courses as well as university business and leadership courses. He's completed a Bachelor's degree in Technical Education and a Master's degree in Administrative Studies. Currently, he provides electrician exam prep and continuing education *Code* classes in South Dakota, Wyoming, and surrounding states using Mike Holt's textbooks and material. He enjoys seeing a student's "lights come on" as they come to a point of understanding and have the "ah-ha" experience of learning something new.

Steve has worked for Mike Holt as a technical editor and video team participant since 2002, and used Mike Holt's books in his classes for a number of years before that. Steve is very thankful to have been associated with an industry leader like Mike who provides excellent training products to help students progress in the electrical industry. Steve has been active in the South Dakota Electrical Council, serving on the Board of the Black Hills Chapter in various capacities and is the current Chapter President.

Steve and his wife Deb live in Rapid City, South Dakota where they're both active in their church and community, and love to spend time with their children and grandchildren. Most of all, Steve and Deb both endeavor to put God first in their lives and in their home.

Technical *Code* Consultant

Ryan Jackson
Electrical Inspector
Draper City, Utah

Ryan Jackson is a combination inspector in the Salt Lake City, Utah, area. He began doing electrical work at the age of 18. At the age of 23 Ryan landed his first job as an electrical inspector, and subsequently became certified in building, plumbing, and mechanical inspection (commercial and residential), as well as building and electrical plan review. Two years after becoming an inspector, he was approached by a friend in the area asking him to fill in at an electrical seminar for him. After his first class he was hooked, and is now a highly sought-after seminar instructor. Ryan has taught in several states, and loves helping people increase their understanding of the *Code*.

In 2005, Ryan met Mike Holt in Salt Lake City, and they became friends immediately. He helped Mike with his *Understanding the NEC, Volume 2* videos and began editing his books as well. Ryan believes that there are only a small handful of opportunities that change a person's life and career, and meeting Mike was one of them.

Ryan can often be found in his garage turning wood on his lathe, and in the autumn you'll find him at as many University of Utah football games as he can attend, which is typically all of them. Ryan married his high school sweetheart, Sharie, and they have two beautiful children together: Kaitlynn and Aaron.

Notes

ARTICLE 90

Introduction to the *National Electrical Code*

INTRODUCTION TO ARTICLE 90—INTRODUCTION TO THE *NATIONAL ELECTRICAL CODE*

Many *NEC* violations and misunderstandings wouldn't occur if people doing the work simply understood Article 90. For example, many people see *Code* requirements as performance standards. In fact, the *NEC* requirements are bare minimums for safety. This is exactly the stance electrical inspectors, insurance companies, and courts take when making a decision regarding electrical design or installation.

Article 90 opens by saying the *NEC* isn't intended as a design specification or instruction manual. The *National Electrical Code* has one purpose only, and that's the "practical safeguarding of persons and property from hazards arising from the use of electricity." It goes on to indicate that the *Code* isn't intended as a design specification or instruction manual. The necessity to carefully study the *NEC* rules can't be overemphasized, and the role of textbooks such as this one is to help in that undertaking. Understanding where to find the rules in the *Code* that apply to the installation is invaluable. Rules in several different articles often apply to even a simple installation.

Article 90 then describes the scope and arrangement of the *NEC*. The balance of Article 90 provides the reader with information essential to understanding those items you do find in the *NEC*.

Typically, electrical work requires you to understand the first four chapters of the *Code* which apply generally, plus have a working knowledge of the Chapter 9 tables. That knowledge begins with Article 90. Chapters 5, 6, and 7 make up a large portion of the *NEC*, but they apply to special occupancies, special equipment, or other special conditions. They build on, modify, or amend the rules in the first four chapters. Chapter 8 contains the requirements for communications systems, such as telephone systems, antenna wiring, CATV, and network-powered broadband systems. Communications systems aren't subject to the general requirements of Chapters 1 through 4, or the special requirements of Chapters 5 through 7, unless there's a specific reference in Chapter 8 to a rule in Chapters 1 through 7.

Essential Rule 1   90.1

90.1 Purpose of the *NEC*.

(A) Practical Safeguarding. The purpose of the *NEC* is to ensure that electrical systems are installed in a manner that protects people and property by minimizing the risks associated with the use of electricity.

(B) Adequacy. The *Code* contains requirements considered necessary for a safe electrical installation. If an electrical installation is installed in compliance with the *NEC*, it will be essentially free from electrical hazards. The *Code* is a safety standard, not a design guide.

NEC requirements aren't intended to ensure the electrical installation will be efficient, convenient, adequate for good service, or suitable for future expansion. Specific items of concern, such as electrical energy management, maintenance, and power quality issues aren't within the scope of the *Code*. **Figure 90–1**

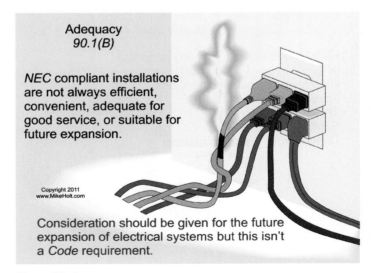

Adequacy
90.1(B)

NEC compliant installations are not always efficient, convenient, adequate for good service, or suitable for future expansion.

Copyright 2011
www.MikeHolt.com

Consideration should be given for the future expansion of electrical systems but this isn't a *Code* requirement.

Figure 90–1

Note: Hazards in electrical systems often occur because circuits are overloaded or not properly installed in accordance with the *NEC*. These often occur if the initial wiring didn't provide reasonable provisions for system changes or for the increase in the use of electricity.

Author's Comments:

- See the definition of "Overload" in Article 100.

- The *NEC* doesn't require electrical systems to be designed or installed to accommodate future loads. However, the electrical designer, typically an electrical engineer, is concerned with not only ensuring electrical safety (*Code* compliance), but also with ensuring the system meets the customers' needs, both of today and in the near future. To satisfy customers' needs, electrical systems are often designed and installed above the minimum requirements contained in the *NEC*. But just remember, if you're taking an exam, licensing exams are based on your understanding of the minimum *Code* requirements.

(C) Intention. The *Code* is intended to be used by those skilled and knowledgeable in electrical theory, electrical systems, construction, and the installation and operation of electrical equipment. It isn't a design specification standard or instruction manual for the untrained and unqualified.

(D) Relation to International Standards. The requirements of the *NEC* address the fundamental safety principles contained in the International Electrotechnical Commission (IEC) standards, including protection against electric shock, adverse thermal effects, overcurrent, fault currents, and overvoltage. **Figure 90–2**

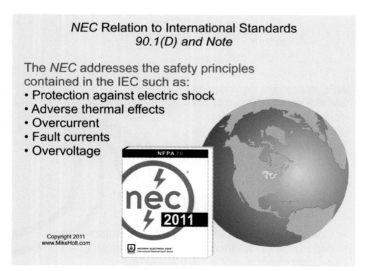

Figure 90–2

Author's Comments:

- See the definition of "Overcurrent" in Article 100.

- The *NEC* is used in Chile, Ecuador, Peru, and the Philippines. It's also the electrical code for Colombia, Costa Rica, Mexico, Panama, Puerto Rico, and Venezuela. Because of these adoptions, the *NEC* is available in Spanish from the National Fire Protection Association, 617.770.3000, or www.NFPA.Org.

Essential Rule 2   90.2

90.2 Scope of the *NEC*.

(A) What is Covered. The *NEC* contains requirements necessary for the proper installation of electrical conductors, equipment, and raceways; signaling and communications conductors, equipment, and raceways; as well as optical fiber cables and raceways for the following locations: **Figure 90–3**

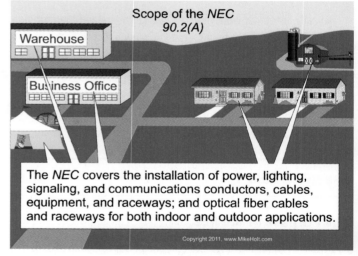

Figure 90–3

(1) Public and private premises, including buildings or structures, mobile homes, recreational vehicles, and floating buildings.

(2) Yards, lots, parking lots, carnivals, and industrial substations.

(3) Conductors and equipment connected to the utility supply.

(4) Installations used by an electric utility, such as office buildings, warehouses, garages, machine shops, recreational buildings, and other electric utility buildings that aren't an integral part of a utility's generating plant, substation, or control center. **Figure 90–4**

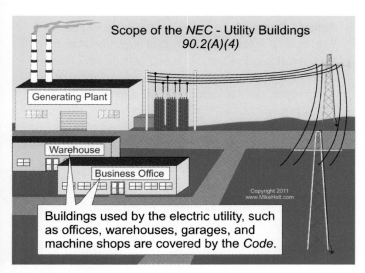

Figure 90–4

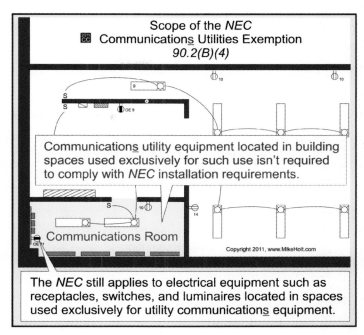

Figure 90–5

(B) What Isn't Covered. The *NEC* doesn't apply to:

(1) Transportation Vehicles. Installations in cars, trucks, boats, ships and watercraft, planes, electric trains, or underground mines.

(2) Mining Equipment. Installations underground in mines and self-propelled mobile surface mining machinery and its attendant electrical trailing cables.

(3) Railways. Railway power, signaling, and communications wiring.

(4) Communications Utilities. The installation requirements of the *NEC* don't apply to communications (telephone), Community Antenna Television (CATV), or network-powered broadband utility equipment located in building spaces used exclusively for these purposes, or outdoors if the installation is under the exclusive control of the communications utility. **Figures 90–5 and 90–6**

> **Author's Comment:** Interior wiring for communications systems, not in building spaces used exclusively for these purposes, must be installed in accordance with the following Chapter 8 Articles:
>
> • Telephone and Data, Article 800
> • CATV, Article 820
> • Network-Powered Broadband, Article 830

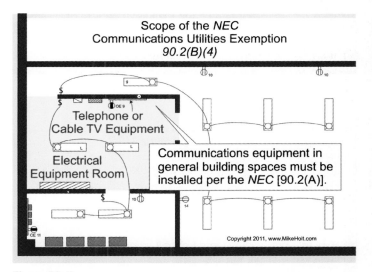

Figure 90–6

(5) Electric Utilities. The *NEC* doesn't apply to installations under the exclusive control of an electric utility where such installations:

a. Consist of service drops or service laterals and associated metering. **Figure 90–7**

b. Are on property owned or leased by the electric utility for the purpose of generation, transformation, transmission, distribution, or metering of electric energy. **Figure 90–8**

Author's Comment: Luminaires located in legally established easements, or rights-of-way, such as at poles supporting transmission or distribution lines, are exempt from the *NEC*. However, if the electric utility provides site and public lighting on private property, then the installation must comply with the *Code* [90.2(A)(4)].

c. Are located on legally established easements, or rights-of-way. **Figure 90–9**

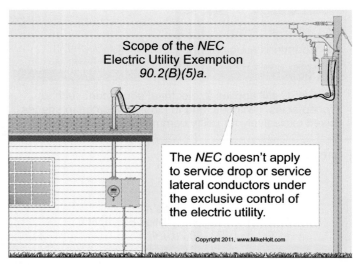

Figure 90–7

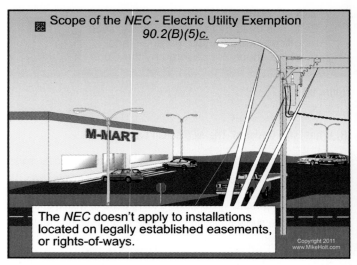

Figure 90–9

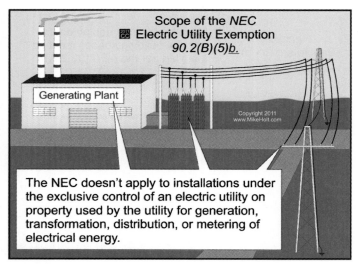

Figure 90–8

d. Are located by other written agreements either designated by or recognized by public service commissions, utility commissions, or other regulatory agencies having jurisdiction for such installations; limited to installations for the purpose of communications, metering, generation, control, transformation, transmission, or distribution of electric energy where legally established easements or rights-of-way can't be obtained. These installations are limited to federal lands, Native American reservations through the U.S. Department of the Interior Bureau of Indian Affairs, military bases, lands controlled by port authorities and state agencies and departments, and lands owned by railroads.

Note to 90.2(B)(4) and (5): Utilities include entities that install, operate, and maintain communications systems (telephone, CATV, Internet, satellite, or data services) or electric supply (generation, transmission, or distribution systems) and are designated or recognized by governmental law or regulation by public service/utility commissions. Utilities may be subject to compliance with codes and standards covering their regulated activities as adopted under governmental law or regulation.

Essential Rule 3   90.3

90.3 *Code* Arrangement. The *Code* is divided into an introduction and nine chapters. **Figure 90–10**

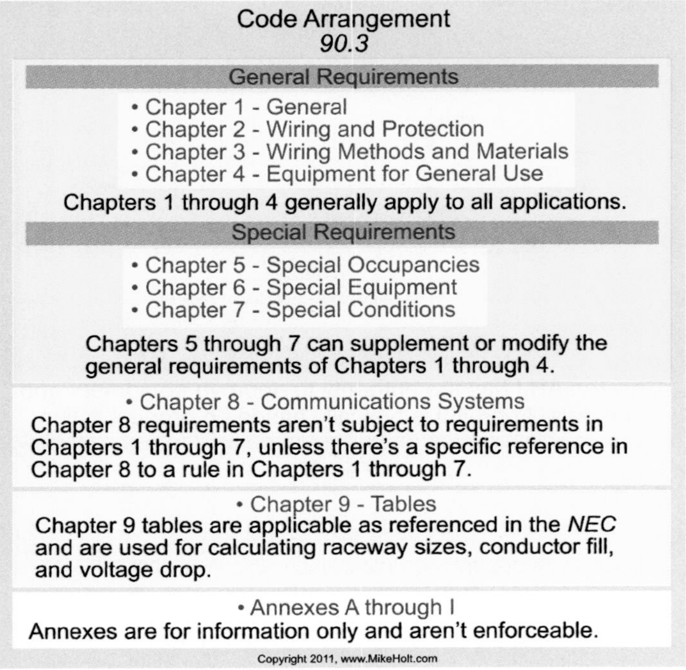

Code Arrangement
90.3

General Requirements
- Chapter 1 - General
- Chapter 2 - Wiring and Protection
- Chapter 3 - Wiring Methods and Materials
- Chapter 4 - Equipment for General Use

Chapters 1 through 4 generally apply to all applications.

Special Requirements
- Chapter 5 - Special Occupancies
- Chapter 6 - Special Equipment
- Chapter 7 - Special Conditions

Chapters 5 through 7 can supplement or modify the general requirements of Chapters 1 through 4.

• Chapter 8 - Communications Systems
Chapter 8 requirements aren't subject to requirements in Chapters 1 through 7, unless there's a specific reference in Chapter 8 to a rule in Chapters 1 through 7.

• Chapter 9 - Tables
Chapter 9 tables are applicable as referenced in the *NEC* and are used for calculating raceway sizes, conductor fill, and voltage drop.

• Annexes A through I
Annexes are for information only and aren't enforceable.

Copyright 2011, www.MikeHolt.com

Figure 90–10

General Requirements. The requirements contained in Chapters 1, 2, 3, and 4 apply to all installations.

> **Author's Comment:** These first four chapters may be thought of as the foundation for the rest of the *Code*, and are the main focus of this textbook.

Special Requirements. The requirements contained in Chapters 5, 6, and 7 apply to special occupancies, special equipment, or other special conditions. These chapters can supplement or modify the requirements in Chapters 1 through 4.

Communications Systems. Chapter 8 contains the requirements for communications systems, such as telephone systems, antenna wiring, CATV, and network-powered broadband systems. Communications systems aren't subject to the general requirements of Chapters 1 through 4, or the special requirements of Chapters 5 through 7, unless there's a specific reference in Chapter 8 to a rule in Chapters 1 through 7.

> **Author's Comment:** An example of how Chapter 8 works is in the rules for working space about equipment. The typical 3 ft working space isn't required in front of communications equipment, because Table 110.26(A)(1) isn't referenced in Chapter 8.

Tables. Chapter 9 consists of tables applicable as referenced in the *NEC*. The tables are used to calculate raceway sizing, conductor fill, the radius of raceway bends, and conductor voltage drop.

Annexes. Annexes aren't part of the *Code*, but are included for informational purposes. There are eight Annexes:

- Annex A. Product Safety Standards
- Annex B. Application Information for Ampacity Calculation
- Annex C. Raceway Fill Tables for Conductors and Fixture Wires of the Same Size
- Annex D. Examples
- Annex E. Types of Construction
- Annex F. Critical Operations Power Systems (COPS)
- Annex G. Supervisory Control and Data Acquisition (SCADA)
- Annex H. Administration and Enforcement

Essential Rule 4   90.4

90.4 Enforcement. The *Code* is intended to be suitable for enforcement by governmental bodies that exercise legal jurisdiction over electrical installations for power, lighting, signaling circuits, and communications systems, such as: **Figure 90–11**

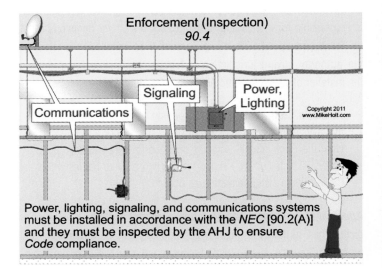

Figure 90–11

Signaling circuits which include:

- Article 725 Class 1, Class 2, and Class 3 Remote-Control, Signaling, and Power-Limited Circuits
- Article 760 Fire Alarm Systems
- Article 770 Optical Fiber Cables and Raceways

Communications systems which include:

- Article 800 Communications Circuits (twisted-pair conductors)
- Article 810 Radio and Television Equipment (satellite dish and antenna)
- Article 820 Community Antenna Television and Radio Distribution Systems (coaxial cable)
- Article 830 Network-Powered Broadband Communications Systems

Author's Comment: The installation requirements for signaling circuits and communications circuits are covered in Mike Holt's *Understanding the National Electrical Code, Volume 2* textbook.

The enforcement of the *NEC* is the responsibility of the authority having jurisdiction (AHJ), who is responsible for interpreting requirements, approving equipment and materials, waiving *Code* requirements, and ensuring equipment is installed in accordance with listing instructions.

Author's Comment: See the definition of "Authority Having Jurisdiction" in Article 100.

Interpretation of the Requirements. The authority having jurisdiction is responsible for interpreting the *NEC*, but his or her decisions must be based on a specific *Code* requirement. If an installation is rejected, the authority having jurisdiction is legally responsible for informing the installer of which specific *NEC* rule was violated.

Author's Comment: The art of getting along with the authority having jurisdiction consists of doing good work and knowing what the *Code* actually says (as opposed to what you only think it says). It's also useful to know how to choose your battles when the inevitable disagreement does occur.

Approval of Equipment and Materials. Only the authority having jurisdiction has authority to approve the installation of equipment and materials. Typically, the authority having jurisdiction will approve equipment listed by a product testing organization, such as Underwriters Laboratories Inc. (UL). The *NEC* doesn't require all equipment to be

listed, but many state and local AHJs do. See 90.7, 110.2, 110.3, and the definitions for "Approved," "Identified," "Labeled," and "Listed" in Article 100. **Figure 90–12**

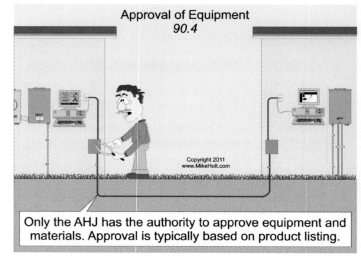

Only the AHJ has the authority to approve equipment and materials. Approval is typically based on product listing.

Figure 90–12

Author's Comment: According to the *NEC*, the authority having jurisdiction determines the approval of equipment. This means he or she can reject an installation of listed equipment and can approve the use of unlisted equipment. Given our highly litigious society, approval of unlisted equipment is becoming increasingly difficult to obtain.

Waiver of Requirements. By special permission, the authority having jurisdiction can waive specific requirements in the *Code* or permit alternative methods where it's assured equivalent safety can be achieved and maintained.

Author's Comment: Special permission is defined in Article 100 as the written consent of the authority having jurisdiction.

Waiver of New Product Requirements. If the 2011 *NEC* requires products that aren't yet available at the time the *Code* is adopted, the authority having jurisdiction can allow products that were acceptable in the previous *Code* to continue to be used.

Author's Comment: Sometimes it takes years before testing laboratories establish product standards for new *NEC* requirements, and then it takes time before manufacturers can design, manufacture, and distribute these products to the marketplace.

Essential Rule 5   90.5

90.5 Mandatory Requirements and Explanatory Material.

(A) Mandatory Requirements. In the *NEC* the words "shall" or "shall not," indicate a mandatory requirement.

> **Author's Comment:** For the ease of reading this textbook, the word "shall" has been replaced with the word "must," and the words "shall not" have been replaced with "must not." Remember that in many places, we will paraphrase the *Code* instead of providing exact quotes, to make it easier to read and understand.

(B) Permissive Requirements. When the *Code* uses "shall be permitted" it means the identified actions are permitted but not required, and the authority having jurisdiction isn't permitted to restrict an installation from being done in that manner. A permissive rule is often an exception to the general requirement.

> **Author's Comment:** For ease of reading, the phrase "shall be permitted," as used in the *Code*, has been replaced in this textbook with the phrase "is permitted" or "are permitted."

(C) Explanatory Material. References to other standards or sections of the *NEC*, or information related to a *Code* rule, are included in the form of <u>Informational Notes</u>. Such notes are for information only and aren't enforceable as a requirement of the *NEC*.

For example, Informational Note 4 in 210.19(A)(1) recommends that the voltage drop of a circuit not exceed 3 percent. This isn't a requirement; it's just a recommendation.

> **Author's Comment:** For convenience and ease of reading in this textbook, I will identify Informational Notes simply as "Note."

(D) <u>Informative</u> **Annexes.** Nonmandatory information annexes contained in the back of the *Code* book are for information only and aren't enforceable as a requirement of the *NEC*.

Essential Rule 6   90.7

90.7 Examination of Equipment for Product Safety.

Product evaluation for safety is typically performed by a testing laboratory, which publishes a list of equipment that meets a nationally recognized test standard. Products and materials that are listed, labeled, or identified by a testing laboratory are generally approved by the authority having jurisdiction.

> **Author's Comment:** See Article 100 for the definition of "Approved."

Listed, factory-installed, internal wiring and construction of equipment need not be inspected at the time of installation, except to detect alterations or damage [300.1(B)]. **Figure 90–13**

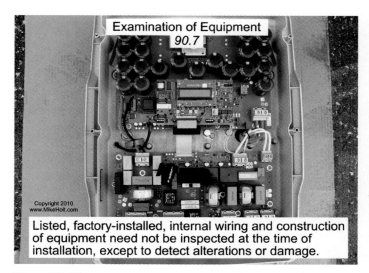

Examination of Equipment 90.7

Copyright 2010
www.MikeHolt.com

Listed, factory-installed, internal wiring and construction of equipment need not be inspected at the time of installation, except to detect alterations or damage.

Figure 90–13

Notes

ARTICLE 110

Requirements for Electrical Installations

INTRODUCTION TO ARTICLE 110—REQUIREMENTS FOR ELECTRICAL INSTALLATIONS

Article 110 sets the stage for how you'll implement the rest of the *NEC*. This article contains a few of the most important and yet neglected parts of the *Code*. For example:

- How should conductors be terminated?
- What kinds of warnings, markings, and identification does a given installation require?
- What's the right working clearance for a given installation?
- What do the temperature limitations at terminals mean?
- What are the *NEC* requirements for dealing with flash protection?

It's critical that you master Article 110. As you read this article, you're building your foundation for correctly applying the *NEC*. In fact, this article itself is a foundation for much of the *Code*. The purpose for the *National Electrical Code* is to provide a safe installation, but Article 110 is perhaps focused a little more on providing an installation that is safe for the installer and maintenance electrician, so time spent in this article is time well spent.

Essential Rule 7	110.2

PART I. GENERAL REQUIREMENTS

110.2 Approval of Conductors and Equipment. The authority having jurisdiction must approve all electrical conductors and equipment. **Figure 110–1**

> **Author's Comment:** For a better understanding of product approval, review 90.4, 90.7, 110.3 and the definitions for "Approved," "Identified," "Labeled," and "Listed" in Article 100.

Essential Rule 8	110.3

110.3 Examination, Identification, Installation, and Use of Equipment.

(A) Guidelines for Approval. The authority having jurisdiction must approve equipment. In doing so, consideration must be given to the following:

(1) Suitability for installation and use in accordance with the *NEC*

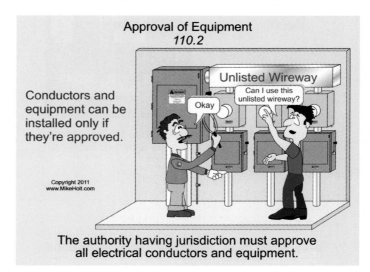

Figure 110–1

Note: Suitability of equipment use may be identified by a description marked on or provided with a product to identify the suitability of the product for a specific purpose, environment, or application. Special conditions of use or other limitations may be marked on the equipment, in the product instructions, or appropriate listing and labeling information. Suitability of equipment may be evidenced by listing or labeling.

(2) Mechanical strength and durability

(3) Wire-bending and connection space

(4) Electrical insulation

(5) Heating effects under all conditions of use

(6) Arcing effects

(7) Classification by type, size, voltage, current capacity, and specific use

(8) Other factors contributing to the practical safeguarding of persons using or in contact with the equipment

(B) Installation and Use. Equipment must be installed and used in accordance with any instructions included in the listing or labeling requirements. **Figure 110–2**

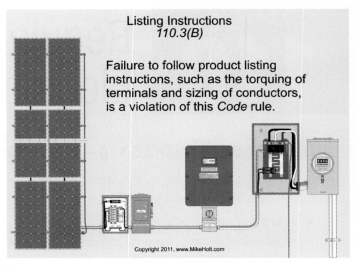

Figure 110–3

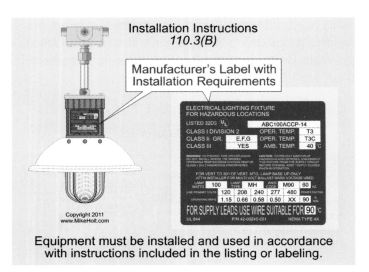

Figure 110–2

Author's Comments:

• See the definitions of "Labeling" and "Listing" in Article 100.

• Failure to follow product listing instructions, such as the torquing of terminals and the sizing of conductors, is a violation of this *Code* rule. **Figure 110–3**

• When an air conditioner nameplate specifies "Maximum Fuse Size," one-time or dual-element fuses must be used to protect the equipment. **Figure 110–4**

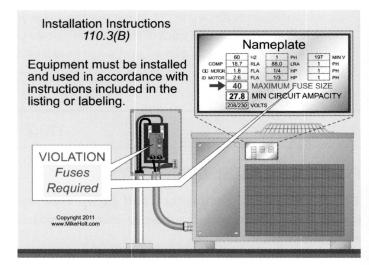

Figure 110–4

Essential Rule 9   110.14

110.14 Conductor Termination and Splicing. Conductor terminal and splicing devices must be identified for the conductor material and they must be properly installed and used. **Figure 110–5**

Connectors and terminals for conductors more finely stranded than Class B and Class C, as shown in Table 10 of Chapter 9, must be identified for the conductor class. **Figure 110–6**

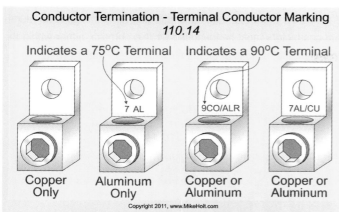

Conductor Termination - Terminal Conductor Marking
110.14

Indicates a 75°C Terminal   Indicates a 90°C Terminal

7 AL   9CO/ALR   7AL/CU

Copper Only   Aluminum Only   Copper or Aluminum   Copper or Aluminum

Copyright 2011, www.MikeHolt.com

Terminals that are suitable only for aluminum must be marked AL. Terminals suitable for both copper and aluminum must be marked CO/ALR or AL/CU.

Figure 110–5

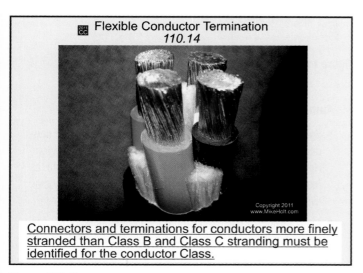

Flexible Conductor Termination
110.14

Copyright 2011
www.MikeHolt.com

Connectors and terminations for conductors more finely stranded than Class B and Class C stranding must be identified for the conductor Class.

Figure 110–6

Author's Comments:

- According to UL Standard 486 A-B, a terminal/lug/connector must be listed and marked for use with conductors stranded in other than Class B. With no marking or factory literature/instructions to the contrary, terminals may only be used with Class B stranded conductors.

- Class D stranding has 37 strands of wire per conductor in sizes 18-2 AWG, 61 strands in sizes 1-4/0 AWG, and 91 strands in sizes 250-500 kcmil.

Switches and receptacles marked CO/ALR are designed to ensure a good connection through the use of the larger contact area and compatible materials. The terminal screws are plated with the element called "Indium." Indium is an extremely soft metal that forms a gas-sealed connection with the aluminum conductor.

Author's Comments:

- See the definition of "Identified" in Article 100.

- Conductor terminations must comply with the manufacturer's instructions as required by 110.3(B). For example, if the instructions for the device state "Suitable for 18-12 AWG Stranded," then only stranded conductors can be used with the terminating device. If the instructions state "Suitable for 18-12 AWG Solid," then only solid conductors are permitted, and if the instructions state "Suitable for 18-12 AWG," then either solid or stranded conductors can be used with the terminating device.

Copper and Aluminum Mixed. Copper and aluminum conductors must not make contact with each other in a device unless the device is listed and identified for this purpose.

Author's Comment: Few terminations are listed for the mixing of aluminum and copper conductors, but if they are, that will be marked on the product package or terminal device. The reason copper and aluminum shouldn't be in contact with each other is because corrosion develops between the two different metals due to galvanic action, resulting in increased contact resistance at the splicing device. This increased resistance can cause the splice to overheat and cause a fire.

Note: Many terminations and equipment are marked with a tightening torque, see Table I.1 in Informative Annex I.

Author's Comment: Conductors must terminate in devices that have been properly tightened in accordance with the manufacturer's torque specifications included with equipment instructions. Failure to torque terminals can result in excessive heating of terminals or splicing devices due to a loose connection. A loose connection can also lead to arcing which increases the heating effect and also may lead to a short circuit or ground fault. Any of these can result in a fire or other failure, including an arc-flash event. In addition, this is a violation of 110.3(B), which requires all equipment to be installed in accordance with listing or labeling instructions. **Figure 110–7**

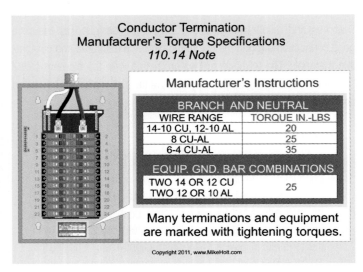

Figure 110–7

> **Question:** *What do you do if the torque value isn't provided with the device?*
>
> **Answer:** *Call the manufacturer, visit the manufacturer's Website, or have the supplier make a copy of the installation instructions.*

Author's Comment: Terminating conductors without a torque tool can result in an improper and unsafe installation. If a torque screwdriver isn't used, there's a good chance the conductors aren't properly terminated.

(A) Terminations. Conductor terminals must ensure a good connection without damaging the conductors and must be made by pressure connectors (including set screw type) or splices to flexible leads.

Author's Comment: See the definition of "Connector, Pressure" in Article 100.

> **Question:** *What if the conductor is larger than the terminal device?*
>
> **Answer:** *This condition needs to be anticipated in advance, and the equipment should be ordered with terminals that will accommodate the larger conductor. However, if you're in the field, you should:*
> - *Contact the manufacturer and have them express deliver you the proper terminals, bolts, washers, and nuts, or*
> - *Order a terminal device that crimps on the end of the larger conductor and reduces the termination size.*

Terminals for more than one conductor and terminals used for aluminum conductors must be identified for this purpose, either within the equipment instructions or on the terminal itself. **Figure 110–8**

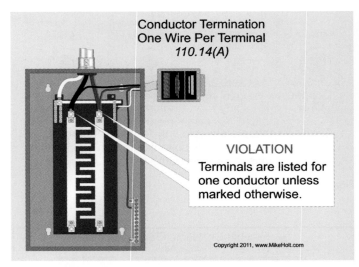

Figure 110–8

Author's Comments:

- Split-bolt connectors are commonly listed for only two conductors, although some are listed for three conductors. However, it's a common industry practice to terminate as many conductors as possible within a split-bolt connector, even though this violates the *NEC.* **Figure 110–9**

- Many devices are listed for more than one conductor per terminal. For example, some circuit breakers rated 30A or less can have two conductors under each lug. Grounding and bonding terminals are also often listed for more than one conductor under the terminal.

- Each neutral conductor within a panelboard must terminate to an individual terminal [408.41].

(B) Conductor Splices. Conductors must be spliced by a splicing device identified for the purpose or by exothermic welding.

Author's Comment: Conductors aren't required to be twisted together prior to the installation of a twist-on wire connector, unless specifically required in the installation instructions. **Figure 110–10**

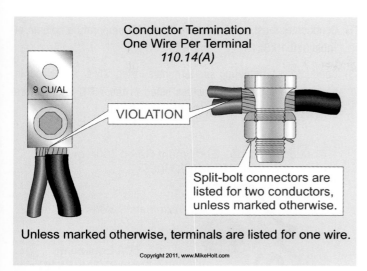

Figure 110–9

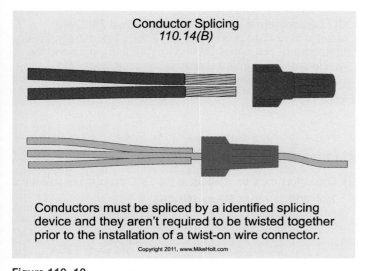

Figure 110–10

Unused circuit conductors aren't required to be removed. However, to prevent an electrical hazard, the free ends of the conductors must be insulated to prevent the exposed end of the conductor from touching energized parts. This requirement can be met by the use of an insulated twist-on or push-on wire connector. **Figure 110–11**

Author's Comment: See the definition of "Energized" in Article 100.

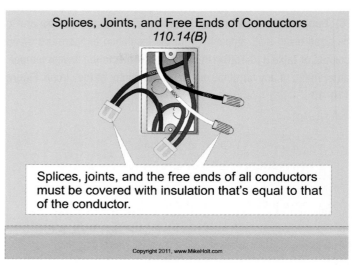

Figure 110–11

Underground Splices:

Single Conductors. Single direct burial conductors of types UF or USE can be spliced underground without a junction box, but the conductors must be spliced with a device listed for direct burial [300.5(E) and 300.15(G)]. **Figure 110–12**

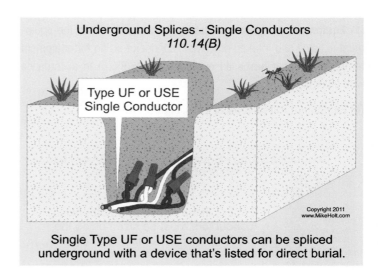

Figure 110–12

Multiconductor Cable. Multiconductor UF or USE cable can have the individual conductors spliced underground without a junction box as long as a listed splice kit that encapsulates the conductors as well as the cable jacket is used.

(C) Temperature Limitations (Conductor Size). Conductors are to be sized using their ampacity from the insulation temperature rating column of Table 310.15(B)(16) that corresponds to the lowest temperature rating of any terminal, device, or conductor of the circuit. **Figure 110–13**

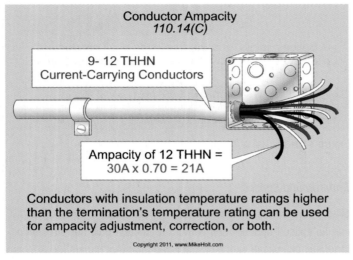

Figure 110–13

(1) Equipment Temperature Rating Provisions. Unless the equipment is listed and marked otherwise, conductor sizing for equipment terminations must be based on Table 310.15(B)(16) in accordance with (a) or (b):

(a) Equipment Rated 100A or Less. Figure 110–14

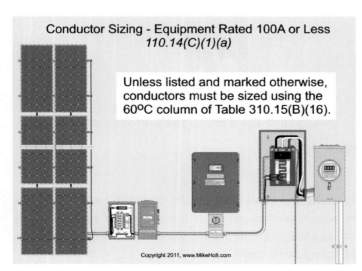

Figure 110–14

(1) Conductors must be sized using the 60°C temperature column of Table 310.15(B)(16).

(3) Conductors terminating on terminals rated 75°C are sized in accordance with the ampacities listed in the 75°C temperature column of Table 310.15(B)(16). **Figure 110–15**

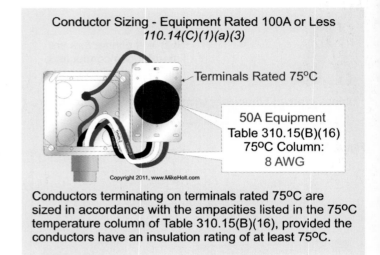

Figure 110–15

(b) Equipment Rated Over 100A.

(1) Conductors must be sized using the 75°C temperature column of Table 310.15(B)(16). **Figure 110–16**

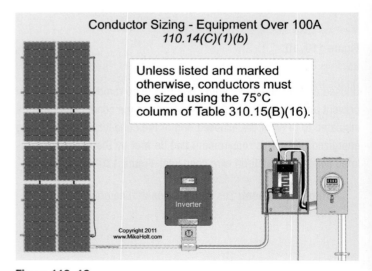

Figure 110–16

(2) Separate Connector Provisions. Conductors can be sized to the 90°C column of Table 310.15(B)(16) if the conductors and pressure connectors are rated at least 90°C. **Figure 110–17**

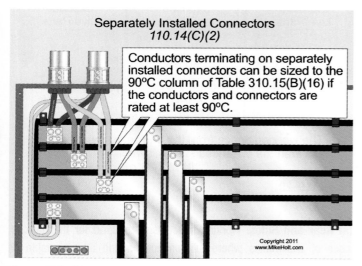

Separately Installed Connectors
110.14(C)(2)

Conductors terminating on separately installed connectors can be sized to the 90°C column of Table 310.15(B)(16) if the conductors and connectors are rated at least 90°C.

Copyright 2011
www.MikeHolt.com

Figure 110–17

Essential Rule 10   **110.16**

110.16 Arc-Flash Hazard Warning. Electrical equipment such as switchboards, panelboards, industrial control panels, meter socket enclosures, and motor control centers in other than dwelling units that are likely to require examination, adjustment, servicing, or maintenance while energized must be field-marked to warn qualified persons of the danger associated with an arc flash from short circuits or ground faults. The field-marking must be clearly visible to qualified persons before they examine, adjust, service, or perform maintenance on the equipment. **Figure 110–18**

Author's Comments:

- See the definition of "Qualified Person" in Article 100.

- This rule is meant to warn qualified persons who work on energized electrical systems that an arc flash hazard exists so they'll select proper personal protective equipment (PPE) in accordance with industry accepted safe work practice standards.

Note 1: NFPA 70E, *Standard for Electrical Safety in the Workplace*, provides assistance in determining the severity of potential exposure, planning safe work practices, and selecting personal protective equipment.

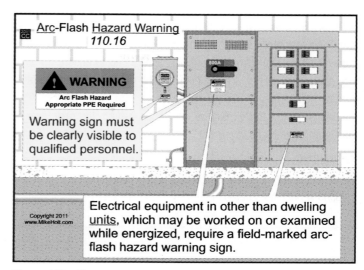

Arc-Flash Hazard Warning
110.16

⚠ **WARNING**
Arc Flash Hazard
Appropriate PPE Required

Warning sign must be clearly visible to qualified personnel.

Copyright 2011
www.MikeHolt.com

Electrical equipment in other than dwelling units, which may be worked on or examined while energized, require a field-marked arc-flash hazard warning sign.

Figure 110–18

Essential Rule 11   **110.24**

110.24 Available Fault Current.

(A) Field Marking. Service equipment in other than dwelling units must be legibly field-marked with the maximum available fault current, including the date the fault current calculation was performed and be of sufficient durability to withstand the environment involved. **Figure 110–19**

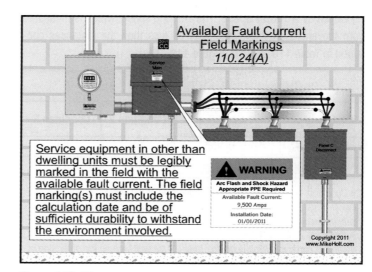

Available Fault Current
Field Markings
110.24(A)

Service equipment in other than dwelling units must be legibly marked in the field with the available fault current. The field marking(s) must include the calculation date and be of sufficient durability to withstand the environment involved.

⚠ **WARNING**
Arc Flash and Shock Hazard
Appropriate PPE Required

Available Fault Current:
9,500 Amps

Installation Date:
01/01/2011

Copyright 2011
www.MikeHolt.com

Figure 110–19

(B) Modifications. When modifications to the electrical installation affect the maximum available fault current at the service, the maximum available fault current must be recalculated to ensure the service equipment ratings are sufficient for the maximum available fault current at the line terminals of the equipment. The required field marking(s) in 110.24(A) must be adjusted to reflect the new level of maximum available fault current.

Ex: Field markings aren't required for industrial installations where conditions of maintenance and supervision ensure that only qualified persons service the equipment.

Essential Rule 12   110.26

PART II. 600V, NOMINAL, OR LESS

110.26 Spaces About Electrical Equipment. For the purpose of safe operation and maintenance of equipment, access and working space must be provided about all electrical equipment.

(A) Working Space. Equipment that may need examination, adjustment, servicing, or maintenance while energized must have working space provided in accordance with (1), (2), and (3):

> **Author's Comment:** The phrase "while energized" is the root of many debates. As always, check with the AHJ to see what equipment he or she believes needs a clear working space.

(1) Depth of Working Space. The working space, which is measured from the enclosure front, must not be less than the distances contained in Table 110.26(A)(1). **Figure 110–20**

Table 110.26(A)(1) Working Space			
Voltage-to-Ground	Condition 1	Condition 2	Condition 3
0–150V	3 ft	3 ft	3 ft
151–600V	3 ft	3½ft	4 ft

- *Condition 1—Exposed live parts on one side of the working space and no live or grounded parts, including concrete, brick, or tile walls are on the other side of the working space.*
- *Condition 2—Exposed live parts on one side of the working space and grounded parts, including concrete, brick, or tile walls are on the other side of the working space.*
- *Condition 3—Exposed live parts on both sides of the working space.*

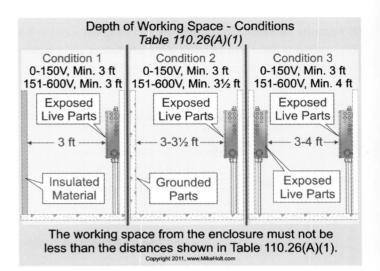

Figure 110–20

(a) Rear and Sides. Working space isn't required for the back or sides of assemblies where all connections and all renewable or adjustable parts are accessible from the front. **Figure 110–21**

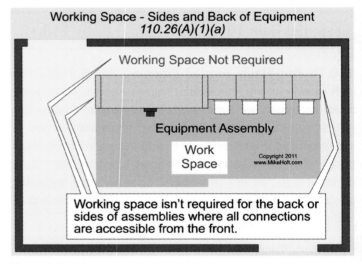

Figure 110–21

(b) Low Voltage. If special permission is granted in accordance with 90.4, working space for equipment that operates at not more than 30V ac or 60V dc can be less than the distance in Table 110.26(A)(1). **Figure 110–22**

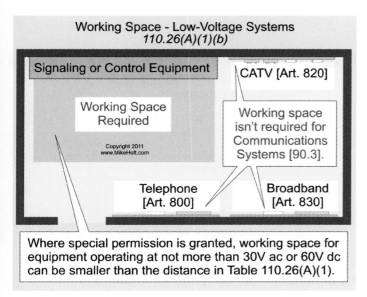

Figure 110–22

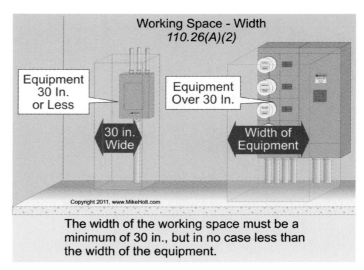

The width of the working space must be a minimum of 30 in., but in no case less than the width of the equipment.

Figure 110–23

Author's Comment: See the definition of "Special Permission" in Article 100.

(c) Existing Buildings. If electrical equipment is being replaced, Condition 2 working space is permitted between dead-front switchboards, panelboards, or motor control centers located across the aisle from each other where conditions of maintenance and supervision ensure that written procedures have been adopted to prohibit equipment on both sides of the aisle from being open at the same time, and only authorized, qualified persons will service the installation.

Author's Comment: The working space requirements of 110.26 don't apply to equipment included in Chapter 8— Communications Circuits [90.3].

(2) Width of Working Space. The width of the working space must be a minimum of 30 in., but in no case less than the width of the equipment. **Figure 110–23**

Author's Comment: The width of the working space can be measured from left-to-right, from right-to-left, or simply centered on the equipment, and the working space can overlap the working space for other electrical equipment. **Figure 110–24**

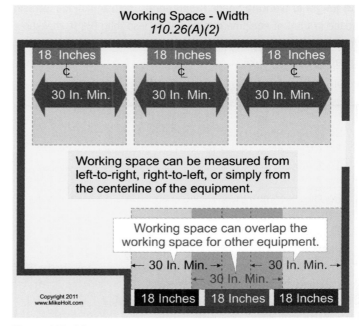

Figure 110–24

In all cases, the working space must be of sufficient width, depth, and height to permit all equipment doors to open 90 degrees. **Figure 110–25**

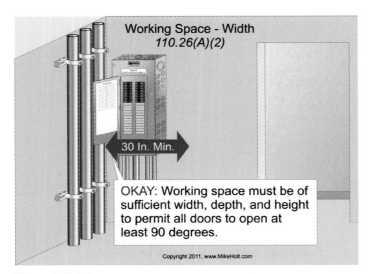

Figure 110–25

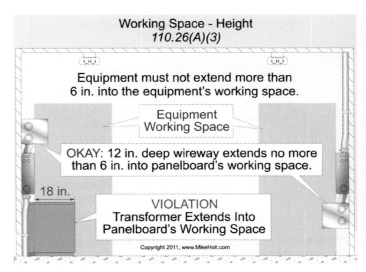

Figure 110–27

(3) Height of Working Space (Headroom). The height of the working space in front of equipment must not be less than 6½ ft, measured from the grade, floor, platform, or the equipment height, whichever is greater. Figure 110–26

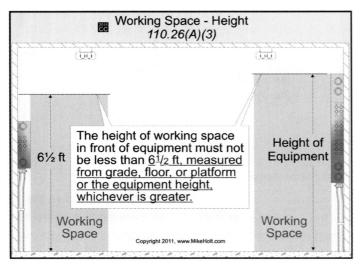

Figure 110–26

Equipment such as raceways, cables, wireways, cabinets, panels, and so on, can be located above or below electrical equipment, but must not extend more than 6 in. into the equipment's working space. Figure 110–27

Ex 1: The minimum headroom requirement doesn't apply to service equipment or panelboards rated 200A or less located in an existing dwelling unit.

Author's Comment: See the definition of "Dwelling Unit" in Article 100.

Ex 2: Meters are permitted to extend beyond the other equipment.

(B) Clear Working Space. The working space required by this section must be clear at all times. Therefore, this space isn't permitted for storage. When normally enclosed live parts are exposed for inspection or servicing, the working space, if in a passageway or general open space, must be suitably guarded.

Author's Comment: When working in a passageway, the working space should be guarded from occupants using the passageway. When working on electrical equipment in a passageway one must be mindful of a fire alarm evacuation with numerous occupants congregated and moving through the passageway.

⚠️ **CAUTION:** *It's very dangerous to service energized parts in the first place, and it's unacceptable to be subjected to additional dangers by working around bicycles, boxes, crates, appliances, and other impediments.* Figure 110–28

Author's Comment: Signaling and communications equipment must not be installed in a manner that encroaches on the working space of the electrical equipment.

(C) Entrance to and Egress from Working Space.

(1) Minimum Required. At least one entrance of sufficient area must provide access to and egress from the working space.

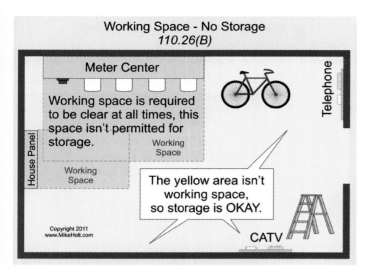

Figure 110–28

Author's Comment: Check to see what the authority having jurisdiction considers "Sufficient Area." Building codes contain minimum dimensions for doors and openings for personnel travel.

(2) Large Equipment. An entrance to and egress from each end of the working space of electrical equipment rated 1,200A or more that's over 6 ft wide is required. The opening must be a minimum of 24 in. wide and 6½ ft high. **Figure 110–29.** A single entrance to and egress from the required working space is permitted where either of the following conditions is met:

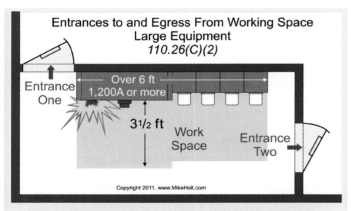

For equipment rated 1,200A or more and over 6 ft wide, an entrance to and egress from (2 ft x 6 ½ ft) is required at each end of the working space.

Figure 110–29

(a) Unobstructed Egress. Only one entrance is required where the location permits a continuous and unobstructed way of egress travel.

(b) Double Workspace. Only one entrance is required where the required working space depth is doubled, and the equipment is located so the edge of the entrance is no closer than the required working space distance. **Figure 110–30**

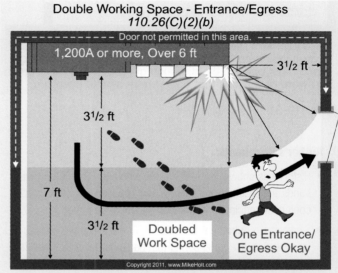

One entrance/egress is permitted where the required working space is doubled, and equipment is located so the edge of the entrance is no closer than the required working space distance.

Figure 110–30

(3) Personnel Doors. If equipment with overcurrent or switching devices rated 1,200A or more is installed, personnel door(s) for entrance to and egress from the working space located less than 25 ft from the nearest edge of the working space must have the door(s) open in the direction of egress and be equipped with panic hardware or other devices that open under simple pressure. **Figure 110–31**

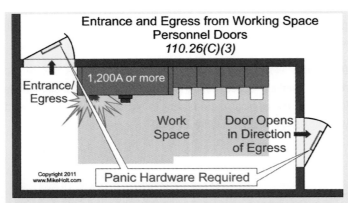

Figure 110–31

Author's Comments:

- History has shown that electricians who suffer burns on their hands in electrical arc flash or arc blast events often can't open doors equipped with knobs that must be turned.

- Since this requirement is in the *NEC*, the electrical contractor is responsible for ensuring that panic hardware is installed where required. Some electrical contractors are offended at being held liable for nonelectrical responsibilities, but this rule is designed to save the lives of electricians. For this and other reasons, many construction professionals routinely hold "pre-construction" or "pre-con" meetings to review potential opportunities for miscommunication—before the work begins.

(D) Illumination. Service equipment, switchboards, panelboards, as well as motor control centers located indoors must have illumination located indoors and must not be controlled by automatic means only. **Figure 110–32**

> **Author's Comment:** The *Code* doesn't provide the minimum foot-candles required to provide proper illumination. Proper illumination of electrical equipment rooms is essential for the safety of those qualified to work on such equipment.

(E) Dedicated Equipment Space. Switchboards, panelboards, and motor control centers must have dedicated equipment space as follows:

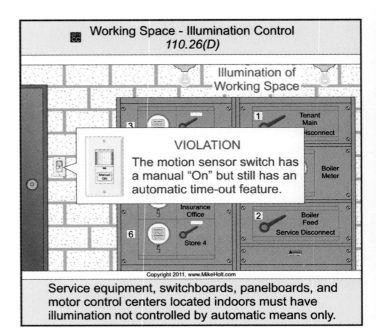

Figure 110–32

(1) Indoors.

(a) Dedicated Electrical Space. The footprint space (width and depth of the equipment) extending from the floor to a height of 6 ft above the equipment or to the structural ceiling, whichever is lower, must be dedicated for the electrical installation. No piping, ducts, or other equipment foreign to the electrical installation can be installed in this dedicated footprint space. **Figure 110–33**

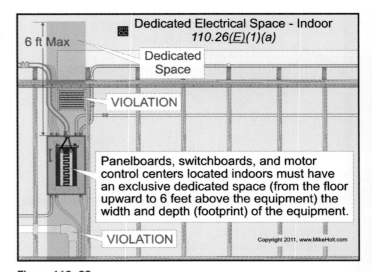

Figure 110–33

Ex: Suspended ceilings with removable panels can be within the dedicated footprint space [110.26(E)(1)(d)].

Author's Comment: Electrical raceways and cables not associated with the dedicated space can be within the dedicated space. These aren't considered "equipment foreign to the electrical installation." **Figure 110–34**

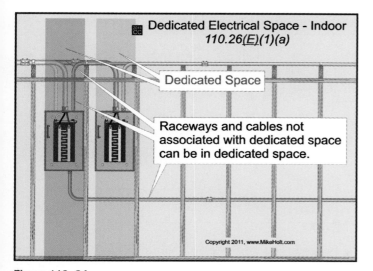

Figure 110–34

(b) Foreign Systems. Foreign systems can be located above the dedicated space if protection is installed to prevent damage to the electrical equipment from condensation, leaks, or breaks in the foreign systems, which can be as simple as a drip-pan. **Figure 110–35**

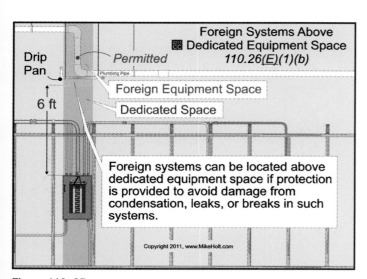

Figure 110–35

(c) Sprinkler Protection. Sprinkler protection piping isn't permitted in the dedicated space, but the *NEC* doesn't prohibit sprinklers from spraying water on electrical equipment.

(d) Suspended Ceilings. A dropped, suspended, or similar ceiling isn't considered a structural ceiling.

(F) Locked Electrical Equipment Rooms or Enclosures. Electrical equipment rooms and enclosures housing electrical equipment can be controlled by locks because they are still considered to be accessible to qualified persons who require access. **Figure 110–36**

Author's Comment: See the definition of "Accessible as it applies to equipment" in Article 100.

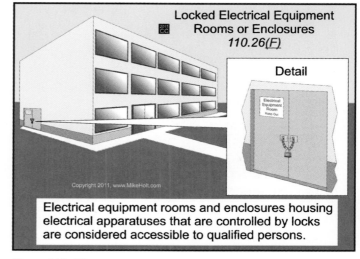

Figure 110–36

Notes

Use and Identification of Grounded Conductors

INTRODUCTION TO ARTICLE 200—USE AND IDENTIFICATION OF GROUNDED CONDUCTORS

This article contains the requirements for the identification of the grounded conductor and its terminals. Article 100 contains definitions for both "Grounded Conductor" and "Neutral Conductor." In some cases, both of these terms apply to the same conductor. Figures 200–1 and 200–2

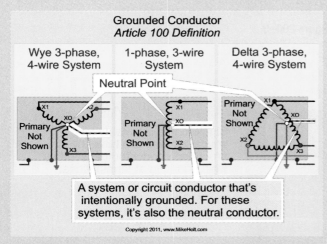

Figure 200–1

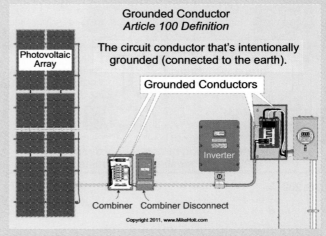

Figure 200–2

In a system that produces direct current, such as a photovoltaic system, the "grounded conductor" is not a neutral conductor. Figure 200–3

Author's Comment: Throughout this book, we will use the term "neutral" when referring to the grounded conductor when the application is not related to PV systems or corner-grounded delta-connected systems.

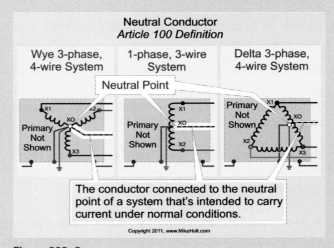

Figure 200–3

Essential Rule 13   200.6

PART I. GENERAL

200.6 Grounded Conductor Identification.

(A) Size 6 AWG or Smaller. Grounded conductors 6 AWG and smaller must be identified by one of the following means: **Figure 200–4**

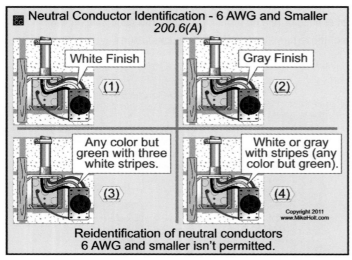

Figure 200–4

(1) By a continuous white outer finish.

(2) By a continuous gray outer finish.

(3) By three continuous white stripes along its entire length on other than green insulation.

(4) Wires that have their outer covering finished to show a white or gray color but have colored tracer threads in the braid identifying the source of manufacture are considered to meet the provisions of this section.

Author's Comment: The use of white tape, paint, or other methods of identification isn't permitted for grounded conductors 6 AWG or smaller. **Figure 200–5**

(6) A single-conductor, sunlight-resistant, outdoor-rated cable used as the grounded conductor in photovoltaic power systems as permitted by 690.31(B) can be identified by distinctive white marking at all terminations. **Figure 200–6**

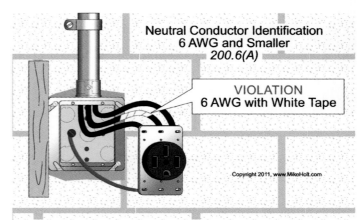

White tape, paint, or other methods of identification aren't permitted for neutral conductors 6 AWG or smaller.

Figure 200–5

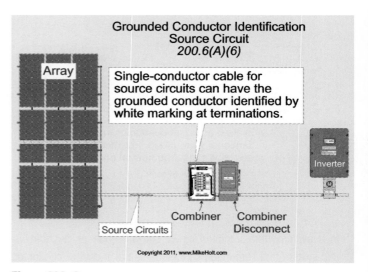

Figure 200–6

(B) Size 4 AWG or Larger. Grounded conductors 4 AWG or larger must be identified by one of the following means: **Figure 200–7**

(1) A continuous white outer finish along its entire length.

(2) A continuous gray outer finish along its entire length.

(3) Three continuous white stripes along its length.

(4) White or gray tape or markings at the terminations.

(D) Grounded Conductors of Different Systems. If grounded conductors of different voltage systems are installed in the same raceway, cable, or enclosure, each system grounded conductor must be identified by:

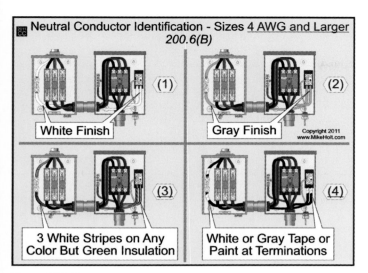

Neutral Conductor Identification - Sizes 4 AWG and Larger
200.6(B)

(1) White Finish

(2) Gray Finish

Copyright 2011
www.MikeHolt.com

(3) 3 White Stripes on Any Color But Green Insulation

(4) White or Gray Tape or Paint at Terminations

Figure 200–7

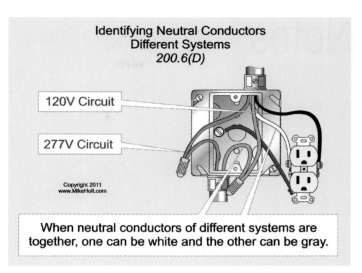

Identifying Neutral Conductors
Different Systems
200.6(D)

120V Circuit

277V Circuit

Copyright 2011
www.MikeHolt.com

When neutral conductors of different systems are together, one can be white and the other can be gray.

Figure 200–8

(1) A continuous white or gray outer finish along its entire length. **Figure 200–8**

(2) The grounded conductor of the other system must have a different outer covering of continuous white or gray outer finish along its entire length or by an outer covering of white or gray with a readily distinguishable color stripe (other than green) along its entire length. **Figure 200–9**

(3) Other identification allowed by 200.6(A) or (B) that distinguishes the grounded conductor from other systems.

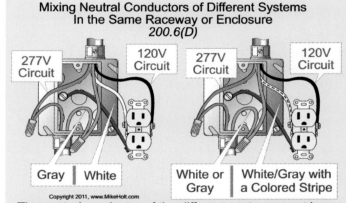

Mixing Neutral Conductors of Different Systems
In the Same Raceway or Enclosure
200.6(D)

277V Circuit   120V Circuit   277V Circuit   120V Circuit

Gray | White   White or Gray | White/Gray with a Colored Stripe

Copyright 2011, www.MikeHolt.com

The neutral conductor of the different systems must have an outer covering of continuous white or gray finish along its entire length or by an outer covering of white or gray with a readily distinguishable colored stripe (other than green) along its entire length.

Figure 200–9

Notes

Branch Circuits

INTRODUCTION TO ARTICLE 210—BRANCH CIRCUITS

This article contains the requirements for branch circuits, such as conductor sizing and identification, GFCI protection, and receptacle and lighting outlet requirements. It consists of three parts:

- Part I. General Provisions
- Part II. Branch-Circuit Ratings
- Part III. Required Outlets

Table 210.2 of this article identifies specific-purpose branch circuits. The provisions for branch circuits that supply equipment listed in Table 210.2 amend or supplement the provisions given in Article 210 for branch circuits, so it's important to be aware of the contents of this table.

The following sections contain a few key items on which to spend extra time as you study Article 210:

- **210.4—Multiwire Branch Circuits.** The conductors of these circuits must originate from the same panel.

- **210.8—GFCI Protection.** Crawl spaces, unfinished basements, and boathouses are just some of the many locations that require GFCI protection.

- **210.11—Branch Circuits Required.** With three subheadings, 210.11 gives summarized requirements for the number of branch circuits in certain situations, states that a load calculated on a VA per area basis must be evenly proportioned, and covers some minimum branch circuit rules for dwelling units.

- **210.12—Arc-Fault Circuit-Interrupter Protection.** An arc-fault circuit interrupter is a device intended to de-energize a circuit when it detects the current waveform characteristics unique to an arcing fault. The purpose of an AFCI is to protect against a fire hazard, whereas the purpose of a GFCI is to protect people against electrocution.

- **210.19—Conductors—Minimum Ampacity and Size.** This section covers the basic rules for sizing branch-circuit conductors, including continuous and noncontinuous loads.

- **210.21—Outlet Devices.** Outlet devices must have an ampere rating at least as large as the load to be served, as well as following the other rules of this section.

- **210.23—Permissible Loads.** This is intended to prevent a circuit overload from occurring because of improper design and planning of circuitry.

- **210.52—Dwelling Unit Receptacle Outlets.** There are some specific receptacle spacing rules and branch-circuit requirements for dwelling units that don't apply to other occupancies.

Mastering the branch-circuit requirements in Article 210 will give you a jump-start toward completing installations that are free of *Code* violations.

Essential Rule 14   210.4

PART I. GENERAL PROVISIONS

210.4 Multiwire Branch Circuits.

Author's Comment: A multiwire branch circuit that consists of two or more ungrounded circuit conductors with a common neutral conductor. There must be a difference of potential (voltage) between the ungrounded conductors and an equal difference of potential (voltage) from each ungrounded conductor to the common neutral conductor. **Figure 210–1**

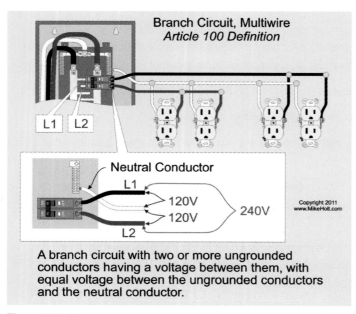

Branch Circuit, Multiwire
Article 100 Definition

Neutral Conductor

L1
120V
120V   240V
L2

Copyright 2011
www.MikeHolt.com

A branch circuit with two or more ungrounded conductors having a voltage between them, with equal voltage between the ungrounded conductors and the neutral conductor.

Figure 210–1

(A) General. A multiwire branch circuit can be considered a single circuit or a multiple circuit.

To prevent inductive heating and to reduce conductor impedance for fault currents, all conductors of a multiwire branch circuit must originate from the same panelboard.

Author's Comment: For more information on the inductive heating of metal parts, see 300.3(B), 300.5(I), and 300.20.

Note: Unwanted and potentially hazardous harmonic neutral currents can cause additional heating of the neutral conductor of a 4-wire, three-phase, 120/208V or 277/480V wye-connected system, which supplies nonlinear loads. To prevent fire or equipment damage from excessive harmonic neutral currents, the designer should consider: (1) increasing the size of the neutral conductor, or (2) installing a separate neutral for each phase. See 220.61(C)(2) and 310.15(B)(5)(c) in this textbook for additional information. **Figures 210–2 and 210–3**

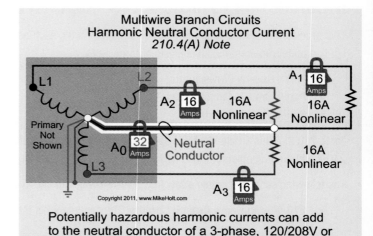

Multiwire Branch Circuits
Harmonic Neutral Conductor Current
210.4(A) Note

L1
L2   A₁ 16 Amps
A₂ 16 Amps   16A   16A
               Nonlinear   Nonlinear
Primary
Not   A₀ 32 Amps   Neutral   16A
Shown   Conductor   Nonlinear
L3
                            A₃ 16 Amps

Copyright 2011. www.MikeHolt.com

Potentially hazardous harmonic currents can add to the neutral conductor of a 3-phase, 120/208V or 277/480V, 4-wire, wye-connected power system.

Figure 210–2

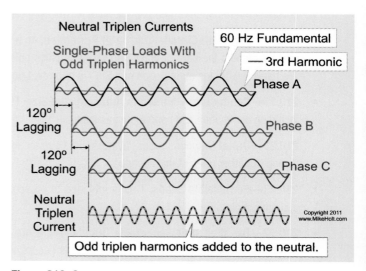

Neutral Triplen Currents

Single-Phase Loads With
Odd Triplen Harmonics

60 Hz Fundamental

— 3rd Harmonic

Phase A

120°
Lagging

Phase B

120°
Lagging

Phase C

Neutral
Triplen
Current

Copyright 2011
www.MikeHolt.com

Odd triplen harmonics added to the neutral.

Figure 210–3

Author's Comments:

- See the definition of "Nonlinear Load" in Article 100.

- For more information, please visit www.MikeHolt.com. Click on "Technical Information" on the left side of the page, and then select "Power Quality."

(B) Disconnecting Means. Each multiwire branch circuit must have a means to simultaneously disconnect all ungrounded conductors at the point where the branch circuit originates. **Figure 210–4**

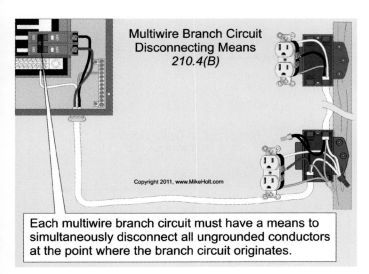

Multiwire Branch Circuit
Disconnecting Means
210.4(B)

Each multiwire branch circuit must have a means to simultaneously disconnect all ungrounded conductors at the point where the branch circuit originates.

Figure 210–4

Note: Individual single-pole circuit breakers with handle ties identified for the purpose can be used for this application [240.15(B)(1)].
Figure 210–5

 CAUTION: *This rule is intended to prevent people from working on energized circuits they thought were disconnected.*

(C) Line-to-Neutral Loads. Multiwire branch circuits must supply only line-to-neutral loads.

Ex 1: A multiwire branch circuit is permitted to supply an individual piece of line-to-line utilization equipment, such as a range or dryer.
Figure 210–6

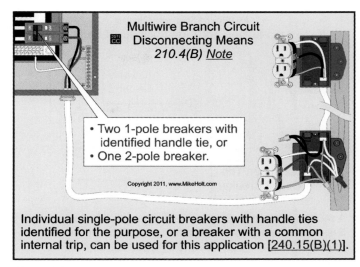

Multiwire Branch Circuit
Disconnecting Means
210.4(B) Note

- Two 1-pole breakers with identified handle tie, or
- One 2-pole breaker.

Individual single-pole circuit breakers with handle ties identified for the purpose, or a breaker with a common internal trip, can be used for this application [240.15(B)(1)].

Figure 210–5

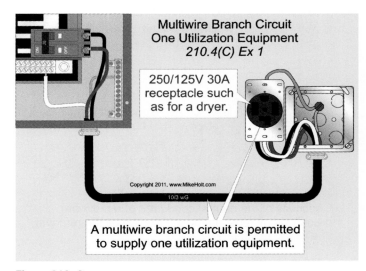

Multiwire Branch Circuit
One Utilization Equipment
210.4(C) Ex 1

250/125V 30A receptacle such as for a dryer.

A multiwire branch circuit is permitted to supply one utilization equipment.

Figure 210–6

Ex 2: A multiwire branch circuit is permitted to supply both line-to-line and line-to-neutral loads if the circuit is protected by a device such as a multipole circuit breaker with a common internal trip that opens all ungrounded conductors of the multiwire branch circuit simultaneously under a fault condition. **Figure 210–7**

> **Note:** See 300.13(B) for the requirements relating to the continuity of the neutral conductor on multiwire branch circuits. **Figure 210–8**

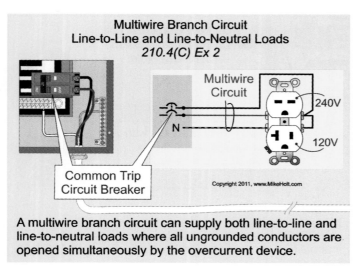

Multiwire Branch Circuit
Line-to-Line and Line-to-Neutral Loads
210.4(C) Ex 2

A multiwire branch circuit can supply both line-to-line and line-to-neutral loads where all ungrounded conductors are opened simultaneously by the overcurrent device.

Figure 210–7

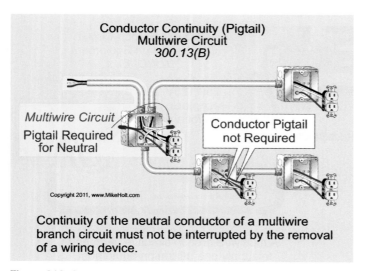

Conductor Continuity (Pigtail)
Multiwire Circuit
300.13(B)

Continuity of the neutral conductor of a multiwire branch circuit must not be interrupted by the removal of a wiring device.

Figure 210–8

⚠️ **CAUTION:** *If the continuity of the neutral conductor of a multiwire circuit is interrupted (opened), the resultant over- or undervoltage can cause a fire and/or destruction of electrical equipment. For details on how this occurs, see 300.13(B) in this textbook.* **Figures 210–9 and 210–10**

(D) Grouping. The ungrounded and neutral conductors of a multiwire branch circuit must be grouped together by cable ties or similar means at the point of origination. **Figure 210–11**

Ex: Grouping isn't required where the circuit conductors are contained in a single raceway or cable unique to that circuit that makes the grouping obvious.

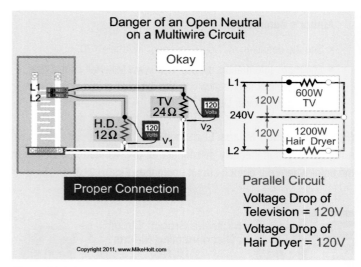

Danger of an Open Neutral
on a Multiwire Circuit

Parallel Circuit

Voltage Drop of
Television = 120V

Voltage Drop of
Hair Dryer = 120V

Figure 210–9

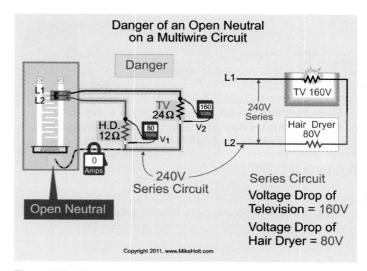

Danger of an Open Neutral
on a Multiwire Circuit

Series Circuit

Voltage Drop of
Television = 160V

Voltage Drop of
Hair Dryer = 80V

Figure 210–10

Author's Comment: Grouping all associated conductors of a multiwire branch circuit together by cable ties or other means within the point of origination makes it easier to visually identify the conductors of the multiwire branch circuit. The grouping will assist in making sure that the correct neutral is used at junction points and in connecting multiwire branch-circuit conductors to circuit breakers correctly, particularly where twin breakers are used. If proper diligence isn't exercised when making these connections, two circuit conductors can be accidentally connected to the same phase.

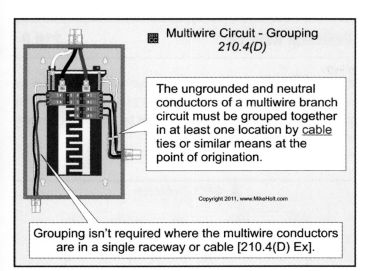

Multiwire Circuit - Grouping
210.4(D)

The ungrounded and neutral conductors of a multiwire branch circuit must be grouped together in at least one location by cable ties or similar means at the point of origination.

Copyright 2011, www.MikeHolt.com

Grouping isn't required where the multiwire conductors are in a single raceway or cable [210.4(D) Ex].

Figure 210–11

CAUTION: *If the ungrounded conductors of a multiwire circuit aren't terminated to different phases or lines, the currents on the neutral conductor won't cancel, but will add, which can cause an overload on the neutral conductor.* Figure 210–12

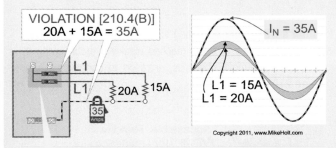

Miswired Multiwire Circuit - Overload on Neutral

VIOLATION [210.4(B)]
20A + 15A = 35A

$I_N = 35A$

L1
L1   20A   15A

L1 = 15A
L1 = 20A

Copyright 2011, www.MikeHolt.com

Caution: If the ungrounded conductors of a multiwire circuit aren't terminated to different phases or lines, the currents on the neutral conductor won't cancel, but will add, which can cause a dangerous overload on the neutral conductor.

Figure 210–12

Essential Rule 15   210.5

210.5 Identification for Branch Circuits.

(A) Neutral Conductor. The neutral conductor of a branch circuit must be identified in accordance with 200.6.

(B) Equipment Grounding Conductor. Equipment grounding conductors can be bare, covered, or insulated. Insulated equipment grounding conductors size 6 AWG and smaller must have a continuous outer finish either green or green with one or more yellow stripes [250.119].

On equipment grounding conductors 4 AWG and larger, insulation can be permanently reidentified with green marking at the time of installation at every point where the conductor is accessible [250.119(A)].

(C) Identification of Ungrounded Conductors—More Than One Voltage System. Ungrounded conductors must be identified as follows: **Figure 210–13**

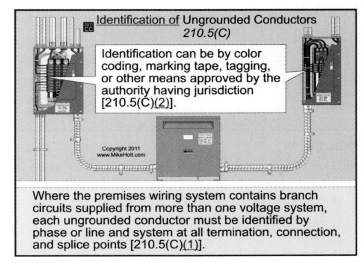

Identification of Ungrounded Conductors
210.5(C)

Identification can be by color coding, marking tape, tagging, or other means approved by the authority having jurisdiction [210.5(C)(2)].

Copyright 2011
www.MikeHolt.com

Where the premises wiring system contains branch circuits supplied from more than one voltage system, each ungrounded conductor must be identified by phase or line and system at all termination, connection, and splice points [210.5(C)(1)].

Figure 210–13

(1) Application. If the premises wiring system contains branch circuits supplied from more than one voltage system, each ungrounded conductor must be identified by phase and system at all termination, connection, and splice points.

(2) Means of Identification. Identification can be by color coding, marking tape, tagging, or other means approved by the authority having jurisdiction.

(3) Posting. The method of identification must be documented in a manner that's readily available or permanently posted at each branch-circuit panelboard.

Author's Comments:

- When a premises has more than one voltage system supplying branch circuits, the ungrounded conductors must be identified by phase and system. This can be done by permanently posting an identification legend that describes the method used, such as color-coded marking tape or color-coded insulation. **Figure 210–14**

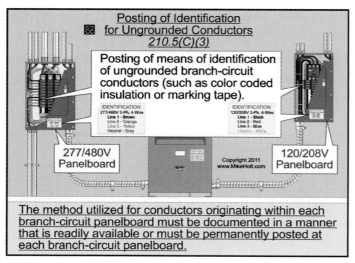

Figure 210–14

- Conductors with insulation that's green or green with one or more yellow stripes can't be used for an ungrounded or neutral conductor [250.119].

- Although the *NEC* doesn't require a specific color code for ungrounded conductors, electricians often use the following color system for power and lighting conductor identification:

  – 120/240V, single-phase—black, red, and white
  – 120/208V, three-phase—black, red, blue, and white
  – 120/240V, three-phase—black, orange, blue, and white
  – 277/480V, three-phase—brown, orange, yellow, and gray; or, brown, purple, yellow, and gray

Essential Rule 16   **210.8**

210.8 GFCI Protection. Ground-fault circuit interruption for personnel must be provided as required in 210.8(A) through (C). The ground-fault circuit-interrupter device must be installed at a readily accessible location. **Figure 210–15**

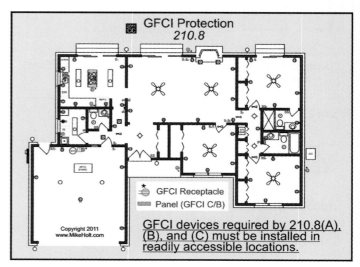

Figure 210–15

Author's Comment: According to Article 100, readily accessible means capable of being reached quickly without having to climb over or remove obstacles, or resort to portable ladders. **Figure 210–16**

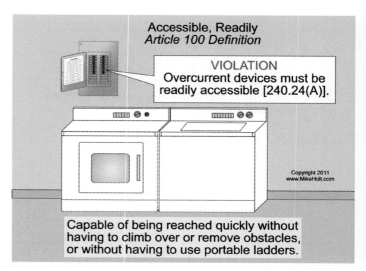

Figure 210–16

(A) Dwelling Units. GFCI protection is required for all 15A and 20A, 125V receptacles located in the following locations:

Author's Comment: See the definitions of "GFCI" and "Dwelling Unit" in Article 100.

(1) Bathroom Area. GFCI protection is required for all 15A and 20A, 125V receptacles in the bathroom area of a dwelling unit. **Figure 210–17**

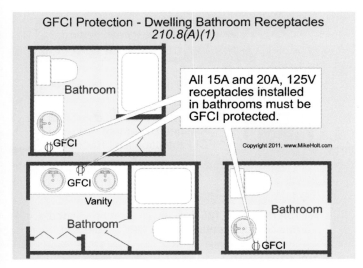

Figure 210–17

Author's Comments:

- See the definition of "Bathroom" in Article 100.
- In the continued interests of safety, proposals to allow receptacles for dedicated equipment in the bathroom area to be exempted from the GFCI protection requirements have been rejected.

(2) Garages and Accessory Buildings. GFCI protection is required for all 15A and 20A, 125V receptacles in garages, and in grade-level portions of accessory buildings used for storage or work areas of a dwelling unit. **Figure 210–18**

Author's Comments:

- See the definition of "Garage" in Article 100.
- A receptacle outlet is required in a dwelling unit attached garage [210.52(G)], but a receptacle outlet isn't required in an accessory building or a detached garage without power. If a 15A or 20A, 125V receptacle is installed in an accessory building, it must be GFCI protected. **Figure 210–19**

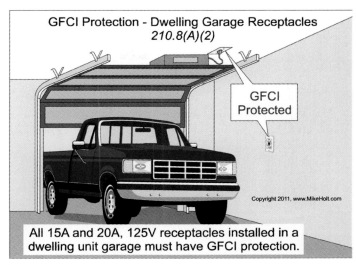

All 15A and 20A, 125V receptacles installed in a dwelling unit garage must have GFCI protection.

Figure 210–18

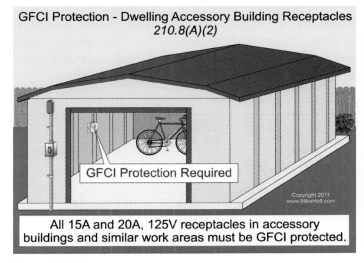

All 15A and 20A, 125V receptacles in accessory buildings and similar work areas must be GFCI protected.

Figure 210–19

(3) Outdoors. All 15A and 20A, 125V receptacles located outdoors of dwelling units, including receptacles installed under the eaves of roofs, must be GFCI protected. **Figure 210–20**

Author's Comments:

- Each dwelling unit of a multifamily dwelling that has an individual entrance at grade level must have at least one GFCI-protected receptacle outlet accessible from grade level located not more than 6½ ft above grade [210.52(E)(2)].
- Balconies, decks, and porches that are attached to the dwelling unit and are accessible from inside the dwelling must have at least one GFCI-protected receptacle outlet accessible from the balcony, deck, or porch [210.52(E)(3)].

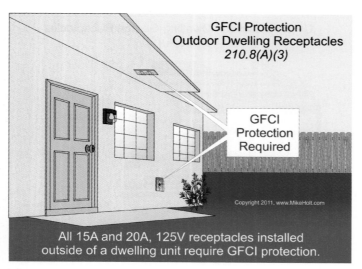

Figure 210–20

Ex: GFCI protection isn't required for a receptacle that's supplied by a branch circuit dedicated to fixed electric snow-melting or deicing or pipeline and vessel heating equipment, if the receptacle isn't readily accessible and the equipment or receptacle has ground-fault protection of equipment (GFPE) [426.28 and 427.22]. **Figure 210–21**

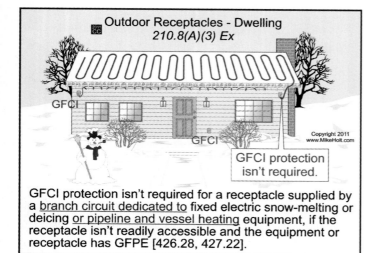

Figure 210–21

(4) Crawl Spaces. All 15A and 20A, 125V receptacles installed in crawl spaces at or below grade of a dwelling unit must be GFCI protected.

Author's Comment: The *Code* doesn't require a receptacle to be installed in a crawl space, except when heating, air-conditioning, and refrigeration equipment is installed there [210.63].

(5) Unfinished Basements. GFCI protection is required for all 15A and 20A, 125V receptacles located in the unfinished portion of a basement not intended as a habitable room and limited to storage and work areas. **Figure 210–22**

Figure 210–22

Ex: A receptacle supplying only a permanently installed fire alarm or burglar alarm system isn't required to be GFCI protected [760.41(B) and 760.121(B)].

Author's Comment: A receptacle outlet is required in each unfinished portion of a dwelling unit basement [210.52(G)].

(6) Kitchen Countertop Surfaces. GFCI protection is required for all 15A and 20A, 125V receptacles that serve countertop surfaces in a dwelling unit. **Figure 210–23**

Author's Comments:

- GFCI protection is required for all receptacles that serve countertop surfaces, but GFCI protection isn't required for receptacles that serve built-in appliances, such as dishwashers or kitchen waste disposals.

- See 210.52(C) for the location requirements of countertop receptacles.

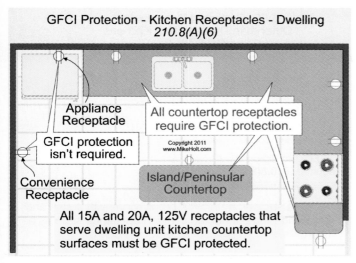

Figure 210–23

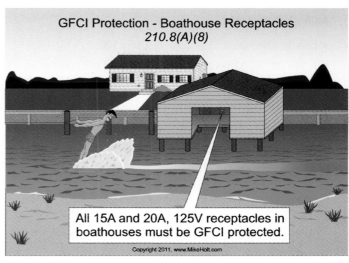

Figure 210–25

(7) Sinks. For other than kitchen sinks, GFCI protection is required for all 15A and 20A, 125V receptacles located within an arc measurement of 6 ft from the outside edge of the sink. **Figure 210–24**

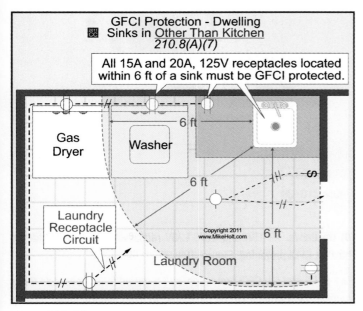

Figure 210–24

(8) Boathouses. GFCI protection is required for all 15A and 20A, 125V receptacles located in a dwelling unit boathouse. **Figure 210–25**

Author's Comment: The *Code* doesn't require a 15A or 20A, 125V receptacle to be installed in a boathouse, but if one is installed, it must be GFCI protected.

(B) Other than Dwelling Units. GFCI protection is required for all 15A and 20A, 125V receptacles installed in the following commercial/industrial locations:

(1) Bathrooms. All 15A and 20A, 125V receptacles installed in commercial or industrial bathrooms must be GFCI protected. **Figure 210–26**

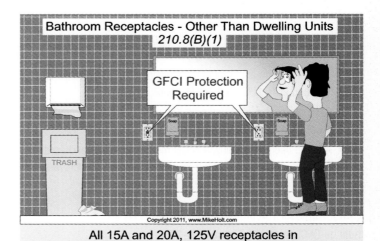

Figure 210–26

Author's Comments:

- See the definition of "Bathroom" in Article 100.

- A 15A or 20A, 125V receptacle isn't required in a commercial or industrial bathroom, but if one is installed, it must be GFCI protected.

(2) Kitchens. All 15A and 20A, 125V receptacles installed in a kitchen, even those that don't supply the countertop surface, must be GFCI protected. **Figure 210–27**

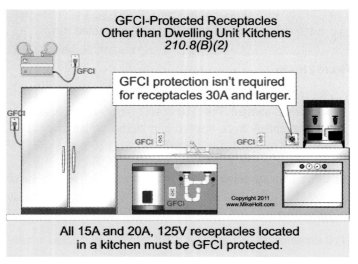

Figure 210–27

Author's Comments:

- A kitchen is an area with a sink and permanent provisions for food preparation and cooking [Article 100]

- GFCI protection isn't required for receptacles rated other than 15A and 20A, 125V in these locations.

- GFCI protection isn't required for hard-wired equipment in these locations.

- An area such an employee break room with a sink and cord-and-plug-connected cooking appliance such as a microwave oven isn't considered a kitchen. **Figure 210–28**

(3) Rooftops. All 15A and 20A, 125V receptacles installed on rooftops must be GFCI protected. **Figure 210–29**

> **Author's Comment:** A 15A or 20A, 125V receptacle outlet must be installed within 25 ft of heating, air-conditioning, and refrigeration equipment [210.63].

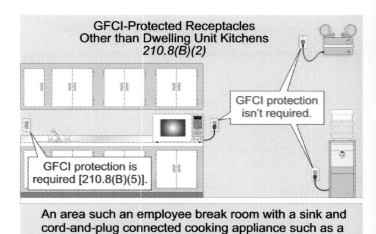

An area such an employee break room with a sink and cord-and-plug connected cooking appliance such as a microwave oven isn't considered a kitchen.

Figure 210–28

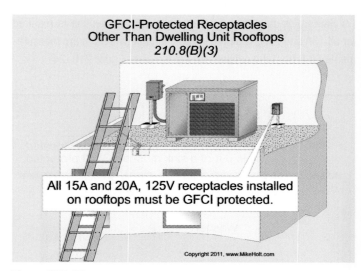

Figure 210–29

(4) Outdoors. All 15A and 20A, 125V receptacles installed outdoors must be GFCI protected. **Figure 210–30**

Ex 1 to (3) and (4): GFCI protection isn't required for a receptacle that's supplied by a branch circuit dedicated to fixed electric snow-melting or deicing or pipeline and vessel heating equipment, if the receptacle isn't readily accessible and the equipment or receptacle has ground-fault protection of equipment (GFPE) [426.28 and 427.22].

(5) Sinks. All 15A and 20A, 125V receptacles installed within 6 ft of the outside edge of a sink must be GFCI protected. **Figure 210–31**

Figure 210–30

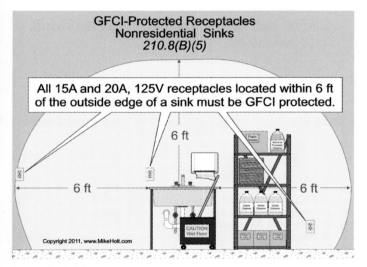

Figure 210–31

Ex 1: In industrial laboratories, receptacles used to supply equipment where removal of power would introduce a greater hazard aren't required to be GFCI protected.

Ex 2: Receptacles located in patient bed locations of general care or critical care areas of health care facilities aren't required to be GFCI protected.

(6) Indoor wet locations. All 15A and 20A, 125V receptacles installed indoors in wet locations must be GFCI protected.

(7) Locker Rooms. All 15A and 20A, 125V receptacles installed in locker rooms with associated showering facilities must be GFCI protected.

(8) Garages. All 15A and 20A, 125V receptacles installed in garages, service bays, and similar areas where electrical diagnostic equipment, electrical hand tools, or portable lighting equipment are to be used must be GFCI protected. **Figure 210–32**

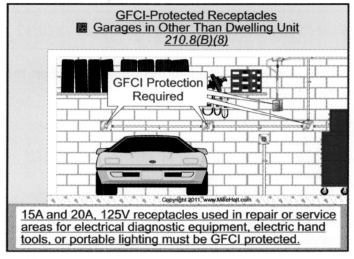

Figure 210–32

(C) Boat Hoists. GFCI protection is required for outlets supplying boat hoists in dwelling unit locations. **Figure 210–33**

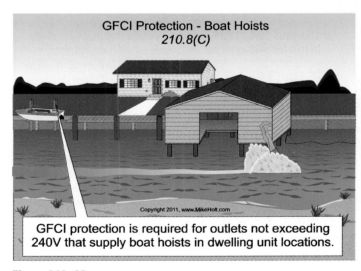

Figure 210–33

Author's Comments:

- See the definition of "Outlet" in Article 100.

- This ensures GFCI protection regardless of whether the boat hoist is cord-and-plug-connected or hard-wired.

Essential Rule 17   210.12

210.12 Arc-Fault Circuit-Interrupter Protection for Dwelling Units

Author's Comment: The combination AFCI is a circuit breaker that protects downstream branch-circuit wiring as well as cord sets and power-supply cords; an outlet branch circuit AFCI (receptacle) is installed as the first outlet in a branch circuit to protect downstream branch-circuit wiring, cord sets, and power-supply cords.

(A) Where Required. All 15A or 20A, 120V branch circuits in dwelling units supplying outlets in family rooms, dining rooms, living rooms, parlors, libraries, dens, bedrooms, sunrooms, recreation rooms, closets, hallways, or similar rooms or areas must be protected by a listed AFCI device of the combination type. **Figure 210–34**

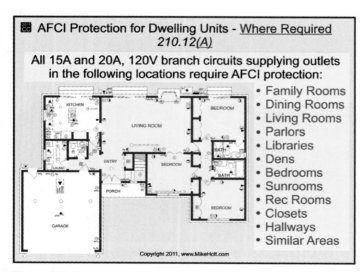

Figure 210–34

Author's Comment: The 120V circuit limitation means AFCI protection isn't required for equipment rated 230V, such as a baseboard heater or room air conditioner. For more information, visit www.MikeHolt.com, click on the "Search" link, and search for "AFCI."

Note 3: See 760.41(B) and 760.121(B) for power-supply requirements for fire alarm systems.

Author's Comment: Smoke alarms connected to a 15A or 20A circuit of a dwelling unit must be AFCI protected if the smoke alarm is located in one of the areas specified in 210.12(A). The exemption from AFCI protection for the "fire alarm circuit" contained in 760.41(B) and 760.121(B) doesn't apply to the single- or multiple-station smoke alarm circuit typically installed in dwelling unit bedroom areas. This is because a smoke alarm circuit isn't a fire alarm circuit as defined in NFPA 72, *National Fire Alarm Code.* Unlike single- or multiple-station smoke alarms, fire alarm systems are managed by a fire alarm control panel. **Figure 210–35**

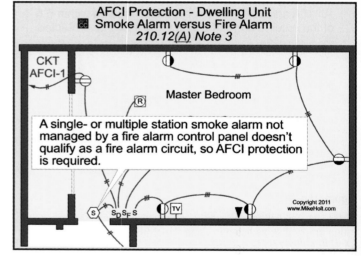

Figure 210–35

Ex 1: AFCI protection can be of the branch-circuit type located at the first outlet if the circuit conductors are installed in RMC, IMC, EMT, or Type MC or steel armored Type AC cable meeting the requirements of 250.118, and the AFCI device is contained in a metal outlet or junction box.

Ex 2: Where a listed metal or nonmetallic conduit or tubing is encased in not less than 2 in. of concrete for the portion of the branch circuit between the branch-circuit overcurrent device and the first outlet, an outlet branch-circuit AFCI at the first outlet is permitted to provide protection for the remaining portion of the branch circuit.

Ex 3: AFCI protection can be omitted for an individual branch circuit to a fire alarm system in accordance with 760.41(B) and 760.121(B), if the circuit conductors are installed in RMC, IMC, EMT, or steel sheath Type AC or MC cable that qualifies as an equipment grounding conductor in accordance with 250.118, with metal outlet and junction boxes.

(B) Branch-Circuit Extensions or Modifications—Dwelling Units. Where branch-circuit wiring is modified, replaced, or extended in any of the areas specified in 210.12(A), the branch circuit must be protected by:

(1) A listed combination AFCI located at the origin of the branch circuit; or

(2) A listed outlet branch circuit AFCI located at the first receptacle outlet of the existing branch circuit.

Essential Rule 18   **210.19**

PART II. BRANCH-CIRCUIT RATINGS

210.19 Conductor Sizing.

(A) Branch Circuits.

(1) Continuous and Noncontinuous Loads. Conductors must be sized no less than 125 percent of the continuous loads, plus 100 percent of the noncontinuous loads, based on the terminal temperature rating ampacities as listed in Table 310.15(B)(16), before any ampacity adjustment [110.14(C)(1)].

Ex 1: If the assembly and the overcurrent device are both listed for operation at 100 percent of its rating, the conductors can be sized at 100 percent of the continuous load.

Author's Comments:

- Equipment suitable for 100 percent continuous loading is rarely available in ratings under 400A.

- See the definition of "Continuous Load" in Article 100.

- See 210.20 for the sizing requirements for the branch-circuit overcurrent device for continuous and noncontinuous loads.

Question: *What size branch-circuit conductors are required for the ungrounded conductors of a 44A continuous load, if the equipment terminals are rated 75°C?* **Figure 210–36**

(a) 10 AWG   (b) 8 AWG   (c) 6 AWG   (d) 4 AWG

Answer: *(c) 6 AWG*

Since the load is 44A continuous, the ungrounded conductors must be sized to have an ampacity of not less than 55A (44A x 1.25). According to the 75°C column of Table 310.15(B)(16), a 6 AWG conductor is suitable, because it has an ampere rating of 65A at 75°C before any conductor ampacity adjustment for ambient temperature [310.15(B)(2)(a)], conductor bundling [310.15(B)(3)(a)], or both.

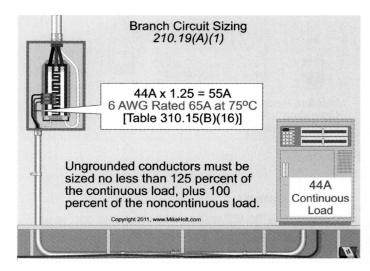

Figure 210–36

Note 4: To provide reasonable efficiency of operation of electrical equipment, branch-circuit conductors should be sized to prevent a voltage drop not to exceed 3 percent. In addition, the maximum total voltage drop on both feeders and branch circuits shouldn't exceed 5 percent. **Figures 210–37 and 210–38**

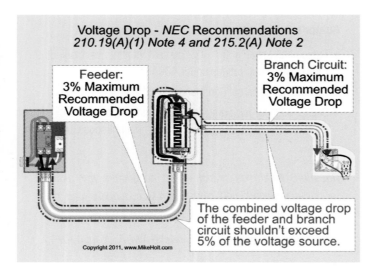

Figure 210–37

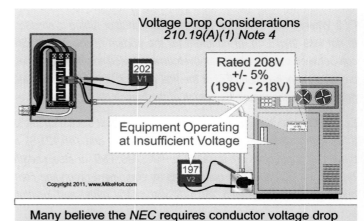

Many believe the *NEC* requires conductor voltage drop to be applied when sizing conductors. Although this is often a good practice, it's not a *Code* requirement.

Figure 210–39

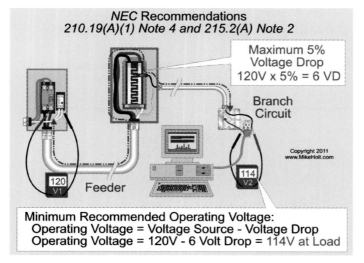

Figure 210–38

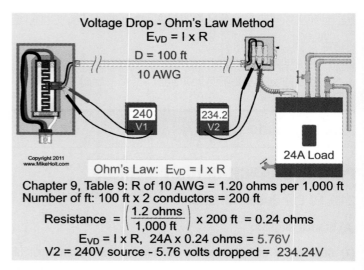

Figure 210–40

Author's Comments:

- Many believe the *NEC* requires conductor voltage drop, as per Note 4 to be applied when sizing conductors. Although this is often a good practice, it's not a *Code* requirement because Notes are only advisory statements [90.5(C)]. **Figures 210–39 and 210–40**

- The *NEC* doesn't consider voltage drop to be a safety issue, except for sensitive electronic equipment [647.4(D)] and fire pumps [695.7].

(2) Branch Circuits Supplying More than One Receptacle. Branch circuits that supply more than one receptacle must have an ampacity not less than the rating of the circuit overcurrent device [210.3].

(3) Household Ranges and Cooking Appliances. Branch-circuit conductors that supply household ranges, wall-mounted ovens or counter-mounted cooking units must have an ampacity not less than the rating of the branch circuit, and not less than the maximum load to be served. For ranges of 8¾ kW or more rating, the minimum branch-circuit ampere rating is 40A.

Ex 1: Conductors tapped from a 50A branch circuit for electric ranges, wall-mounted electric ovens and counter-mounted electric cooking units must have an ampacity not less than 20A, and must have sufficient ampacity for the load to be served. The taps must not be longer than necessary for servicing the appliances.

Essential Rule 19	210.20

210.20 Overcurrent Protection.

(A) Continuous and Noncontinuous Loads. Branch-circuit overcurrent devices must have a rating of not less than 125 percent of the continuous loads, plus 100 percent of the noncontinuous loads. **Figure 210–41**

> **Author's Comment:** See 210.19(A)(1) for branch-circuit conductor sizing requirements.

Ex: If the assembly and the overcurrent devices are both listed for operation at 100 percent of their rating, the branch-circuit overcurrent device can be sized at 100 percent of the continuous load.

> **Author's Comment:** Equipment suitable for 100 percent continuous loading is rarely available in ratings under 400A.

(B) Conductor Protection. Branch-circuit conductors must be protected against overcurrent in accordance with 240.4.

(C) Equipment Protection. Branch-circuit equipment must be protected in accordance with 240.3.

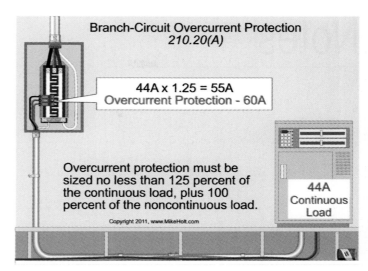

Branch-Circuit Overcurrent Protection
210.20(A)

44A x 1.25 = 55A
Overcurrent Protection - 60A

Overcurrent protection must be sized no less than 125 percent of the continuous load, plus 100 percent of the noncontinuous load.

Copyright 2011, www.MikeHolt.com

44A Continuous Load

Figure 210–41

Notes

Mike Holt's Illustrated Guide to Essential Rules of the National Electrical Code, Based on the 2011 NEC

ARTICLE 225

Outside Branch Circuits and Feeders

INTRODUCTION TO ARTICLE 225—OUTSIDE BRANCH CIRCUITS AND FEEDERS

This article covers the installation requirements for equipment, including conductors, located outdoors on or between buildings, poles, and other structures on the premises. Conductors installed outdoors can serve many purposes such as area lighting, power for outdoor equipment, or providing power to a separate building or structure. It's important to remember that the power supply for buildings or structures aren't always service conductors, but in many cases may be feeders or branch-circuit conductors originating in another building. Be careful not to assume that the conductors supplying power to a building are service conductors until you've identified where the utility service point is and reviewed the Article 100 Definitions for feeders, branch circuits, and service conductors. If they're service conductors, use Article 230. For outside branch circuit and feeder conductors, whatever they feed, use this article.

Section 225.2 provides a listing of other articles that may furnish additional requirements, then Part I of Article 225 goes on to address installation methods intended to provide a secure installation of outside conductors while providing sufficient conductor size, support, attachment means, and maintaining safe clearances.

Part II of the article limits the number of supplies (branch circuits or feeders) permitted to a building or structure and provides rules regarding disconnects for them. These rules include the disconnect rating, construction characteristics, labeling, and where to locate the disconnecting means and the grouping of multiple disconnects.

Outside branch circuits and feeders over 600V are the focus of Part III of Article 225.

Essential Rule 20	225.32

225.32 Disconnect Location. The disconnecting means for a building/structure must be installed at a readily accessible location either outside or inside nearest the point of entrance of the conductors. **Figure 225–1**

Supply conductors are considered outside of a building or other structure where they're encased or installed under not less than 2 in. of concrete or brick [230.6]. **Figure 225–2**

Ex 1: If documented safe switching procedures are established and maintained, the building/structure disconnecting means can be located elsewhere on the premises, if monitored by qualified persons.

> **Author's Comment:** A "Qualified Person" is one who has skills and knowledge related to the construction and operation of the electrical equipment and installation, and has received safety training to recognize and avoid the hazards involved with electrical systems [Article 100].

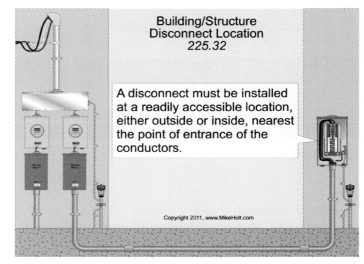

Building/Structure
Disconnect Location
225.32

A disconnect must be installed at a readily accessible location, either outside or inside, nearest the point of entrance of the conductors.

Copyright 2011, www.MikeHolt.com

Figure 225–1

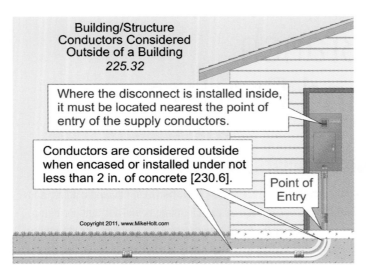

Figure 225–2

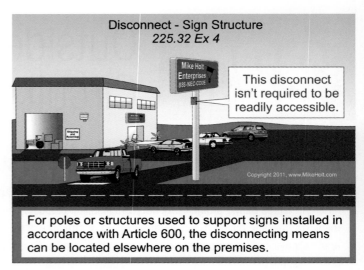

Figure 225–4

Ex 3: A disconnecting means isn't required within sight of poles that support luminaires. **Figure 225–3**

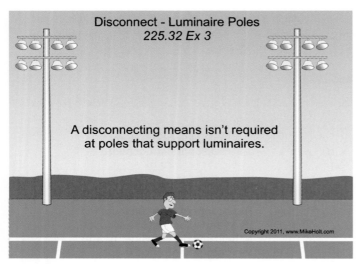

Figure 225–3

Author's Comment: According to Article 100, within sight means that it's visible and not more than 50 ft from one to the other.

Ex 4: The disconnecting means for a sign must be controlled by an externally operable switch or circuit breaker that opens all ungrounded conductors to the sign. The sign disconnecting means must be within sight of the sign, or the disconnecting means must be capable of being locked in the open position [600.6(A)]. **Figure 225–4**

225.33 Maximum Number of Disconnects.

(A) General. The building/structure disconnecting means can consist of no more than six switches or six circuit breakers in a single enclosure, or separate enclosures for each supply grouped in one location as permitted by 225.30. **Figure 225–5**

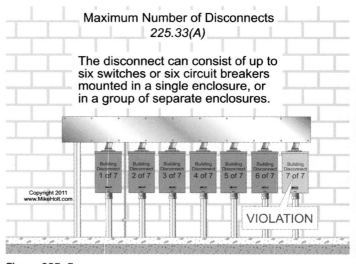

Figure 225–5

Essential Rule 22	225.34

225.34 Grouping of Disconnects.

(A) General. The building/structure disconnecting means must be grouped in one location, and they must be marked to indicate the loads they serve [110.22].

(B) Additional Disconnects. To minimize the possibility of accidental interruption of the critical power systems, the disconnecting means for a fire pump or for standby power must be located remotely away from the normal power disconnect.

Notes

Services

INTRODUCTION TO ARTICLE 230—SERVICES

This article covers the installation requirements for service conductors and service equipment. The requirements for service conductors differ from those for other conductors. For one thing, service conductors for one building/structure can't pass through the interior of another building or structure [230.3], and you apply different rules depending on whether a service conductor is inside or outside a building/structure. When are they "outside" as opposed to "inside?" The answer may seem obvious, but Section 230.6 should be consulted before making this decision.

Let's review the following definitions in Article 100 to understand when the requirements of Article 230 apply:

- Service Point—The point of connection between the serving utility and the premises wiring.
- Service Conductors—The conductors from the service point to the service disconnecting means. Service-entrance conductors can either be overhead or underground.
- Service Equipment—The necessary equipment, usually consisting of circuit breakers or switches and fuses and their accessories, connected to the load end of service conductors at a building or other structure, and intended to constitute the main control and cutoff of the electrical supply. Service equipment doesn't include individual meter socket enclosures [230.66].

After reviewing these definitions, you should understand that service conductors originate at the serving utility (service point) and terminate on the line side of the service disconnecting means. Conductors and equipment on the load side of service equipment are considered feeder conductors or branch circuits, and must be installed in accordance with Articles 210 and 215. They must also comply with Article 225 if they're outside branch circuits and feeders, such as the supply to a building/structure. Feeder conductors include: **Figures 230–1 and 230–2**

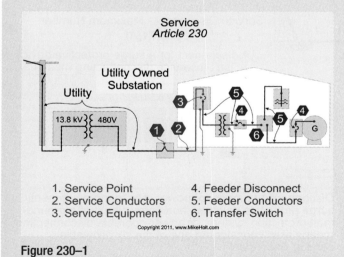

Service
Article 230

1. Service Point
2. Service Conductors
3. Service Equipment
4. Feeder Disconnect
5. Feeder Conductors
6. Transfer Switch

Copyright 2011, www.MikeHolt.com

Figure 230–1

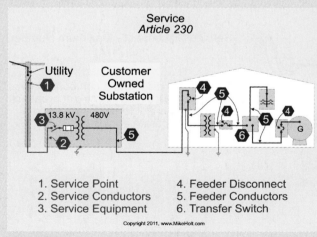

Service
Article 230

1. Service Point
2. Service Conductors
3. Service Equipment
4. Feeder Disconnect
5. Feeder Conductors
6. Transfer Switch

Copyright 2011, www.MikeHolt.com

Figure 230–2

- Secondary conductors from customer-owned transformers,
- Conductors from generators, UPS systems, or photovoltaic systems, and
- Conductors to remote buildings or structures

Article 230 consists of seven parts:

- Part I. General
- Part II. Overhead Service Conductors
- Part III. Underground Service Conductors
- Part IV. Service-Entrance Conductors
- Part V. Service Equipment
- Part VI. Disconnecting Means
- Part VIII. Overcurrent Protection

Essential Rule 23   230.71

230.71 Number of Disconnects.

(A) Maximum. There must be no more than six service disconnects for each service permitted by 230.2, or each set of service-entrance conductors permitted by 230.40 Ex 1, 3, 4, or 5. 230-71A0 02

The service disconnecting means for <u>each</u> service grouped in one location [230.72(A)] can consist of up to six switches or six circuit breakers mounted in a single enclosure, in a group of separate enclosures, or in or on a switchboard. **Figure 230–3**

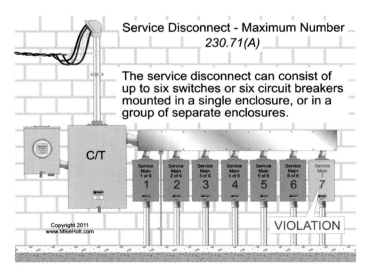

Figure 230–3

⚠️ **CAUTION:** *The rule is six disconnecting means for each service, not for each building. If the building has two services, then there can be a total of 12 service disconnects (six disconnects per service).* **Figure 230–4**

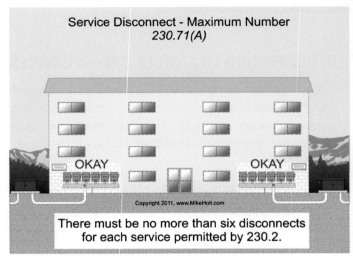

Figure 230–4

Disconnecting means used for the following are not considered a service disconnecting means:

(1) Power monitoring equipment

(2) Surge protective device(s). **Figure 230–5**

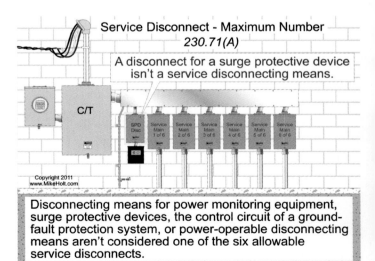

Figure 230–5

(3) Control circuit of the ground-fault protection system

(4) Power-operable service disconnecting means

> **Author's Comment:** A photovoltaic system disconnect connected to the supply-side of service equipment as permitted by 230.82(6) and 705.12(A) is not considered a service disconnecting means. **Figure 230–6**

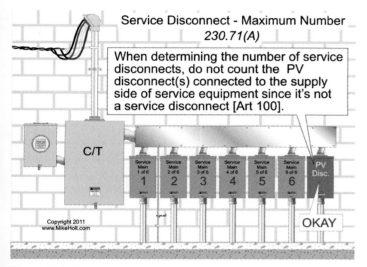

Service Disconnect - Maximum Number
230.71(A)

When determining the number of service disconnects, do not count the PV disconnect(s) connected to the supply side of service equipment since it's not a service disconnect [Art 100].

C/T

Service Main 1 of 6 **1**
Service Main 2 of 6 **2**
Service Main 3 of 6 **3**
Service Main 4 of 6 **4**
Service Main 5 of 6 **5**
Service Main 6 of 6 **6**
PV Disc.

OKAY

Copyright 2011
www.MikeHolt.com

Figure 230–6

Essential Rule 24   230.72

230.72 Grouping of Disconnects.

(A) Two to Six Disconnects. The service disconnecting means for each service must be grouped.

(B) Additional Service Disconnecting Means. To minimize the possibility of accidental interruption of power, the disconnecting means for fire pumps [Article 695], emergency [Article 700], legally required standby [Article 701], or optional standby [Article 702] systems must be located remote from the one to six service disconnects for normal service.

> **Author's Comment:** Because emergency systems are just as important as fire pumps and standby systems, they need to have the same safety precautions to prevent unintended interruption of the supply of electricity.

(C) Access to Occupants. In a multiple-occupancy building, each occupant must have access to their service disconnecting means.

Ex: In multiple-occupancy buildings where electrical maintenance is provided by continuous building management, the service disconnecting means can be accessible only to building management personnel.

Notes

ARTICLE 240

Overcurrent Protection

INTRODUCTION TO ARTICLE 240—OVERCURRENT PROTECTION

This article provides the requirements for selecting and installing overcurrent devices. Overcurrent exists when current exceeds the rating of equipment or the ampacity of a conductor. This can be due to an overload, short circuit, or ground fault [Article 100].

Overload. An overload is a condition where equipment or conductors carry current exceeding their current rating [Article 100]. A fault, such as a short circuit or ground fault, isn't an overload. An example of an overload is plugging two 12.50A (1,500W) hair dryers into a 20A branch circuit.

Ground Fault. A ground fault is an unintentional, electrically conducting connection between an ungrounded conductor of an electrical circuit and the normally noncurrent-carrying conductors, metallic enclosures, metallic raceways, metallic equipment, or the earth [Article 100]. During the period of a ground fault, dangerous voltages will be present on metal parts until the circuit overcurrent device opens.

Short Circuit. A short circuit is the unintentional electrical connection between any two normally current-carrying conductors of an electrical circuit, either line-to-line or line-to-neutral.

Overcurrent Devices Protect Conductors and Equipment. Selecting the proper overcurrent protection for a specific circuit can become more complicated than it sounds. The general rule for overcurrent protection is that conductors must be protected in accordance with their ampacities at the point where they receive their supply [240.4and 240.21]. There are many special cases that deviate from this basic rule, such as the overcurrent protection limitations for small conductors [240.4(D)] and the rules for specific conductor applications found in other articles, as listed in Table 240.4(G). There are also a number of rules allowing tap conductors in specific situations [240.21(B)]. Article 240 even has limits on where overcurrent devices are allowed to be located [240.24].

An overcurrent device must be capable of opening a circuit when an overcurrent situation occurs, and must also have an interrupting rating sufficient to avoid damage in fault conditions [110.9]. Carefully study the provisions of this article to be sure you provide sufficient overcurrent protection in the correct location.

Essential Rule 25	240.4

240.4 Protection of Conductors. Except as permitted by (A) through (G), conductors must be protected against overcurrent in accordance with their ampacity after ampacity correction and adjustment as specified in 310.15. **Figure 240–1**

(A) Power Loss Hazard. Conductor overload protection isn't required, but short-circuit protection is required where the interruption of the circuit will create a hazard; such as in a material-handling electromagnet circuit or fire pump circuit.

(B) Overcurrent Devices Rated 800A or Less. The next higher standard rating of overcurrent device listed in 240.6 (above the ampacity of the ungrounded conductors being protected) is permitted, provided all of the following conditions are met:

(1) The conductors aren't part of a branch circuit supplying more than one receptacle for cord-and-plug-connected loads.

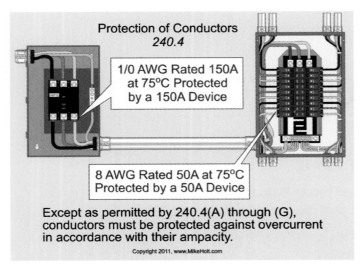

Figure 240-1

(2) The ampacity of a conductor, after the application of ambient temperature correction [310.15(B)(2)(a)], conductor bundling adjustment [310.15(B)(3)(a)], or both, doesn't correspond with the standard rating of a fuse or circuit breaker in 240.6(A).

(3) The overcurrent device rating doesn't exceed 800A.

Example: A 400A overcurrent device can protect 500 kcmil conductors, where each conductor has an ampacity of 380A at 75°C, in accordance with Table 310.15(B)(16). **Figure 240-2**

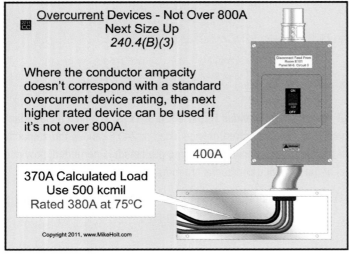

Figure 240-2

Author's Comment: This "next size up" rule doesn't apply to feeder tap conductors [240.21(B)] or transformer secondary conductors [240.21(C)].

(C) Overcurrent Devices Rated Over 800A. If the circuit's overcurrent device exceeds 800A, the conductor ampacity (after the application of ambient temperature correction [310.15(B)(2)(a)], conductor bundling adjustment [310.15(B)(3)(a)], or both, must have a rating of not less than the rating of the overcurrent device defined in 240.6.

Example: A 1,200A overcurrent device can protect three sets of 600 kcmil conductors per phase, where each conductor has an ampacity of 420A at 75°C, in accordance with Table 310.15(B)(16). **Figure 240-3**

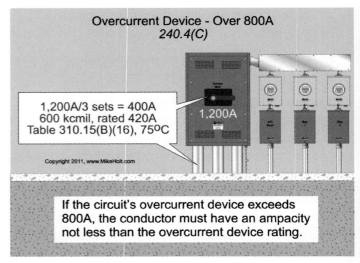

Figure 240-3

(D) Small Conductors. Unless specifically permitted in 240.4(E) or (G), overcurrent protection must not exceed the following: **Figure 240-4**

(1) 18 AWG Copper—7A

(2) 16 AWG Copper—10A

(3) 14 AWG Copper—15A

(4) 12 AWG Aluminum/Copper-Clad Aluminum—15A

(5) 12 AWG Copper—20A

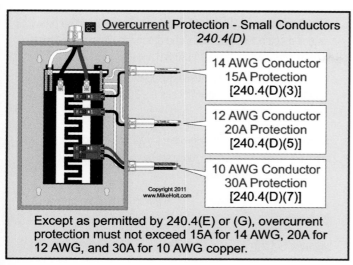

Figure 240–4

(6) 10 AWG Aluminum/Copper-Clad Aluminum—25A

(7) 10 AWG Copper—30A

(E) Tap Conductors. Tap conductors must be protected against overcurrent as follows:

(1) Household Ranges and Cooking Appliances and Other Loads, 210.19(A)(3) and (4)

(2) Fixture Wire, 240.5(B)(2)

(3) Location in Circuit, 240.21

(4) Reduction in Ampacity Size of Busway, 368.17(B)

(5) Feeder or Branch Circuits (busway taps), 368.17(C)

(6) Single Motor Taps, 430.53(D)

(F) Transformer Secondary Conductors. The primary overcurrent device sized in accordance with 450.3(B) is considered suitable to protect the secondary conductors of a 2-wire (single voltage) system, provided the primary overcurrent device doesn't exceed the value determined by multiplying the secondary conductor ampacity by the secondary-to-primary transformer voltage ratio.

Question: What's the minimum secondary conductor size required for a 2-wire, 480V to 120V transformer rated 1.50 kVA? **Figure 240–5**

(a) 16 AWG   (b) 14 AWG   (c) 12 AWG   (d) 10 AWG

Answer: (b) 14 AWG

Primary Current = VA/E

VA = 1,500 VA

E = 480V

Primary Current = 1,500 VA/480V
Primary Current = 3.13A

Primary Protection [450.3(B)] = 3.13A x 1.67
Primary Protection = 5.22A or 5A Fuse

Secondary Current = 1,500 VA/120V
Secondary Current = 12.50A

Secondary Conductor = 14 AWG, rated 20A at 75°C,
[Table 310.15(B)(16)]

The 5A primary overcurrent device can be used to protect 14 AWG secondary conductors because it doesn't exceed the value determined by multiplying the secondary conductor ampacity by the secondary-to-primary transformer voltage ratio (5A = 20A x 120V/480V).

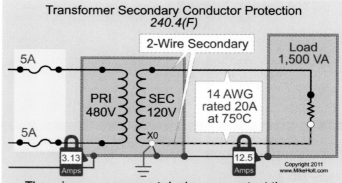

Figure 240–5

(G) Overcurrent Protection for Specific Applications. Overcurrent protection for specific equipment and conductors must comply with the requirements referenced in Table 240.4(G).

Air-Conditioning and Refrigeration [Article 440]. Air-conditioning and refrigeration equipment, and their circuit conductors, must be protected against overcurrent in accordance with 440.22.

> **Author's Comment:** Typically, the branch-circuit ampacity and protection size is marked on the equipment nameplate [440.4(A)].

> **Question:** What size branch-circuit overcurrent device is required for an air conditioner (18A) when the nameplate indicates the minimum circuit ampacity is 23A, with maximum overcurrent protection of 40A? **Figure 240–6**
>
> (a) 12 AWG, 40A protection   (b) 12 AWG, 50A protection
> (c) 12 AWG, 60A protection   (d) 12 AWG, 70A protection
>
> **Answer:** (a) 12 AWG, 40A protection

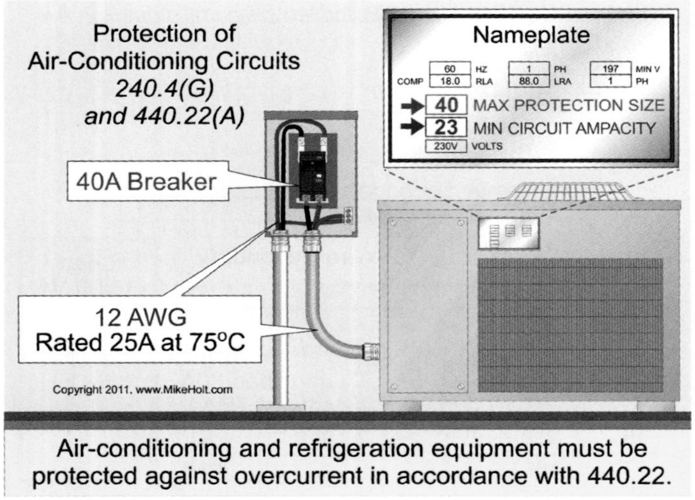

Protection of Air-Conditioning Circuits 240.4(G) and 440.22(A)

Nameplate

COMP 60 HZ | 18.0 RLA | 1 PH | 88.0 LRA | 197 MIN V | 1 PH

→ **40** MAX PROTECTION SIZE
→ **23** MIN CIRCUIT AMPACITY
230V VOLTS

40A Breaker

12 AWG Rated 25A at 75°C

Copyright 2011, www.MikeHolt.com

Air-conditioning and refrigeration equipment must be protected against overcurrent in accordance with 440.22.

Figure 240–6

> **Author's Comment:** Air-conditioning and refrigeration nameplate values are calculated by the manufacturer according to the following:
>
> • Branch-Circuit Conductor Size [440.32]
>   18A x 1.25 = 22.50A, 12 AWG rated 25A at 75°C
> • Branch-Circuit Protection Size [440.22(A)]
>   18A x 2.25 = 40.50A, 40A maximum overcurrent protection size [240.6(A)]

• Motors [Article 430]. Motor circuit conductors must be protected against short circuits and ground faults in accordance with 430.52 and 430.62 [430.51].

If the nameplate calls for fuses, fuses must be used to comply with the manufacturer's instructions [110.3(B)].

> **Question:** What size branch-circuit conductor and overcurrent device (circuit breaker) is required for a 7½ hp, 230V, three-phase motor? **Figure 240–7**
>
> (a) 10 AWG, 50A breaker   (b) 10 AWG, 60A breaker
> (c) a or b   (d) none of these
>
> **Answer:** (c) a or b
>
> Step 1: Determine the branch-circuit conductor size [Table 310.15(B)(16), 430.22, and Table 430.250]:
>
>   FLC = 28A [Table 430-250]
>
>   22A x 1.25 = 28A, 10 AWG, rated 35A at 75°C
>
> Step 2: Determine the branch-circuit protection size [240.6(A), 430.52(C)(1) Ex 1, and Table 430.250].
>
>   Inverse Time Breaker: 22A x 2.50 = 55A
>   Next size up = 60A

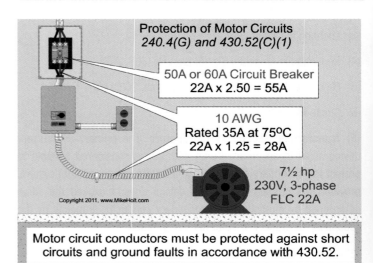

Protection of Motor Circuits
240.4(G) and 430.52(C)(1)

50A or 60A Circuit Breaker
22A x 2.50 = 55A

10 AWG
Rated 35A at 75°C
22A x 1.25 = 28A

7½ hp
230V, 3-phase
FLC 22A

Copyright 2011, www.MikeHolt.com

Motor circuit conductors must be protected against short circuits and ground faults in accordance with 430.52.

Figure 240–7

Motor Control [Article 430]. Motor control circuit conductors must be sized and protected in accordance with 430.72.

Remote-Control, Signaling, and Power-Limited Circuits [Article 725]. Remote-control, signaling, and power-limited circuit conductors must be protected against overcurrent in accordance with 725.43.

Essential Rule 26   240.21

PART II. LOCATION

240.21 Overcurrent Protection Location in Circuit.

Except as permitted by (A) through (H), overcurrent devices must be placed at the point where the branch circuit or feeder conductors receive their power. Taps and transformer secondary conductors aren't permitted to supply another conductor (tapping a tap isn't permitted). **Figure 240–8**

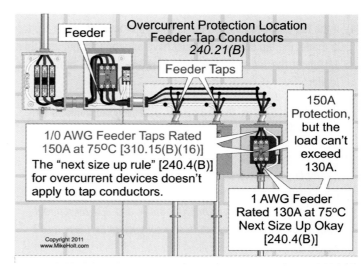

Figure 240-9

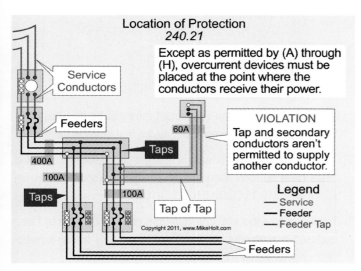

Figure 240–8

(A) Branch-Circuit Taps. Branch-circuit taps are permitted in accordance with 210.19.

(B) Feeder Taps. Conductors can be tapped to a feeder as specified in 240.21(B)(1) through (B)(5). The "next size up protection rule" of 240.4(B) is not permitted for tap conductors. **Figure 240-9**

(1) 10-Foot Feeder Tap. Feeder tap conductors up to 10 ft long are permitted without overcurrent protection at the tap location if the tap conductors comply with the following:

(1) The ampacity of the tap conductor must not be less than: **Figure 240–10**

   a. The calculated load in accordance with Article 220, and

   b. The rating of the device or overcurrent device supplied by the tap conductors.

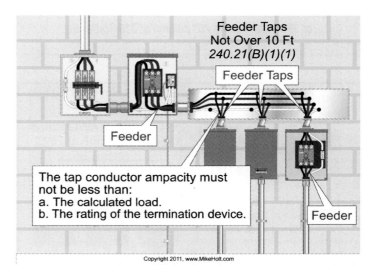

Figure 240–10

(2) The tap conductors must not extend beyond the equipment they supply.

(3) The tap conductors are installed in a raceway if they leave the enclosure.

(4) If the tap conductors leave the enclosure or vault in which the tap is made, the tap conductors must have an ampacity not less than 1/10th of the rating of the overcurrent device that protects the feeder.

Note: See 408.36 for the overcurrent protection requirements for panelboards.

> *Example: A 400A breaker protects a set of 500 kcmil feeder conductors. There are three taps fed from the 500 kcmil feeders that supply disconnects with 200A, 150A, and 30A overcurrent devices. What are the minimum size conductors for these taps?* **Figure 240–11**
>
> - *200A: 3/0 AWG is rated 200A at 75°, and is greater than 10 percent of the ampacity of 500 kcmil, which is rated 380A at 75°.*
>
> - *150A: 1/0 AWG is rated 150A at 75°, and is greater than 10 percent of the ampacity of 500 kcmil, which is rated 380A at 75°.*
>
> - *30A: 8 AWG is rated 50A at 75°, and is greater than 10 percent of the ampacity of 500 kcmil, which is rated 380A at 75°. Anything smaller than 8 AWG can't be used, as it will have an ampacity of less than 10 percent of 380A (38A) in the 75° column of 310.15(B)(16).*

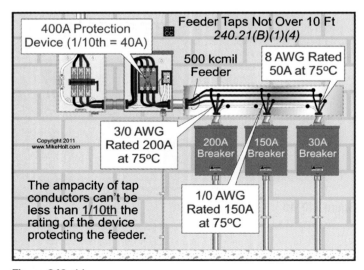

Figure 240–11

(2) 25-Foot Feeder Tap. Feeder tap conductors up to 25 ft long are permitted without overcurrent protection at the tap location if the tap conductors comply with the following: **Figure 240–12**

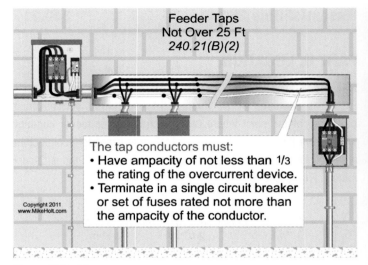

Figure 240–12

(1) The ampacity of the tap conductors must not be less than one-third the rating of the overcurrent device that protects the feeder.

(2) The tap conductors terminate in a single circuit breaker, or set of fuses rated no more than the tap conductor ampacity in accordance with 310.15 [Table 310.15(B)(16)].

(3) The tap conductors are protected from physical damage by being enclosed in a manner approved by the authority having jurisdiction, such as within a raceway.

(3) Taps Supplying a Transformer. Feeder tap conductors that supply a transformer are permitted if the tap complies with the following:

(1) The primary tap conductors must have an ampacity not less than one-third the rating of the overcurrent device.

(2) The secondary conductors must have an ampacity that, when multiplied by the ratio of the primary-to-secondary voltage, is at least one-third the rating of the overcurrent device that protects the feeder conductors.

(3) The total length of the primary and secondary conductors must not exceed 25 ft.

(4) Primary and secondary conductors are protected from physical damage by being enclosed in a manner approved by the authority having jurisdiction, such as within a raceway.

(5) Secondary conductors terminate in a single circuit breaker or set of fuses rated no more than the tap conductor ampacity in accordance with 310.15 [Table 310.15(B)(16)].

(5) Outside Feeder Taps of Unlimited Length. Outside feeder tap conductors can be of unlimited length, without overcurrent protection at the point they receive their supply, if they comply with the following: **Figure 240–13**

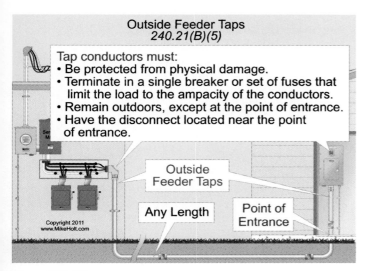

Outside Feeder Taps
240.21(B)(5)

Tap conductors must:
• Be protected from physical damage.
• Terminate in a single breaker or set of fuses that limit the load to the ampacity of the conductors.
• Remain outdoors, except at the point of entrance.
• Have the disconnect located near the point of entrance.

Outside Feeder Taps

Any Length

Point of Entrance

Copyright 2011
www.MikeHolt.com

Figure 240–13

(1) The tap conductors are suitably protected from physical damage in a raceway or manner approved by the authority having jurisdiction.

(2) The tap conductors must terminate at a single circuit breaker or a single set of fuses that limits the load to the ampacity of the conductors.

(3) The overcurrent device for the tap conductors is an integral part of the disconnecting means, or it's located immediately adjacent to it.

(4) The disconnecting means is located at a readily accessible location, either outside the building/structure, or nearest the point of entry of the conductors.

(C) Transformer Secondary Conductors. A set of conductors supplying single or separate loads is permitted to be connected to a transformer secondary without overcurrent protection in accordance with (1) through (6).

Author's Comment: The permission of the 'next size up' protection rule when the conductor ampacity does not correspond with the standard size overcurrent device of 240.4(B) does not apply to transformer secondary conductors. **Figure 240–14**

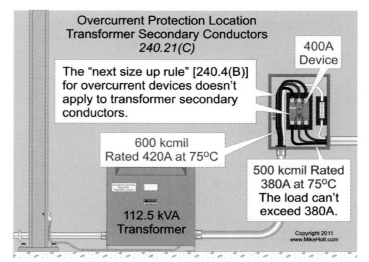

Overcurrent Protection Location
Transformer Secondary Conductors
240.21(C)

400A Device

The "next size up rule" [240.4(B)] for overcurrent devices doesn't apply to transformer secondary conductors.

600 kcmil
Rated 420A at 75°C

500 kcmil Rated 380A at 75°C
The load can't exceed 380A.

112.5 kVA
Transformer

Copyright 2011
www.MikeHolt.com

Figure 240–14

(1) Protection by Primary Overcurrent Device. The primary overcurrent device sized in accordance with 450.3(B) is considered suitable to protect the secondary conductors of a 2-wire (single-voltage) system, provided the primary overcurrent device doesn't exceed the value determined by multiplying the secondary conductor ampacity by the secondary-to-primary transformer voltage ratio.

Question: What's the minimum size secondary conductor required for a 2-wire, 480V to 120V transformer rated 1.50 kVA? **Figure 240–15**

(a) 16 AWG   (b) 14 AWG   (c) 12 AWG   (d) 10 AWG

Answer: (b) 14 AWG

Primary Current = VA/E

VA = 1,500 VA

E = 480V

Primary Current = 1,500 VA/480V

Primary Current = 3.13A

Primary Protection [450.3(B)] = 3.13A x 1.67

Primary Protection [450.3(B)] = 5.22A or 5A Fuse

Secondary Current = 1,500 VA/120V

Secondary Current = 12.50A

Secondary Conductor = 14 AWG, rated 20A at 60°C, [Table 310.15(B)(16)]

The 5A primary overcurrent device can be used to protect 14 AWG secondary conductors because it doesn't exceed the value determined by multiplying the secondary conductor ampacity by the secondary-to-primary transformer voltage ratio (5A = 20A x 120V/480V).

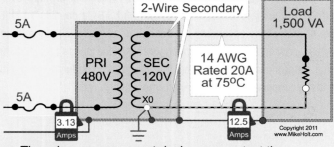

The primary overcurrent device can protect the secondary conductors of a 2-wire system if the primary device doesn't exceed the value determined by multiplying the secondary conductor ampacity by the secondary-to-primary voltage ratio.

Figure 240–15

(2) 10 Ft Secondary Conductors. Secondary conductors can be run up to 10 ft without overcurrent protection if installed as follows:

(1) The ampacity of the secondary conductor must not be less than: **Figure 240–16**

   a. The calculated load in accordance with Article 220,

   b. The rating of the device supplied by the secondary conductors or the overcurrent device at the termination of the secondary conductors, and

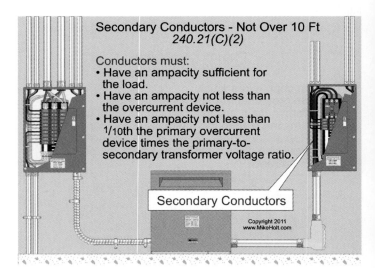

Figure 240–16

(2) The secondary conductors must not extend beyond the switchboard, panelboard, disconnecting means, or control devices they supply.

(3) The secondary conductors are enclosed in a raceway.

(4) Not less than one-tenth the rating of the overcurrent device protecting the primary of the transformer, multiplied by the primary-to-secondary transformer voltage ratio.

(4) Outside Secondary Conductors of Unlimited Length. Outside secondary conductors can be of unlimited length, without overcurrent protection at the point they receive their supply, if they're installed as follows: **Figure 240–17**

(1) The conductors are suitably protected from physical damage in a raceway or manner approved by the authority having jurisdiction.

(2) The conductors must terminate at a single circuit breaker or a single set of fuses that limit the load to the ampacity of the conductors.

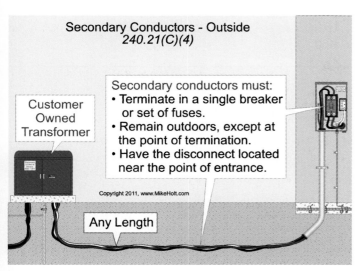

Secondary Conductors - Outside
240.21(C)(4)

Customer Owned Transformer

Secondary conductors must:
• Terminate in a single breaker or set of fuses.
• Remain outdoors, except at the point of termination.
• Have the disconnect located near the point of entrance.

Copyright 2011, www.MikeHolt.com

Any Length

Figure 240–17

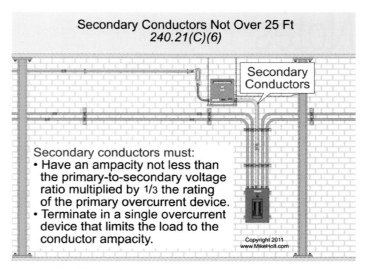

Secondary Conductors Not Over 25 Ft
240.21(C)(6)

Secondary Conductors

Secondary conductors must:
• Have an ampacity not less than the primary-to-secondary voltage ratio multiplied by 1/3 the rating of the primary overcurrent device.
• Terminate in a single overcurrent device that limits the load to the conductor ampacity.

Copyright 2011 www.MikeHolt.com

Figure 240–18

(3) The overcurrent device for the ungrounded conductors is an integral part of a disconnecting means or it's located immediately adjacent thereto.

(4) The disconnecting means is located at a readily accessible location that complies with one of the following:

a. Outside of a building/structure.

b. Inside, nearest the point of entrance of the conductors.

c. If installed in accordance with 230.6, nearest the point of entrance of the conductors.

(5) Secondary Conductors from a Feeder Tapped Transformer. Transformer secondary conductors must be installed in accordance with 240.21(B)(3).

(6) 25-Foot Secondary Conductor. Secondary conductors can be run up to 25 ft without overcurrent protection if they comply with all of the following: **Figure 240–18**

(1) The secondary conductors have an ampacity not less than the value of the primary-to-secondary voltage ratio multiplied by one-third of the rating of the overcurrent device that protects the primary of the transformer.

(2) Secondary conductors terminate in a single circuit breaker or set of fuses rated no more than the tap conductor ampacity in accordance with 310.15 [Table 310.15(B)(16)].

(3) The secondary conductors are protected from physical damage by being enclosed in a manner approved by the authority having jurisdiction, such as within a raceway.

(D) Service Conductors. Service conductors are protected against overload by the service disconnect overcurrent device in accordance with 230.91.

(H) Battery Conductors. Overcurrent protection is installed as close as practicable to the storage battery terminals.

Notes

Grounding and Bonding

INTRODUCTION TO ARTICLE 250—GROUNDING AND BONDING

No other article can match Article 250 for misapplication, violation, and misinterpretation. Terminology used in this article has been a source for much confusion, but that has improved during the last few *NEC* revisions. It's very important to understand the difference between grounding and bonding in order to correctly apply the provisions of Article 250. Pay careful attention to the definitions that apply to grounding and bonding both here and in Article 100 as you begin the study of this important article. Article 250 covers the grounding requirements for providing a path to the earth to reduce overvoltage from lightning, and the bonding requirements for a low-impedance fault current path back to the source of the electrical supply to facilitate the operation of overcurrent devices in the event of a ground fault.

Over the past five Code cycles, this article was extensively revised to organize it better and make it easier to understand and implement. It's arranged in a logical manner, so it's a good idea to just read through Article 250 to get a big picture view—after you review the definitions. Next, study the article closely so you understand the details. The illustrations will help you understand the key points.

Essential Rule 27	250.2

250.2 Definitions.

Bonding Jumper, Supply-Side. A conductor on the supply side or within a service or separately derived system to ensure the electrical conductivity between metal parts required to be electrically connected. **Figures 250–1 and 250–2**

Effective Ground-Fault Current Path. An intentionally constructed low-impedance conductive path designed to carry fault current from the point of a ground fault on a wiring system to the electrical supply source. **Figure 250–3**

> **Author's Comment:** In **Figure 250–3**, EGC represents the equipment grounding conductor [259.118], MBJ represents the main bonding jumper, SNC represents the service neutral conductor (grounded service conductor), GEC represents the grounding electrode conductor.

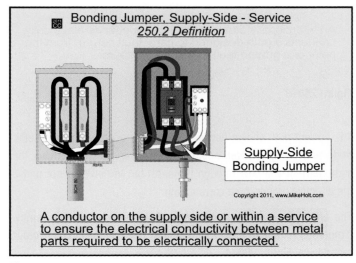

Bonding Jumper, Supply-Side - Service
250.2 Definition

Supply-Side Bonding Jumper

Copyright 2011, www.MikeHolt.com

A conductor on the supply side or within a service to ensure the electrical conductivity between metal parts required to be electrically connected.

Figure 250–1

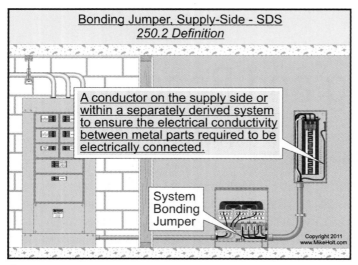

Figure 250–2

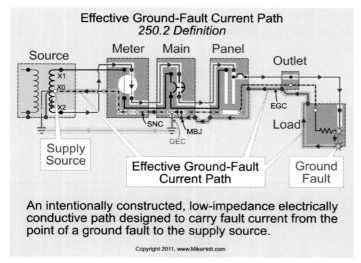

Figure 250–3

The current path shown between the supply source grounding electrode and the grounding electrode at the service main shows that some current will flow through the earth but the earth is not part of the effective ground-fault current path.

The effective ground-fault current path is intended to help remove dangerous voltage from a ground fault by opening the circuit overcurrent device. **Figure 250–4**

Ground-Fault Current Path. An electrically conductive path from a ground fault to the electrical supply source.

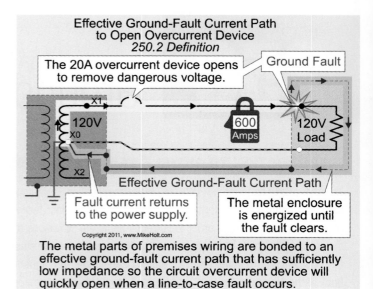

Figure 250–4

Note: The ground-fault current path could be metal raceways, cable sheaths, electrical equipment, or other electrically conductive materials, such as metallic water or gas piping, steel-framing members, metal ducting, reinforcing steel, or the shields of communications cables. **Figure 250–5**

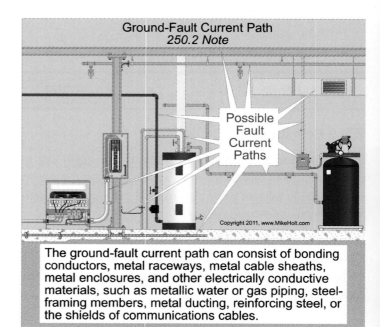

Figure 250–5

Author's Comment: The difference between an "effective ground-fault current path" and a "ground-fault current path" is the effective ground-fault current path is "intentionally" constructed to provide a low-impedance fault current path to the electrical supply source for the purpose of clearing a ground fault. A ground-fault current path is all of the available conductive paths over which fault current flows on its return to the electrical supply source during a ground fault.

Essential Rule 28   250.4

250.4 General Requirements for Grounding and Bonding.

(A) Solidly Grounded Systems.

(1) Electrical System Grounding. Electrical power systems, such as the secondary winding of a transformer are grounded (connected to the earth) to limit the voltage induced by lightning, line surges, or unintentional contact by higher-voltage lines. **Figure 250–6**

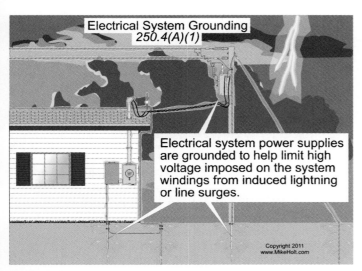

Figure 250–6

Author's Comment: System grounding helps reduce fires in buildings as well as voltage stress on electrical insulation, thereby ensuring longer insulation life for motors, transformers, and other system components. **Figure 250–7**

Note: An important consideration for limiting imposed voltage is to remember that grounding electrode conductors shouldn't be any longer than necessary and unnecessary bends and loops should be avoided. **Figure 250–8**

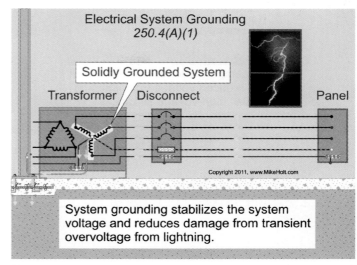

Figure 250–7

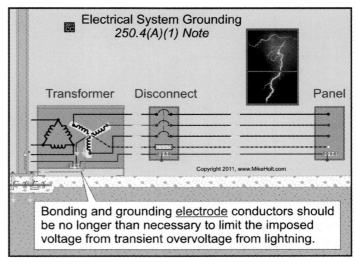

Figure 250–8

(2) Equipment Grounding. Metal parts of electrical equipment are grounded (connected to the earth) to reduce induced voltage on metal parts from exterior lightning so as to prevent fires from an arc within the building/structure. **Figure 250–9**

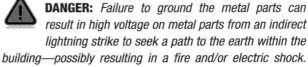 **DANGER:** *Failure to ground the metal parts can result in high voltage on metal parts from an indirect lightning strike to seek a path to the earth within the building—possibly resulting in a fire and/or electric shock.* **Figure 250–10**

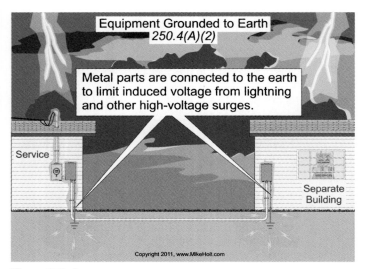

Figure 250–9

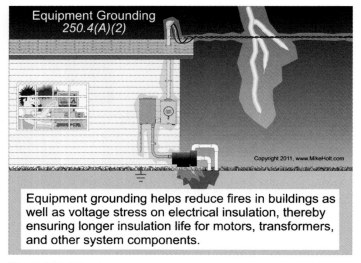

Figure 250–10

Author's Comment: Grounding metal parts helps drain off static electricity charges before flashover potential is reached. Static grounding is often used in areas where the discharge (arcing) of the voltage buildup (static) can cause dangerous or undesirable conditions [500.4 Note 3].

⚠ **DANGER:** *Because the contact resistance of an electrode to the earth is so high, very little fault current returns to the power supply if the earth is the only fault current return path. Result—the circuit overcurrent device won't open and clear the ground fault, and all metal parts associated with the electrical installation, metal piping, and structural building steel will become and remain energized.* **Figure 250–11**

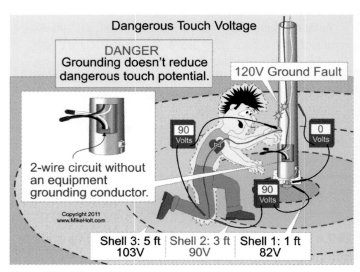

Figure 250–11

(3) Equipment Bonding. Metal parts of electrical raceways, cables, enclosures, and equipment must be connected to the supply source via the effective ground-fault current path. **Figures 250–12 and 250–13**

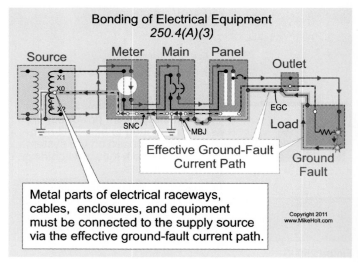

Figure 250–12

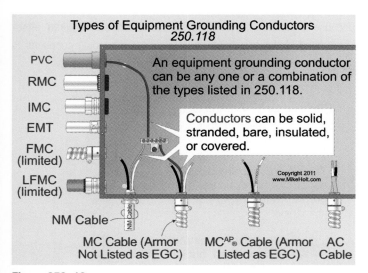

Types of Equipment Grounding Conductors
250.118

PVC
RMC
IMC
EMT
FMC (limited)
LFMC (limited)

An equipment grounding conductor can be any one or a combination of the types listed in 250.118.

Conductors can be solid, stranded, bare, insulated, or covered.

Copyright 2011
www.MikeHolt.com

NM Cable
MC Cable (Armor Not Listed as EGC)
MC^AP® Cable (Armor Listed as EGC)
AC Cable

Figure 250–13

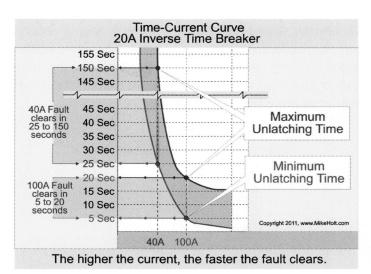

Time-Current Curve
20A Inverse Time Breaker

155 Sec
150 Sec
145 Sec

40A Fault clears in 25 to 150 seconds
45 Sec
40 Sec
35 Sec
30 Sec
25 Sec

Maximum Unlatching Time

100A Fault clears in 5 to 20 seconds
20 Sec
15 Sec
10 Sec
5 Sec

Minimum Unlatching Time

Copyright 2011, www.MikeHolt.com

40A   100A

The higher the current, the faster the fault clears.

Figure 250–15

Author's Comments:

- To quickly remove dangerous touch voltage on metal parts from a ground fault, the fault current path must have sufficiently low impedance to the source so that fault current will quickly rise to a level that will open the branch-circuit overcurrent device. **Figure 250–14**

- The time it takes for an overcurrent device to open is inversely proportional to the magnitude of the fault current. This means the higher the ground-fault current value, the less time it will take for the overcurrent device to open and clear the fault. For example, a 20A circuit with an overload of 40A (two times the 20A rating) takes 25 to 150 seconds to open the overcurrent device. At 100A (five times the 20A rating) the 20A breaker trips in 5 to 20 seconds. **Figure 250–15**

(4) Bonding Conductive Materials. Electrically conductive materials such as metal water piping systems, metal sprinkler piping, metal gas piping, and other metal-piping systems, as well as exposed structural steel members likely to become energized, must be connected to the supply source via an equipment grounding conductor of a type recognized in 250.118. **Figure 250–16**

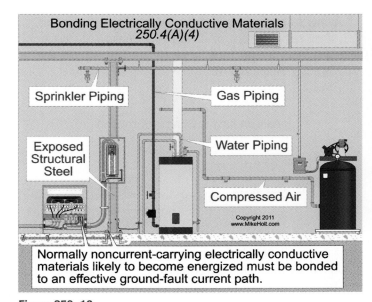

Bonding Electrically Conductive Materials
250.4(A)(4)

Sprinkler Piping
Gas Piping
Exposed Structural Steel
Water Piping
Compressed Air

Copyright 2011
www.MikeHolt.com

Normally noncurrent-carrying electrically conductive materials likely to become energized must be bonded to an effective ground-fault current path.

Figure 250–16

Author's Comment: The phrase "likely to become energized" is subject to interpretation by the authority having jurisdiction.

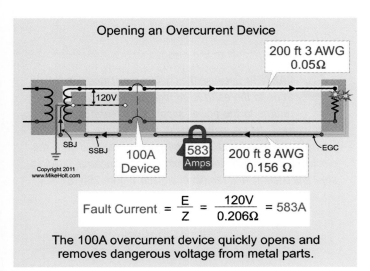

Opening an Overcurrent Device

200 ft 3 AWG
0.05Ω

120V

SBJ   SSBJ
100A Device
583 Amps
200 ft 8 AWG
0.156 Ω
EGC

Copyright 2011
www.MikeHolt.com

$$\text{Fault Current} = \frac{E}{Z} = \frac{120V}{0.206\Omega} = 583A$$

The 100A overcurrent device quickly opens and removes dangerous voltage from metal parts.

Figure 250–14

(5) Effective Ground-Fault Current Path. Metal parts of electrical raceways, cables, enclosures, or equipment must be bonded together and to the supply system in a manner that creates a low-impedance path for ground-fault current that facilitates the operation of the circuit overcurrent device. **Figure 250–17**

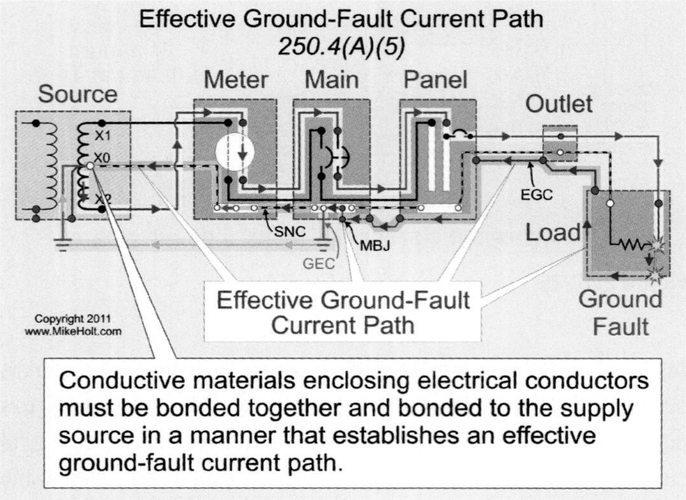

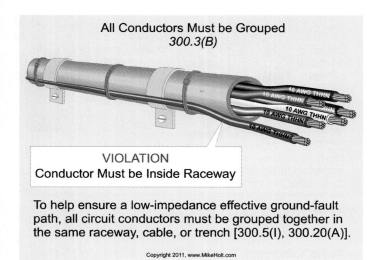

Effective Ground-Fault Current Path
250.4(A)(5)

Conductive materials enclosing electrical conductors must be bonded together and bonded to the supply source in a manner that establishes an effective ground-fault current path.

Figure 250–17

Author's Comment: To ensure a low-impedance ground-fault current path, all circuit conductors must be grouped together in the same raceway, cable, or trench [300.3(B), 300.5(I), and 300.20(A)]. **Figure 250–18**

All Conductors Must be Grouped
300.3(B)

VIOLATION
Conductor Must be Inside Raceway

To help ensure a low-impedance effective ground-fault path, all circuit conductors must be grouped together in the same raceway, cable, or trench [300.5(I), 300.20(A)].

Figure 250–18

Because the earth isn't suitable to serve as the required effective ground-fault current path, an equipment grounding conductor is required to be installed with all circuits. **Figure 250–19**

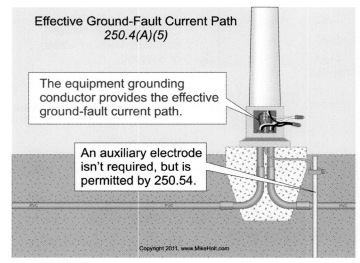

Effective Ground-Fault Current Path
250.4(A)(5)

The equipment grounding conductor provides the effective ground-fault current path.

An auxiliary electrode isn't required, but is permitted by 250.54.

Figure 250–19

Question: *What's the maximum fault current that can flow through the earth to the power supply from a 120V ground fault to metal parts of a light pole that's grounded (connected to the earth) via a ground rod having a contact resistance to the earth of 25 ohms?* **Figure 250–20**

(a) 4.80A   (b) 20A   (c) 40A   (d) 100A

Answer: *(a) 4.80A*

$I = E/R$
$I = 120V/25\ ohms$
$I = 4.80A$

⚠ **DANGER:** *Because the contact resistance of an electrode to the earth is so high, very little fault current returns to the power supply if the earth is the only fault current return path. Result—the circuit overcurrent device won't open and all metal parts associated with the electrical installation, metal piping, and structural building steel will become and remain energized.* **Figure 250–21**

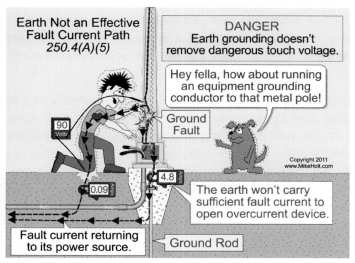

Figure 250–20

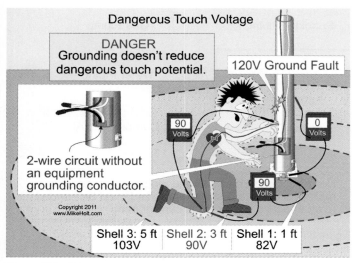

Figure 250–21

EARTH SHELLS

According to ANSI/IEEE 142, *Recommended Practice for Grounding of Industrial and Commercial Power Systems* (Green Book) [4.1.1], the resistance of the soil outward from a ground rod is equal to the sum of the series resistances of the earth shells. The shell nearest the rod has the highest resistance and each successive shell has progressively larger areas and progressively lower resistances. Don't be concerned if you don't understand this statement; just review the table below. **Figure 250–22**

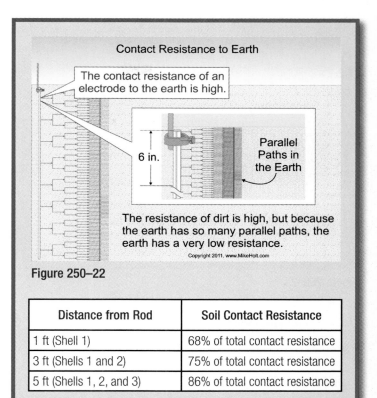

Figure 250–22

Distance from Rod	Soil Contact Resistance
1 ft (Shell 1)	68% of total contact resistance
3 ft (Shells 1 and 2)	75% of total contact resistance
5 ft (Shells 1, 2, and 3)	86% of total contact resistance

Since voltage is directly proportional to resistance, the voltage gradient of the earth around an energized ground rod will be as follows, assuming a 120V ground fault:

Distance from Rod	Soil Contact Resistance	Voltage Gradient
1 ft (Shell 1)	68%	82V
3 ft (Shells 1 and 2)	75%	90V
5 ft (Shells 1, 2, and 3)	86%	103V

(B) Ungrounded Systems.

Author's Comment: Ungrounded systems are those systems with no connection to the ground or to a conductive body that extends the ground connection [Article 100]. **Figure 250–23**

(1) Equipment Grounding. Metal parts of electrical equipment are grounded (connected to the earth) to reduce induced voltage on metal parts from exterior lightning so as to prevent fires from an arc within the building/structure. **Figure 250–24**

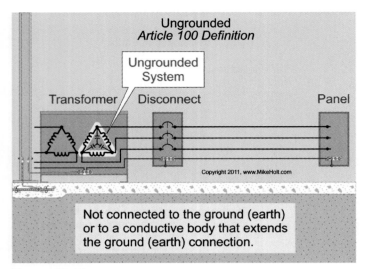

Figure 250–23

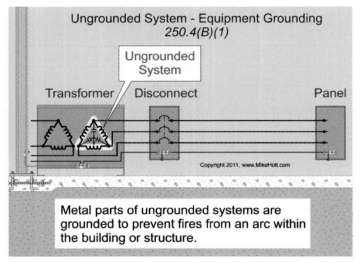

Figure 250–24

Author's Comment: Grounding metal parts helps drain off static electricity charges before an electric arc takes place (flashover potential). Static grounding is often used in areas where the discharge (arcing) of the voltage buildup (static) can cause dangerous or undesirable conditions [500.4 Note 3].

 CAUTION: *Connecting metal parts to the earth (grounding) serves no purpose in electrical shock protection.*

(2) Equipment Bonding. Metal parts of electrical raceways, cables, enclosures, or equipment must be bonded together in a manner that creates a low-impedance path for ground-fault current to facilitate the operation of the circuit overcurrent device.

The fault current path must be capable of safely carrying the maximum ground-fault current likely to be imposed on it from any point on the wiring system where a ground fault may occur to the electrical supply source.

(3) Bonding Conductive Materials. Conductive materials such as metal water piping systems, metal sprinkler piping, metal gas piping, and other metal-piping systems, as well as exposed structural steel members likely to become energized must be bonded together in a manner that creates a low-impedance fault current path that's capable of carrying the maximum fault current likely to be imposed on it. **Figure 250–25**

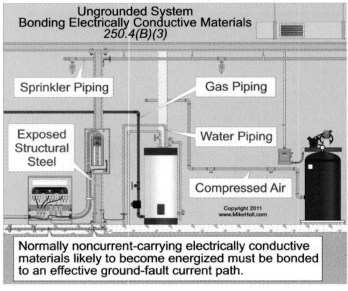

Figure 250–25

Author's Comment: The phrase "likely to become energized" is subject to interpretation by the authority having jurisdiction.

(4) Fault Current Path. Electrical equipment, wiring, and other electrically conductive material likely to become energized must be installed in a manner that creates a low-impedance fault current path to facilitate the operation of overcurrent devices should a second ground fault from a different phase occur. **Figure 250–26**

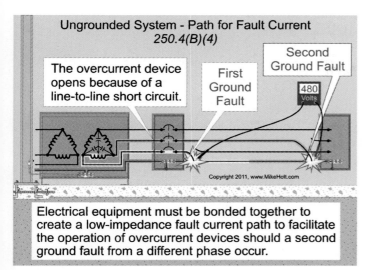

Ungrounded System - Path for Fault Current
250.4(B)(4)

The overcurrent device opens because of a line-to-line short circuit.

First Ground Fault

Second Ground Fault

480 Volts

Electrical equipment must be bonded together to create a low-impedance fault current path to facilitate the operation of overcurrent devices should a second ground fault from a different phase occur.

Figure 250–26

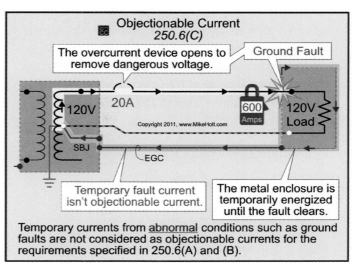

Objectionable Current
250.6(C)

The overcurrent device opens to remove dangerous voltage.

Ground Fault

120V   20A   600 Amps   120V Load

Copyright 2011, www.MikeHolt.com

SBJ   EGC

Temporary fault current isn't objectionable current.

The metal enclosure is temporarily energized until the fault clears.

Temporary currents from abnormal conditions such as ground faults are not considered as objectionable currents for the requirements specified in 250.6(A) and (B).

Figure 250–27

Author's Comment: A single ground fault can't be cleared on an ungrounded system because there's no low-impedance fault current path to the power source. The first ground fault simply grounds the previously ungrounded system. However, a second ground fault on a different phase results in a line-to-line short circuit between the two ground faults. The conductive path, between the ground faults, provides the low-impedance fault current path necessary so the overcurrent device will open.

Essential Rule 29   250.6

250.6 Objectionable Current.

(A) Preventing Objectionable Current. To prevent a fire, electric shock, or improper operation of circuit overcurrent devices or electronic equipment, electrical systems and equipment must be installed in a manner that prevents objectionable neutral current from flowing on metal parts.

(C) Temporary Currents Not Classified as Objectionable Currents. Temporary currents from abnormal conditions, such as ground faults, aren't to be classified as objectionable current. **Figure 250–27**

(D) Limitations to Permissible Alterations. Currents that introduce noise or data errors in electronic equipment are not considered objectionable currents for the purposes of this section. Circuits that supply electronic equipment must be connected to an equipment grounding conductor.

OBJECTIONABLE CURRENT

Objectionable neutral current occurs because of improper neutral-to-case connections or wiring errors that violate 250.142(B).

Improper Neutral-to-Case Connection [250.142]

Panelboards. Objectionable neutral current will flow when the neutral conductor is connected to the metal case of a panelboard that's not used as service equipment. **Figure 250–28**

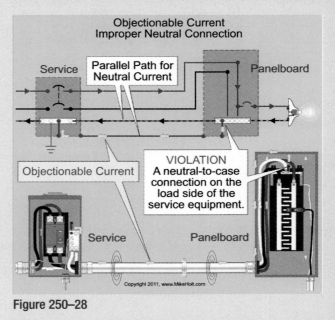

Objectionable Current
Improper Neutral Connection

Service

Parallel Path for Neutral Current

Panelboard

Objectionable Current

VIOLATION
A neutral-to-case connection on the load side of the service equipment.

Service   Panelboard

Copyright 2011, www.MikeHolt.com

Figure 250–28

Separately Derived Systems. Objectionable neutral current will flow on conductive metal parts and conductors if the neutral conductor is connected to the circuit equipment grounding conductor on the load side of the system bonding jumper for a separately derived system. **Figures 250–29 and 250–30**

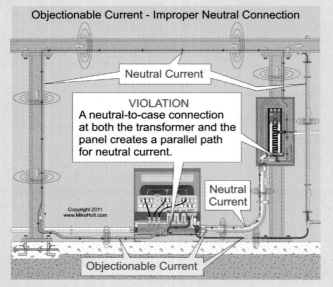

Figure 250-29

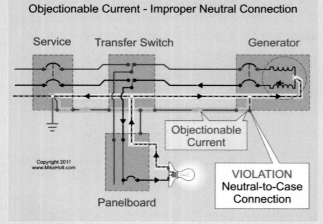

Figure 250-30

Disconnects. Objectionable neutral current will flow when the neutral conductor is connected to the metal case of a disconnecting means that's not part of the service equipment. **Figure 250–31**

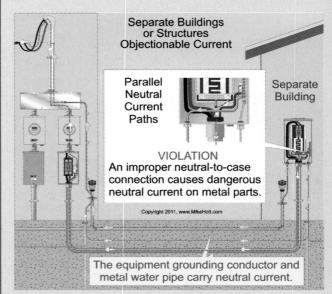

Figure 250-31

Wiring Errors. Objectionable neutral current will flow when the neutral conductor from one system is connected to a circuit of a different system. **Figure 250–32**

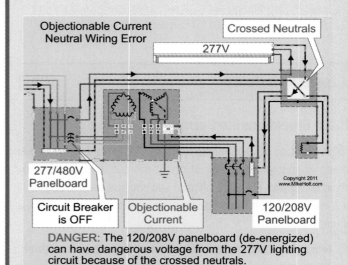

Figure 250-32

Objectionable neutral current will flow on metal parts when the circuit equipment grounding conductor is used as a neutral conductor such as where:

- A 230V time-clock motor is replaced with a 115V time-clock motor, and the circuit equipment grounding conductor is used for neutral return current.

- A 115V water filter is wired to a 240V well-pump motor circuit, and the circuit equipment grounding conductor is used for neutral return current. **Figure 250–33**

- The circuit equipment grounding conductor is used for neutral return current. **Figure 250–34**

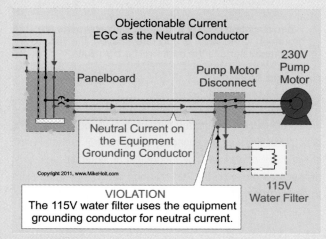

Objectionable Current
EGC as the Neutral Conductor

Panelboard — Pump Motor Disconnect — 230V Pump Motor

Neutral Current on the Equipment Grounding Conductor

Copyright 2011, www.MikeHolt.com

115V Water Filter

VIOLATION
The 115V water filter uses the equipment grounding conductor for neutral current.

Figure 250–33

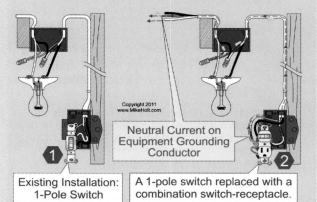

Objectionable Current - EGC as Neutral Conductor

Copyright 2011
www.MikeHolt.com

Neutral Current on Equipment Grounding Conductor

❶ Existing Installation: 1-Pole Switch

❷ A 1-pole switch replaced with a combination switch-receptacle.

Figure 250–34

DANGERS OF OBJECTIONABLE CURRENT

Objectionable neutral current on metal parts can cause electric shock, fires, and improper operation of electronic equipment and overcurrent devices such as GFPs, GFCIs, and AFCIs.

Shock Hazard. When objectionable neutral current flows on metal parts, electric shock and even death can occur from the elevated voltage on those metal parts. **Figures 250–35 and 250–36**

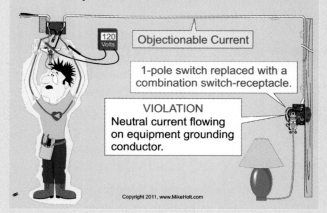

Objectionable Current - Shock Hazard

120 Volts

Objectionable Current

1-pole switch replaced with a combination switch-receptacle.

VIOLATION
Neutral current flowing on equipment grounding conductor.

Copyright 2011, www.MikeHolt.com

Figure 250–35

Objectionable Current - Shock Hazard

Open Raceway

120 Volts

DANGER
Improper Neutral-to-Case Connection

Copyright 2011, www.MikeHolt.com

Service Equipment

If the equipment grounding conductor opens and a person becomes in series with the raceway, they can be electrocuted.

A neutral-to-case bond can't be made on the load side of the service disconnect.

Figure 250–36

Fire Hazard. When objectionable neutral current flows on metal parts, a fire can ignite adjacent combustible material. Heat is generated whenever current flows, particularly over high-resistance parts. In addition, arcing at loose connections is especially dangerous in areas containing easily ignitible and explosive gases, vapors, or dust. **Figure 250–37**

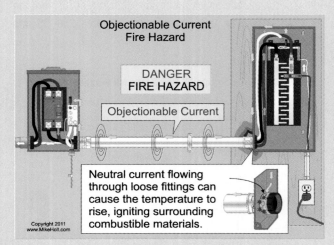

Objectionable Current
Fire Hazard

DANGER
FIRE HAZARD

Objectionable Current

Neutral current flowing through loose fittings can cause the temperature to rise, igniting surrounding combustible materials.

Copyright 2011
www.MikeHolt.com

Figure 250–37

Improper Operation of Electronic Equipment. Objectionable neutral current flowing on metal parts of electrical equipment and building parts can cause electromagnetic fields which negatively affect the performance of electronic devices, particularly medical equipment. For more information, visit www.MikeHolt.com, click on the "Technical Link," and then on "Power Quality." **Figure 250–38**

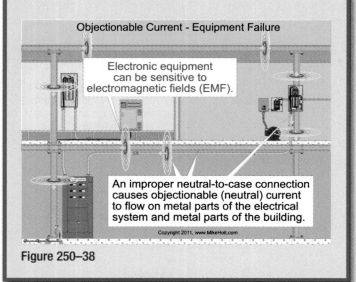

Objectionable Current - Equipment Failure

Electronic equipment can be sensitive to electromagnetic fields (EMF).

An improper neutral-to-case connection causes objectionable (neutral) current to flow on metal parts of the electrical system and metal parts of the building.

Copyright 2011, www.MikeHolt.com

Figure 250–38

When a system is properly grounded and bonded, the voltage of all metal parts to the earth and to each other will be zero. **Figure 250–39**

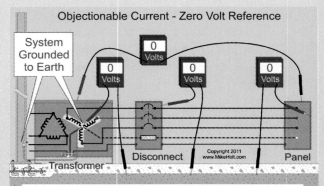

Objectionable Current - Zero Volt Reference

System Grounded to Earth

0 Volts
0 Volts
0 Volts
0 Volts

Transformer   Disconnect   Panel

Copyright 2011
www.MikeHolt.com

When a system neutral and metal electrical parts are grounded to the earth at only one location, the voltage of all metal parts to the earth will be zero volts.

Figure 250–39

When objectionable neutral current travels on metal parts because of the improper bonding of the neutral to metal parts in violation of the *NEC*, a difference of potential will exist between all metal parts. This situation can cause some electronic equipment to operate improperly. **Figure 250–40**

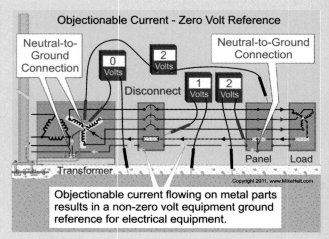

Objectionable Current - Zero Volt Reference

Neutral-to-Ground Connection

Neutral-to-Ground Connection

0 Volts
2 Volts
1 Volts
2 Volts

Disconnect

Transformer   Panel   Load

Copyright 2011, www.MikeHolt.com

Objectionable current flowing on metal parts results in a non-zero volt equipment ground reference for electrical equipment.

Figure 250–40

Operation of Overcurrent Devices. When objectionable neutral current travels on metal parts, tripping of electronic overcurrent devices equipped with ground-fault protection can occur because some neutral current flows on the circuit equipment grounding conductor instead of the neutral conductor.

Essential Rule 30 **250.24**

PART II. SYSTEM GROUNDING AND BONDING

250.24 Service Equipment—Grounding and Bonding.

(A) Grounded System. Service equipment supplied from a grounded system must have the neutral conductor terminate in accordance with (1) through (5).

(1) Grounding Location. A grounding electrode conductor must connect the service neutral conductor to the grounding electrode at any accessible location, from the load end of the service drop or service lateral, up to and including the service disconnecting means. **Figure 250–41**

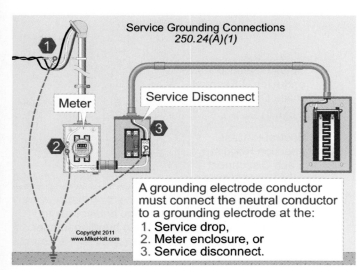

Service Grounding Connections
250.24(A)(1)

Meter

Service Disconnect

A grounding electrode conductor must connect the neutral conductor to a grounding electrode at the:
1. Service drop,
2. Meter enclosure, or
3. Service disconnect.

Copyright 2011
www.MikeHolt.com

Figure 250–41

Author's Comment: Some inspectors require the service neutral conductor to be grounded (connected to the earth) from the meter socket enclosure, while other inspectors insist that the service neutral conductor be grounded (connected to the earth) only from the service disconnect.

(4) Grounding Termination. When the service neutral conductor is connected to the service disconnecting means [250.24(B)] by a wire or busbar [250.28], the grounding electrode conductor is permitted to terminate to either the neutral terminal or the equipment grounding terminal within the service disconnect.

(5) Neutral-to-Case Connection. A neutral-to-case connection isn't permitted on the load side of service equipment, except as permitted by 250.142(B). **Figure 250–42**

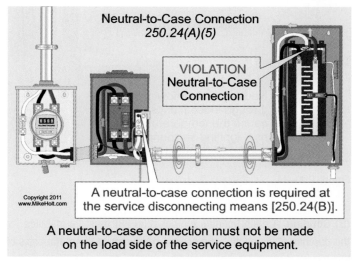

Neutral-to-Case Connection
250.24(A)(5)

VIOLATION
Neutral-to-Case
Connection

A neutral-to-case connection is required at the service disconnecting means [250.24(B)].

Copyright 2011
www.MikeHolt.com

A neutral-to-case connection must not be made on the load side of the service equipment.

Figure 250–42

Author's Comment: If a neutral-to-case connection is made on the load side of service equipment, dangerous objectionable neutral current will flow on conductive metal parts of electrical equipment [250.6(A)]. Objectionable neutral current on metal parts of electrical equipment can cause electric shock and even death from ventricular fibrillation, as well as a fire. **Figures 250–43 and 250–44**

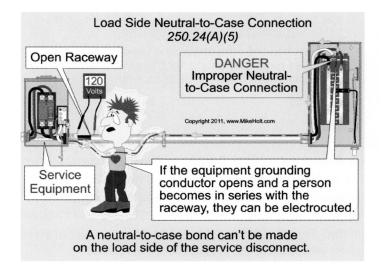

Load Side Neutral-to-Case Connection
250.24(A)(5)

Open Raceway

120 Volts

DANGER
Improper Neutral-to-Case Connection

Copyright 2011, www.MikeHolt.com

Service Equipment

If the equipment grounding conductor opens and a person becomes in series with the raceway, they can be electrocuted.

A neutral-to-case bond can't be made on the load side of the service disconnect.

Figure 250–43

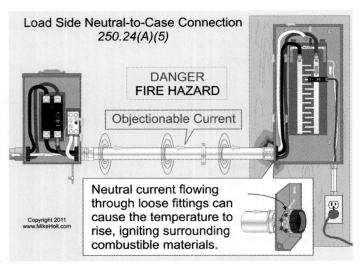

Figure 250–44

(B) Bonding. A main bonding jumper [250.28] must be installed for the purpose of connecting the neutral conductor to the metal parts of the service disconnecting means. **Figure 250–45**

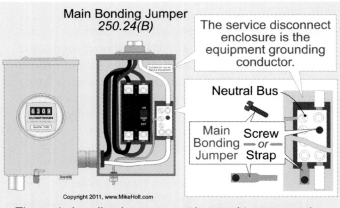

The main bonding jumper must be used to connect the equipment grounding conductor (metal enclosure) to the neutral conductor in a service disconnect.

Figure 250–45

(C) Grounded Conductor Brought to Service Equipment. A service neutral conductor from the electric utility must be <u>routed with the ungrounded conductors</u> and terminate to the service disconnecting means via a main bonding jumper [250.24(B)] that's installed between the service neutral conductor and the service disconnecting means enclosure [250.28]. **Figures 250–46 and 250–47**

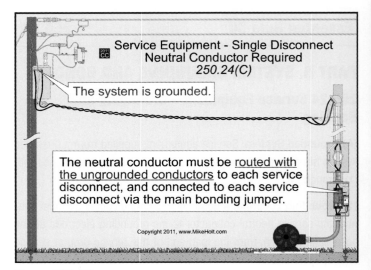

Figure 250–46

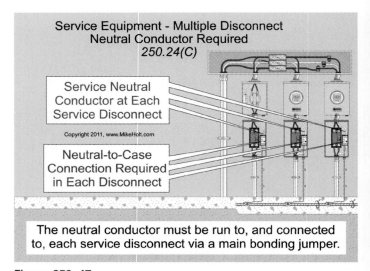

Figure 250–47

Author's Comment: The service neutral conductor provides the effective ground-fault current path to the power supply to ensure that dangerous voltage from a ground fault will be quickly removed by opening the overcurrent device [250.4(A)(3) and 250.4(A)(5)]. **Figure 250–48**

DANGER: *Dangerous voltage from a ground fault won't be removed from metal parts, metal piping, and structural steel if the service disconnecting means enclosure isn't connected to the service neutral conductor. This is because the contact resistance of a grounding electrode to the earth is so great that insufficient fault current returns to the power supply if the earth is the only fault current return path to open the circuit overcurrent device.* **Figure 250–49**

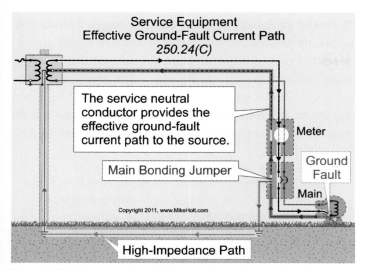

Figure 250–48

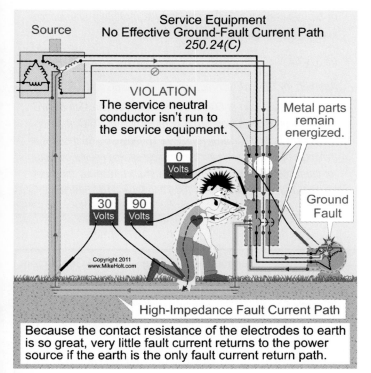

Because the contact resistance of the electrodes to earth is so great, very little fault current returns to the power source if the earth is the only fault current return path.

Figure 250–49

Author's Comment: For example, if the neutral conductor is opened, dangerous voltage will be present on metal parts under normal conditions, providing the potential for electric shock. If the earth's ground resistance is 25 ohms and the load's resistance is 25 ohms, the voltage drop across each of these resistors will be half of the voltage source. Since the neutral is connected to the service disconnect, all metal parts will be elevated to 60V above the earth's potential for a 120/240V system. **Figure 250–50**

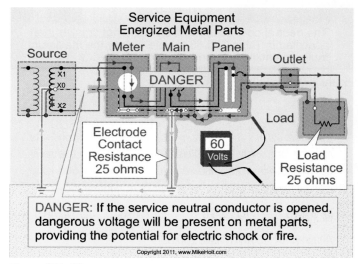

Figure 250–50

To determine the actual voltage on the metal parts from an open service neutral conductor, you need to do some complex math calculations. Visit www.MikeHolt.com and go to the "Free Stuff" link to download a spreadsheet for this purpose.

(1) Single Raceway. Because the service neutral conductor serves as the effective ground-fault current path to the source for ground faults, the neutral conductor must be sized so it can safely carry the maximum fault current likely to be imposed on it [110.10 and 250.4(A)(5)]. This is accomplished by sizing the neutral conductor not smaller than specified in Table 250.66, based on the cross-sectional area of the largest ungrounded service conductor. **Figure 250–51**

> **Author's Comment:** In addition, the neutral conductors must have the capacity to carry the maximum unbalanced neutral current in accordance with 220.61.

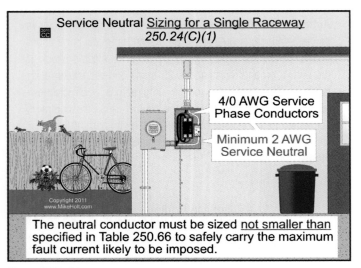

The neutral conductor must be sized not smaller than specified in Table 250.66 to safely carry the maximum fault current likely to be imposed.

Figure 250–51

Question: *What's the minimum size service neutral conductor required for a 240V, single-phase service installed in one raceway where the ungrounded service conductors are 500 kcmil and the maximum unbalanced load is 100A?* **Figure 250–52**

(a) 3 AWG   (b) 2 AWG   (c) 1 AWG   (d) 1/0 AWG

Answer: *(d) 1/0 AWG [Table 250.66]*

The unbalanced load of 100A requires a 3 AWG service neutral conductor, which is rated 100A at 75ºC in accordance with Table 310.15(B)(16) [220.61]. Table 250.66 requires a minimum of 1/0 AWG based on 500 kcmil ungrounded conductors.

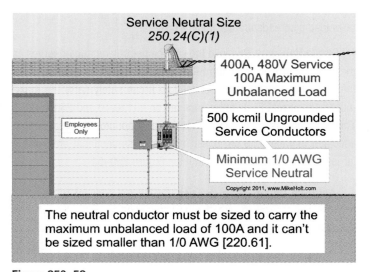

The neutral conductor must be sized to carry the maximum unbalanced load of 100A and it can't be sized smaller than 1/0 AWG [220.61].

Figure 250–52

(2) Parallel Conductors in Two or More Raceways. If service conductors are paralleled in two or more raceways, a neutral conductor must be installed in each of the parallel raceways. The size of the neutral conductor in each raceway must not be smaller than specified in Table 250.66, based on the cross-sectional area of the largest ungrounded service conductor in each raceway. In no case can the neutral conductor in each parallel set be sized smaller than 1/0 AWG [310.10(H)(1)].

Author's Comment: In addition, the neutral conductors must have the capacity to carry the maximum unbalanced neutral current in accordance with 220.61.

Question: *What's the minimum size service neutral conductor required for a 250V, single-phase service installed in parallel in two raceways where the ungrounded service conductors in each of the raceways are 350 kcmil and the maximum unbalanced load is 100A?* **Figure 250–53**

(a) 3 AWG   (b) 2 AWG   (c) 1 AWG   (d) 1/0 AWG

Answer: *(d) 1/0 AWG per raceway [Table 250.66 and 310.10(H)]*

The unbalanced load of 50A in each raceway requires an 8 AWG service neutral conductor, which is rated 50A at 75ºC in accordance with Table 310.15(B)(16) [220.61]. Table 250.66 requires a minimum of 2 AWG, however, the smallest service neutral conductor permitted to be installed in parallel in each raceway must not be smaller than 1/0 AWG [310.10(H) and Table 310.15(B)(16)].

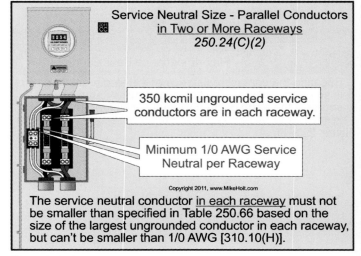

The service neutral conductor in each raceway must not be smaller than specified in Table 250.66 based on the size of the largest ungrounded conductor in each raceway, but can't be smaller than 1/0 AWG [310.10(H)].

Figure 250–53

(D) Grounding Electrode Conductor. A grounding electrode conductor, sized in accordance with 250.66 based on the area of the ungrounded service conductor, must connect the metal parts of service equipment enclosures to a grounding electrode in accordance with Part III of Article 250.

> **Question:** What's the minimum size grounding electrode conductor for a 400A service where the ungrounded service conductors are sized at 500 kcmil? **Figure 250–54**
>
> (a) 3 AWG   (b) 2 AWG   (c) 1 AWG   (d) 1/0 AWG
>
> **Answer:** (d) 1/0 AWG [Table 250.66]

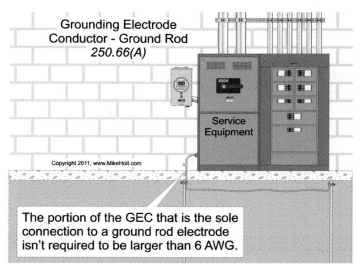

Grounding Electrode
Conductor - Ground Rod
250.66(A)

Service
Equipment

The portion of the GEC that is the sole connection to a ground rod electrode isn't required to be larger than 6 AWG.

Figure 250–55

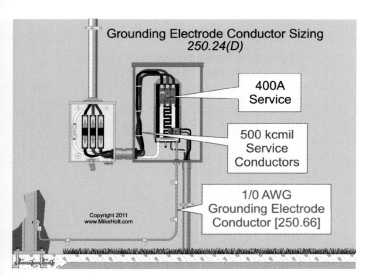

Grounding Electrode Conductor Sizing
250.24(D)

400A
Service

500 kcmil
Service
Conductors

1/0 AWG
Grounding Electrode
Conductor [250.66]

Figure 250–54

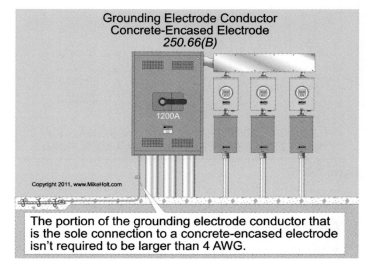

Grounding Electrode Conductor
Concrete-Encased Electrode
250.66(B)

1200A

The portion of the grounding electrode conductor that is the sole connection to a concrete-encased electrode isn't required to be larger than 4 AWG.

Figure 250–56

Author's Comment: If the grounding electrode conductor is connected to a ground rod, the portion of the conductor that's the sole connection to the ground rod isn't required to be larger than 6 AWG copper [250.66(A)]. **Figure 250–55**. If the grounding electrode conductor is connected to a concrete-encased electrode, the portion of the conductor that's the sole connection to the concrete-encased electrode isn't required to be larger than 4 AWG copper [250.66(B)]. **Figure 250–56**

Essential Rule 31   250.30

250.30 Separately Derived Systems—Grounding and Bonding.

Note 1: An alternate alternating-current power source such as an on-site generator isn't a separately derived system if the neutral conductor is solidly interconnected to a service-supplied system neutral conductor. An example is a generator provided with a transfer switch that includes a neutral conductor that's not switched. **Figure 250–57**

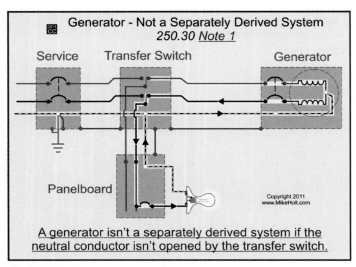

Figure 250–57

Author's Comments:

- According to Article 100, a separately derived system is a wiring system whose power is derived from a source where there's no direct electrical connection to the supply conductors of another system.

- Transformers are considered separately derived when the primary conductors have no direct electrical connection from circuit conductors of one system to circuit conductors of another system, other than connections through the earth, metal enclosures, metallic raceways, or equipment grounding conductors. **Figure 250-58**

- A generator having transfer equipment that switches the neutral conductor, or one that has no neutral conductor at all, is a separately derived system and must be grounded and bonded in accordance with 250.30(A). **Figure 250–59**

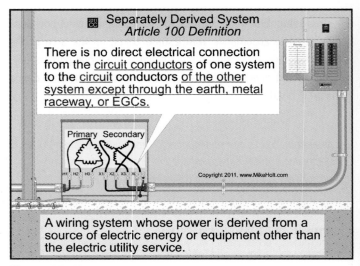

Figure 250–58

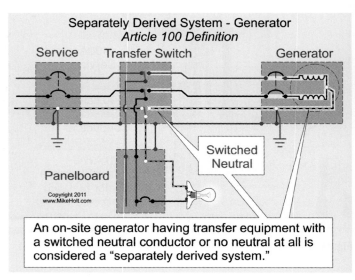

Figure 250–59

Note 2: For nonseparately derived systems, see 445.13 for the minimum size neutral conductors necessary to carry fault current. **Figures 250–60 and 250–61**

(A) Grounded Systems. Separately derived systems must be grounded and bonded in accordance with (A)(1) through (A)(8).

A neutral-to-case connection must not be made on the load side of the system bonding jumper, except as permitted by 250.142(B).

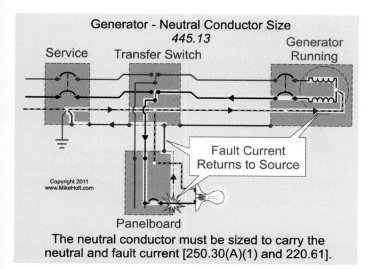

Generator - Neutral Conductor Size
445.13

The neutral conductor must be sized to carry the neutral and fault current [250.30(A)(1) and 220.61].

Figure 250–60

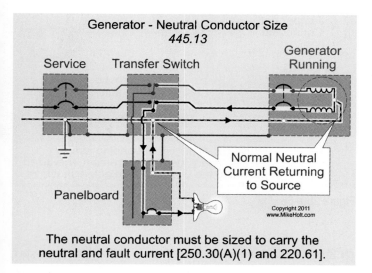

Generator - Neutral Conductor Size
445.13

The neutral conductor must be sized to carry the neutral and fault current [250.30(A)(1) and 220.61].

Figure 250–61

⚠️ **CAUTION:** *Dangerous objectionable neutral current will flow on conductive metal parts of electrical equipment as well as metal piping and structural steel, in violation of 250.6(A), if more than one system bonding jumper is installed, or if it's not located where the grounding electrode conductor terminates to the neutral conductor.* **Figure 250–62**

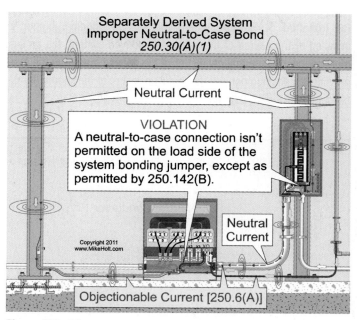

Separately Derived System
Improper Neutral-to-Case Bond
250.30(A)(1)

Neutral Current

VIOLATION
A neutral-to-case connection isn't permitted on the load side of the system bonding jumper, except as permitted by 250.142(B).

Neutral Current

Objectionable Current [250.6(A)]

Figure 250–62

(1) System Bonding Jumper. An unspliced system bonding jumper must be installed at the same location where the grounding electrode conductor terminates to the neutral terminal of the separately derived system; either at the separately derived system or the system disconnecting means, but not at both locations [250.30(A)(5)].

Author's Comment: A system bonding jumper is the connection between the neutral conductor and supply-side bonding jumper or equipment grounding conductor or both at a separately derived system [Article 100]. **Figure 250–63**

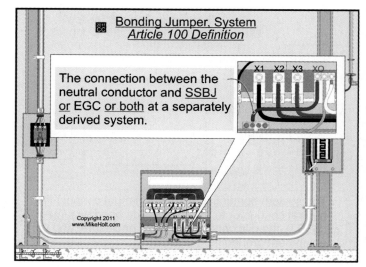

Bonding Jumper, System
Article 100 Definition

The connection between the neutral conductor and SSBJ or EGC or both at a separately derived system.

Figure 250–63

(a) Installed at Source. Where the system bonding jumper is installed at the source of the separately derived system, the jumper must connect the neutral conductor of the derived system to the supply-side bonding jumper and the metal enclosure of the source (transformer case). **Figure 250–64**

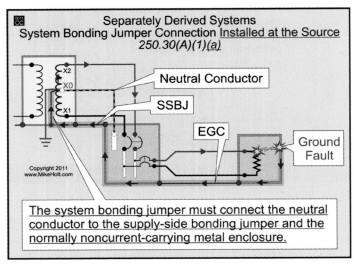

Figure 250–64

(b) Installed at First Disconnecting Means. Where the system bonding jumper is installed at the first disconnecting means of a separately derived system, the jumper must connect the neutral conductor of the derived system to the supply-side bonding jumper and the metal disconnecting means enclosure. **Figure 250–65**

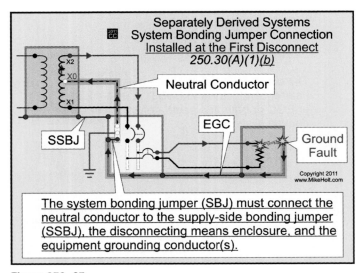

Figure 250–65

Author's Comment: A system bonding jumper is a conductor, screw, or strap that bonds the metal parts of a separately derived system to the system neutral point [Article 100 Bonding Jumper, System], and it's sized to Table 250.66 in accordance with 250.28(D).

DANGER: *During a ground fault, metal parts of electrical equipment, as well as metal piping and structural steel, will become and remain energized providing the potential for electric shock and fire if the system bonding jumper isn't installed.* **Figure 250–66**

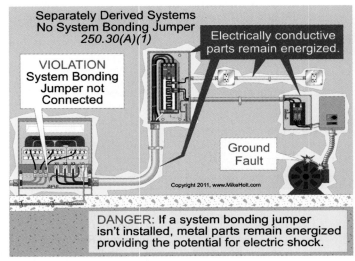

Figure 250–66

(2) Supply-Side Bonding Jumper. If the separately derived system and the first disconnecting means are located in separate enclosures, a supply-side bonding jumper must be run to the derived system disconnecting means. The supply-side bonding jumper can be a nonflexible metal raceway, a wire, or a bus.

(a) If the supply-side bonding jumper is of the wire type, it must be sized in accordance with Table 250.66, based on the area of the largest ungrounded derived system conductor in the raceway or cable.

Question: What size supply-side bonding jumper is required for flexible metal conduit containing 300 kcmil secondary conductors? **Figure 250–67**

(a) 3 AWG (b) 2 AWG (c) 1 AWG (d) 1/0 AWG

Answer: (b) 2 AWG [Table 250.66]

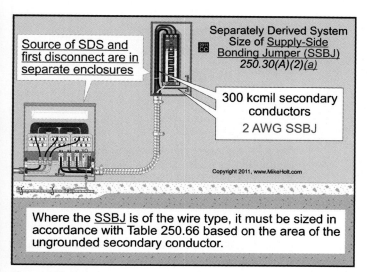

Figure 250–67

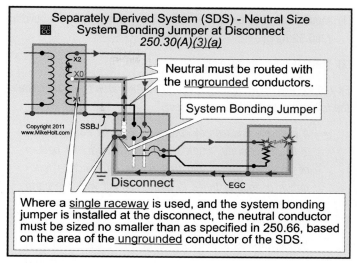

Figure 250–68

Author's Comment: If the system bonding jumper is installed at the disconnecting means instead of at the source, an equipment bonding conductor must connect the metal parts of the separately derived system to the neutral conductor at the disconnecting means in accordance with 250.30(A)(2).

(4) Grounding Electrode. The grounding electrode must be as near as practicable, and preferably in the same area where the system bonding jumper is installed and be one of the following: **Figure 250–69**

(b) If the supply-side bonding jumper is a bus, it must have a cross-sectional area no smaller than required by Table 250.66.

(3) System Neutral Conductor Size. If the system bonding jumper is installed at the disconnecting means instead of at the source, the following requirements apply:

(a) Sizing for Single Raceway. Because the neutral conductor of a derived system serves as the effective ground-fault current path for ground-fault current, it must be routed with the ungrounded conductors of the derived system and be sized not smaller than specified in Table 250.66, based on the area of the ungrounded conductor of the derived system. **Figure 250–68**

(b) Parallel Conductors in Two or More Raceways. If the conductors from the derived system are installed in parallel in two or more raceways, the neutral conductor of the derived system in each raceway or cable must be sized not smaller than specified in Table 250.66, based on the area of the largest ungrounded conductor of the derived system in the raceway or cable. In no case is the neutral conductor of the derived system permitted to be smaller than 1/0 AWG [310.10(H)].

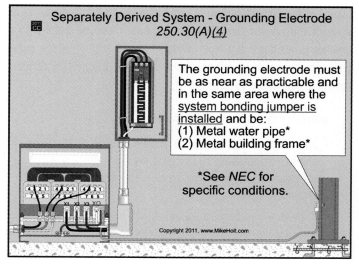

Figure 250–69

(1) Metal water pipe electrode, within 5 ft of the entry to the building [250.52(A)(1)].

(2) Metal building frame electrode [250.52(A)(2)].

Ex 1: If the electrodes specified in 250.30(A)(4) aren't available, one of the following electrodes can be used:

- *A concrete-encased electrode encased by not less than 2 in. of concrete, located horizontally near the bottom or vertically, and within that portion of concrete foundation or footing that's in direct contact with the earth [250.52(A)(3)].*

- *A ground ring electrode encircling the building/structure, buried not less than 30 in. below grade, consisting of at least 20 ft of bare copper conductor not smaller than 2 AWG [250.52(A)(4) and 250.53(F)].*

- *A ground rod electrode having not less than 8 ft of contact with the soil meeting the requirements of 250.52(A)(5) and 250.53(G)].*

- *Other metal underground systems, piping systems, or underground tanks [250.52(A)(8)].*

Note 1: Interior metal water piping in the area served by separately derived systems must be bonded to the separately derived system in accordance with 250.104(D).

(5) Grounding Electrode Conductor, Single Separately Derived System. The grounding electrode conductor must be sized in accordance with 250.66, based on the area of the largest <u>ungrounded</u> conductor of the derived system. A grounding electrode conductor must connect the neutral terminal of a separately derived system to a grounding electrode of a type identified in 250.30(A)(4) at the same point on the separately derived system where the system bonding jumper is connected. **Figure 250–70**

Author's Comments:

- System grounding also helps reduce fires in buildings as well as voltage stress on electrical insulation, thereby ensuring longer insulation life for motors, transformers, and other system components.

- To prevent objectionable neutral current from flowing [250.6] onto metal parts, the grounding electrode conductor must originate at the same point on the separately derived system where the system bonding jumper is connected [250.30(A)(1)].

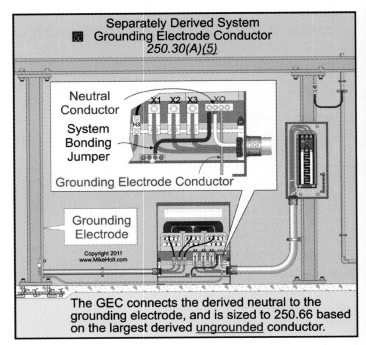

The GEC connects the derived neutral to the grounding electrode, and is sized to 250.66 based on the largest derived <u>ungrounded</u> conductor.

Figure 250–70

Ex 1: If the system bonding jumper is a wire or busbar, the grounding electrode conductor is permitted to terminate to either the neutral terminal or the equipment grounding terminal, bar, or bus in accordance with 250.30(A)(1). **Figure 250–71**

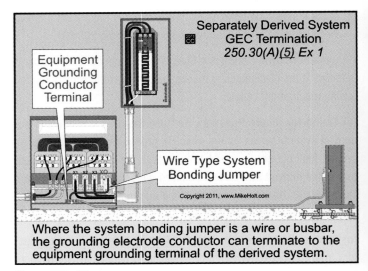

Where the system bonding jumper is a wire or busbar, the grounding electrode conductor can terminate to the equipment grounding terminal of the derived system.

Figure 250–71

Ex 3: Separately derived systems rated 1 kVA or less aren't required to be grounded (connected to the earth).

(6) Grounding Electrode Conductor, Multiple Separately Derived Systems. Where there are multiple separately derived systems, a grounding electrode conductor tap from each separately derived system to a common grounding electrode conductor is permitted. This connection is to be made at the same point on the separately derived system where the system bonding jumper is connected [250.30(A)(1)]. **Figure 250–72**

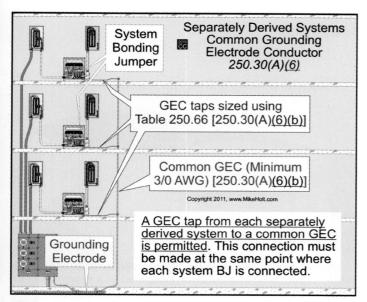

Figure 250–72

Ex 1: If the system bonding jumper is a wire or busbar, the grounding electrode conductor tap can terminate to either the neutral terminal or the equipment grounding terminal, bar, or bus in accordance with 250.30(A)(1).

Ex 2: Separately derived systems rated 1 kVA or less aren't required to be grounded (connected to the earth).

(a) Common Grounding Electrode Conductor. The common grounding electrode conductor can be one of the following:

(1) A conductor not smaller than 3/0 AWG copper or 250 kcmil aluminum.

(2) The metal frame of the building/structure that complies with 250.52(A)(2) or is connected to the grounding electrode system by a conductor not smaller than 3/0 AWG copper or 250 kcmil aluminum.

(b) Tap Conductor Size. Grounding electrode conductor taps must be sized in accordance with Table 250.66, based on the area of the largest ungrounded conductor of the given derived system.

(c) Connections. All tap connections to the common grounding electrode conductor must be made at an accessible location by one of the following methods:

(1) A connector listed as grounding and bonding equipment.

(2) Listed connections to aluminum or copper busbars not less than ¼ in. x 2 in.

(3) Exothermic welding.

Grounding electrode conductor taps must be connected to the common grounding electrode conductor so the common grounding electrode conductor isn't spliced.

(7) Installation. The grounding electrode conductor must comply with the following:

- Be of copper where within 18 in. of the earth [250.64(A)].

- Securely fastened to the surface on which it's carried [250.64(B)].

- Adequately protected if exposed to physical damage [250.64(B)].

- Metal enclosures enclosing a grounding electrode conductor must be made electrically continuous from the point of attachment to cabinets or equipment to the grounding electrode [250.64(E)].

(8) Structural Steel and Metal Piping. To ensure dangerous voltage from a ground fault is removed quickly, structural steel and metal piping in the area served by a separately derived system must be connected to the neutral conductor at the separately derived system in accordance with 250.104(D).

(C) Outdoor Source. If the separately derived system is located outside the building/structure, a connection to the grounding electrode must be made at the separately derived system location. **Figure 250–73**

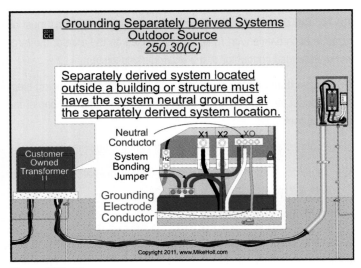

Figure 250–73

Essential Rule 32 — 250.32

250.32 Buildings or Structures Supplied by a Feeder or Branch Circuit.

(A) Grounding Electrode. Each building/structure's disconnect must be connected to an electrode of a type identified in 250.52. **Figure 250–74**

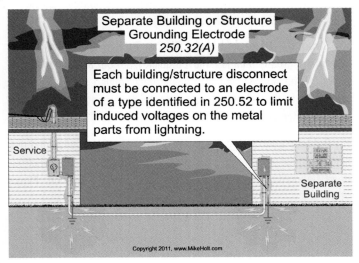

Figure 250–74

Author's Comments:

- The grounding of the building/structure disconnecting means to the earth is intended to help in limiting induced voltages on the metal parts from nearby lightning strikes [250.4(A)(1)].
- The *Code* prohibits the use of the earth to serve as an effective ground-fault current path [250.4(A)(5) and 250.4(B)(4)].

Ex: A grounding electrode isn't required where the building/structure is served with a 2-wire, 3-wire, or 4-wire multiwire branch circuit. **Figure 250–75**

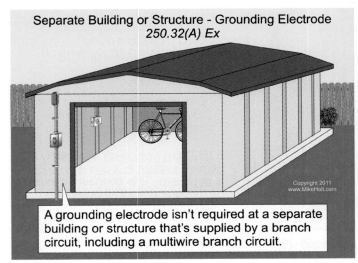

Figure 250–75

(B) Equipment Grounding Conductor.

(1) Supplied by a Feeder or Branch Circuit. To quickly clear a ground fault and remove dangerous voltage from metal parts, the building/structure disconnecting means must be connected to the circuit equipment grounding conductor, which must be one of the types described in 250.118. If the supply circuit equipment grounding conductor is of the wire type, it must be sized in accordance with 250.122, based on the rating of the overcurrent device. **Figure 250–76**

⚠ **CAUTION:** *To prevent dangerous objectionable neutral current from flowing onto metal parts [250.6(A)], the supply circuit neutral conductor isn't permitted to be connected to the remote building/structure disconnecting means [250.142(B)].* **Figure 250–77**

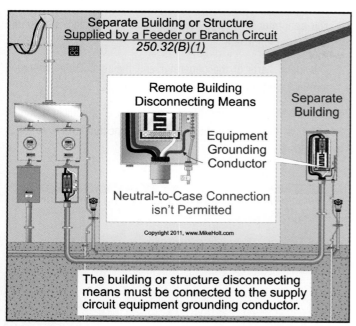

**Separate Building or Structure
Supplied by a Feeder or Branch Circuit
250.32(B)(1)**

Remote Building
Disconnecting Means

Separate
Building

Equipment
Grounding
Conductor

Neutral-to-Case Connection
isn't Permitted

Copyright 2011, www.MikeHolt.com

The building or structure disconnecting
means must be connected to the supply
circuit equipment grounding conductor.

Figure 250–76

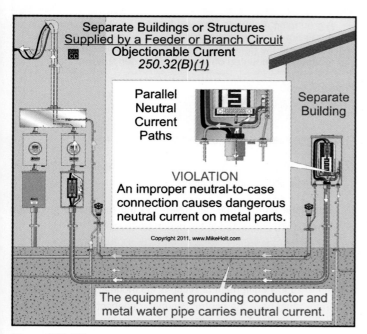

**Separate Buildings or Structures
Supplied by a Feeder or Branch Circuit
Objectionable Current
250.32(B)(1)**

Parallel
Neutral
Current
Paths

Separate
Building

VIOLATION
An improper neutral-to-case
connection causes dangerous
neutral current on metal parts.

Copyright 2011, www.MikeHolt.com

The equipment grounding conductor and
metal water pipe carries neutral current.

Figure 250–77

Ex: The neutral conductor <u>can serve as the ground-fault return path</u> for the building/structure disconnecting means for <u>existing installations in compliance with previous editions of the Code</u> where there are no continuous metallic paths between buildings and structures, ground-fault protection of equipment isn't installed on the supply side of the circuit, and the neutral conductor is sized no smaller than the larger of:

(1) The maximum unbalanced neutral load in accordance with 220.61.

(2) The minimum equipment grounding conductor size in accordance with 250.122.

(2) Supplied by Separately Derived System.

(a) With Overcurrent Protection. If overcurrent protection is provided where the conductors originate, the supply conductors must contain an equipment grounding conductor in accordance with 250.32(B)(1).

(b) Without Overcurrent Protection. If overcurrent protection isn't provided for the supply conductors to the building/structure as permitted by 240.21(C)(4), the installation must be grounded and bonded in accordance with 250.30(A).

(E) Grounding Electrode Conductor. The grounding electrode conductor must terminate to the grounding terminal of the disconnecting means, and it must be sized in accordance with 250.66, based on the conductor area of the ungrounded feeder conductor.

> **Question:** What size grounding electrode conductor is required for a building disconnect supplied with a 3/0 AWG feeder?
> **Figure 250–78**
>
> (a) 4 AWG   (b) 3 AWG   (c) 2 AWG   (d) 1 AWG
>
> **Answer:** (a) 4 AWG [Table 250.66]

Author's Comment: If the grounding electrode conductor is connected to a ground rod, the portion of the conductor that's the sole connection to the ground rod isn't required to be larger than 6 AWG copper [250.66(A)]. If the grounding electrode conductor is connected to a concrete-encased electrode, the portion of the conductor that's the sole connection to the concrete-encased electrode isn't required to be larger than 4 AWG copper [250.66(B)].

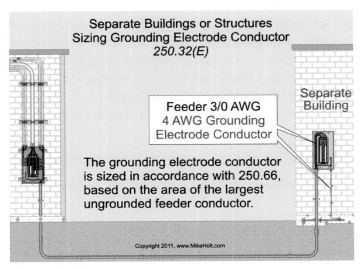

Figure 250–78

Essential Rule 33   250.34

250.34 Generators—Portable and Vehicle-Mounted.

(A) Portable Generators. The frame of a portable generator isn't required to be grounded (connected to the earth) if: **Figure 250–79**

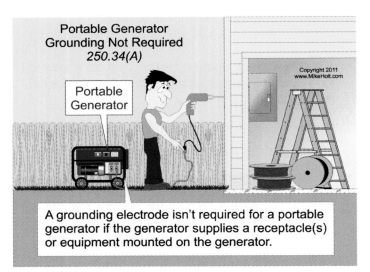

Figure 250–79

(1) The generator only supplies equipment or receptacles mounted on the generator, and

(2) The metal parts of the generator and the receptacle grounding terminal are connected to the generator frame.

(B) Vehicle-Mounted Generators. The frame of a vehicle-mounted generator isn't required to be grounded (connected to the earth) if: **Figure 250–80**

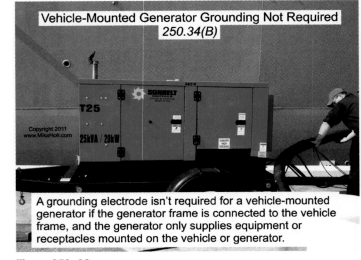

Figure 250–80

(1) The generator frame is bonded to the vehicle frame,

(2) The generator only supplies equipment or receptacles mounted on the vehicle or generator, and

(3) The metal parts of the generator and the receptacle grounding terminal are connected to the generator frame.

(C) Separately Derived Portable or Vehicle-Mounted Generator. A portable or vehicle-mounted generator used as a separately derived system to supply equipment or receptacles mounted on the vehicle or generator must have the neutral conductor connected to the generator frame.

> **Note:** A portable or vehicle-mounted generator supplying fixed wiring for a premises must be grounded (connected to the earth) and bonded in accordance with 250.30 for separately derived systems and 250.35 for nonseparately derived systems.

Essential Rule 34   250.50

PART III. GROUNDING ELECTRODE SYSTEM AND GROUNDING ELECTRODE CONDUCTOR

250.50 Grounding Electrode System. Any grounding electrode described in 250.52(A)(1) through (A)(8) that's present at a building/structure must be bonded together to form the grounding electrode system. **Figure 250–81**

- Underground metal water pipe [250.52(A)(1)]
- Metal frame of the building/structure [250.52(A)(2)]
- Concrete-encased electrode [250.52(A)(3)]
- Ground ring [250.52(A)(4)]
- Ground rod [250.52(A)(5)]
- Other listed electrodes [250.52(A)(6)]
- Grounding plate [250.52(A)(7)]
- Metal underground systems, piping systems, or underground tanks [250.52(A)(8)].

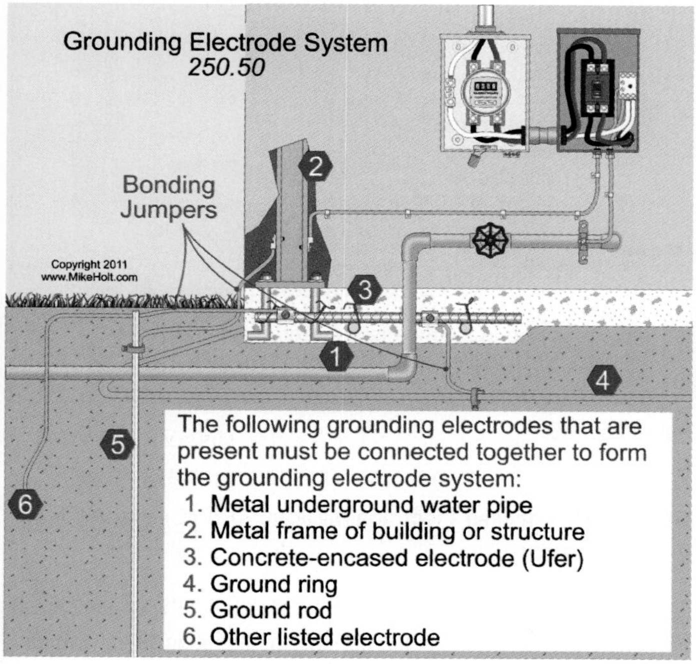

Ex: Concrete-encased electrodes aren't required for existing buildings or structures where the conductive steel reinforcing bars aren't accessible without chipping up the concrete. **Figure 250–82**

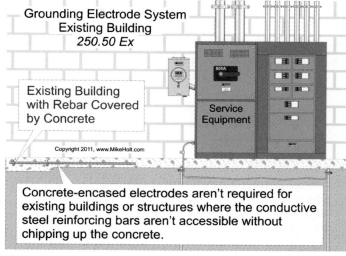

Grounding Electrode System
Existing Building
250.50 Ex

Existing Building
with Rebar Covered
by Concrete

Service
Equipment

Copyright 2011, www.MikeHolt.com

Concrete-encased electrodes aren't required for existing buildings or structures where the conductive steel reinforcing bars aren't accessible without chipping up the concrete.

Figure 250–82

Author's Comment: When a concrete-encased electrode is used at a building/structure that doesn't have an underground metal water pipe electrode, no additional electrode is required. **Figure 250–83**

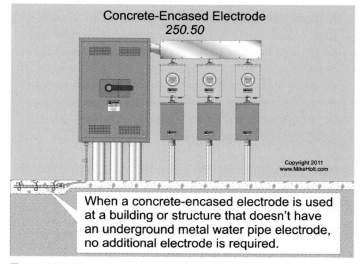

Concrete-Encased Electrode
250.50

Copyright 2011
www.MikeHolt.com

When a concrete-encased electrode is used at a building or structure that doesn't have an underground metal water pipe electrode, no additional electrode is required.

Figure 250–83

Grounding Electrode System
250.50

Bonding
Jumpers

Copyright 2011
www.MikeHolt.com

The following grounding electrodes that are present must be connected together to form the grounding electrode system:
1. Metal underground water pipe
2. Metal frame of building or structure
3. Concrete-encased electrode (Ufer)
4. Ground ring
5. Ground rod
6. Other listed electrode

Figure 250–81

Essential Rule 35   250.52

250.52 Grounding Electrode Types.

(A) Electrodes Permitted for Grounding.

(1) Underground Metal Water Pipe Electrode. Underground metal water pipe in direct contact with the earth for 10 ft or more can serve as a grounding electrode. **Figure 250–84**

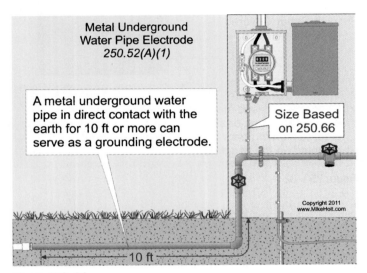

Figure 250–84

Author's Comment: Controversy about using metal underground water supply piping as a grounding electrode has existed since the early 1900s. The water industry believes that neutral current flowing on water piping corrodes the metal. For more information, contact the American Water Works Association about their report—*Effects of Electrical Grounding on Pipe Integrity and Shock Hazard*, Catalog No. 90702, 1.800.926.7337. **Figure 250–85**

(2) Metal Frame Electrode. The metal frame of a building/structure can serve as a grounding electrode when it meets at least one of the following conditions:

(1) At least one structural metal member is in direct contact with the earth for 10 ft or more, with or without concrete encasement.

(2) The bolts securing the structural steel column are connected to a concrete-encased electrode [250.52(A)(3)] by welding, exothermic welding, steel tie wires, or other approved means. **Figure 250–86**

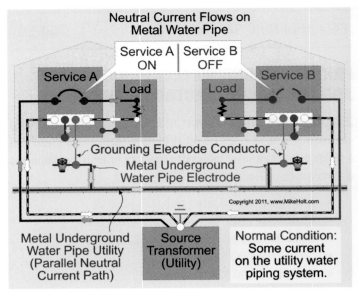

Figure 250–85

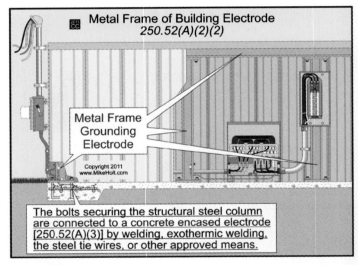

Figure 250–86

(3) Concrete-Encased Electrode. At least 20 ft of either (1) or (2): **Figure 250–87**

(1) One or more of bare, zinc-galvanized, or otherwise electrically conductive steel reinforcing bars of not less than ½ in. diameter, mechanically connected together by steel tie wires, welding, or other effective means, to create a 20 ft or greater length.

(2) Bare copper conductor not smaller than 4 AWG.

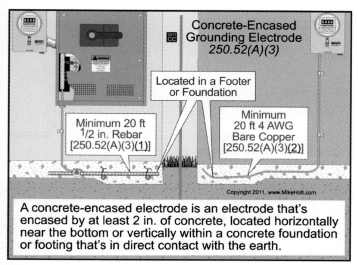

Figure 250–87

The reinforcing bars or bare copper conductor must be encased by at least 2 in. of concrete located horizontally near the bottom of a concrete footing or vertically within a concrete foundation that's in direct contact with the earth.

If multiple concrete-encased electrodes are present at a building/structure, only one is required to serve as a grounding electrode. **Figure 250–88**

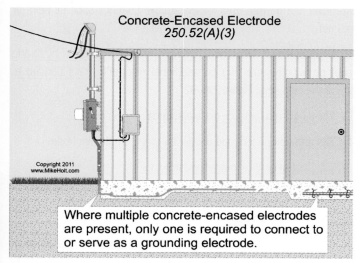

Figure 250–88

Note: Concrete containing insulation, vapor barriers, films or similar items separating it from the earth isn't considered to be in "direct contact" with the earth.

Author's Comments:

• The grounding electrode conductor to a concrete-encased grounding electrode isn't required to be larger than 4 AWG copper [250.66(B)].

• The concrete-encased grounding electrode is also called a "Ufer Ground," named after a consultant working for the U.S. Army during World War II. The technique Mr. Ufer came up with was necessary because the site needing grounding had no underground water table and little rainfall. The desert site was a series of bomb storage vaults in the area of Flagstaff, Arizona. This type of grounding electrode generally offers the lowest ground resistance for the cost.

(4) Ground Ring Electrode. A ground ring consisting of at least 20 ft of bare copper conductor not smaller than 2 AWG buried in the earth encircling a building/structure, can serve as a grounding electrode. **Figure 250–89**

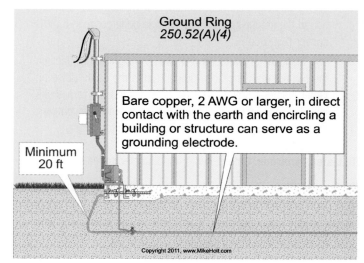

Figure 250–89

Author's Comment: The ground ring must be buried not less than 30 in. [250.53(F)], and the grounding electrode conductor to a ground ring isn't required to be larger than the ground ring conductor size [250.66(C)].

(5) Ground Rod and Pipe Electrode. Ground rod electrodes must not be less than 8 ft in length in contact with the earth [250.53(G)].

(b) Rod-type electrodes must have a diameter of at least ⅝ in., unless listed. **Figure 250–90**

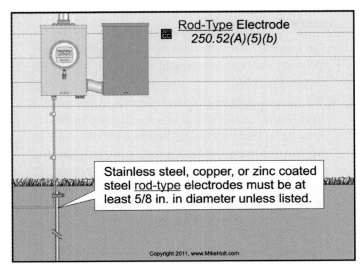

Rod-Type Electrode
250.52(A)(5)(b)

Stainless steel, copper, or zinc coated steel <u>rod-type</u> electrodes must be at least 5/8 in. in diameter unless listed.

Copyright 2011, www.MikeHolt.com

Figure 250–90

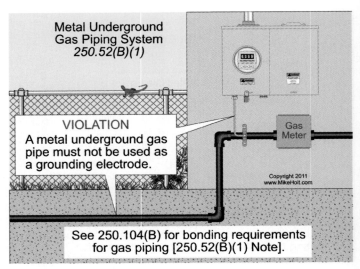

Metal Underground Gas Piping System
250.52(B)(1)

VIOLATION
A metal underground gas pipe must not be used as a grounding electrode.

Gas Meter

Copyright 2011
www.MikeHolt.com

See 250.104(B) for bonding requirements for gas piping [250.52(B)(1) Note].

Figure 250–91

Author's Comments:

- The grounding electrode conductor, if it's the sole connection to the ground rod, isn't required to be larger than 6 AWG copper [250.66(A)].

- The diameter of a ground rod has an insignificant effect on the contact resistance of a ground rod to the earth. However, larger diameter ground rods (¾ in. and 1 in.) are sometimes installed where mechanical strength is desired, or to compensate for the loss of the electrode's metal due to corrosion.

(6) Listed Electrode. Other listed grounding electrodes.

(7) Ground Plate Electrode. A <u>bare or conductively coated</u> iron or steel plate with not less than ¼ in. of thickness, or a <u>solid uncoated</u> copper metal plate not less than 0.06 in. of thickness, with an exposed surface area of not less than 2 sq ft.

(8) Metal Underground Systems Electrode. Metal underground piping systems, underground tanks, and underground metal well casings can serve as a grounding electrode.

> **Author's Comment:** The grounding electrode conductor to the metal underground system must be sized in accordance with Table 250.66.

(B) Not Permitted for Use as a Grounding Electrode.

(1) Underground metal gas-piping systems. **Figure 250–91**

(2) Aluminum

Essential Rule 36   250.53

250.53 Grounding Electrode Installation Requirements.

(A) Rod, Pipe, or Plate Electrodes.

(1) Below Permanent Moisture Level. If practicable, rod, pipe, and plate electrodes must be embedded below the permanent moisture level and be free from nonconductive coatings such as paint or enamel.

(2) Supplemental Electrode. A single rod, pipe or plate electrode must be supplemented by an additional electrode that's bonded to one of the following: **Figure 250–92**

(1) The single rod, pipe, or plate electrode

(2) The grounding electrode conductor of the single electrode

(3) The neutral service-entrance conductor

(4) The nonflexible grounded service raceway

(5) The service enclosure

Ex: If a single rod, pipe, or plate grounding electrode has an earth contact resistance of 25 ohms or less, the supplemental electrode isn't required. **Figure 250–93**

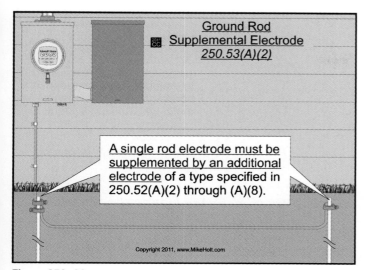

Figure 250–92

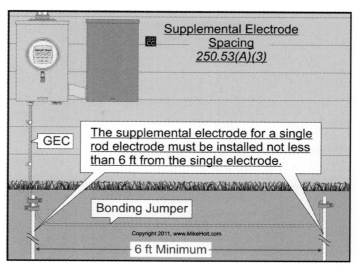

Figure 250–94

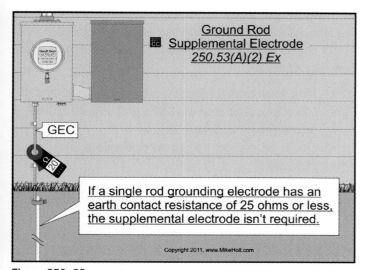

Figure 250–93

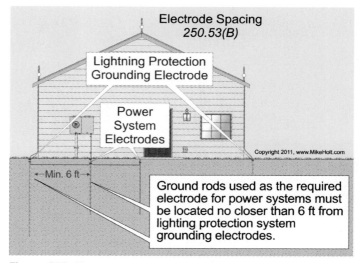

Figure 250–95

(3) Spacing. The supplemental electrode for a single rod, pipe, or plate electrode must be installed not less than 6 ft from the single electrode. **Figure 250–94**

> **Note:** The efficiency of paralleling electrodes is improved by spacing them at least twice the length of the longest rod.

(B) Electrode Spacing. Ground rods used as the required electrode for power systems must be located no closer than 6 ft from lighting protection or photovoltaic system grounding electrodes. Two or more grounding electrodes that are bonded together are considered a single grounding electrode system. **Figure 250–95**

(C) Grounding Electrode Bonding Jumper. Grounding electrode bonding jumpers must be copper when within 18 in. of the earth [250.64(A)], be securely fastened to the surface, and be protected if exposed to physical damage [250.64(B)]. The bonding jumper to each electrode must be sized in accordance with 250.66. **Figure 250–96**

The grounding electrode bonding jumpers must terminate by the use of listed pressure connectors, terminal bars, exothermic welding, or other listed means [250.8(A)]. When the termination is encased in concrete or buried, the termination fittings must be listed for this purpose [250.70]. **Figure 250–97**

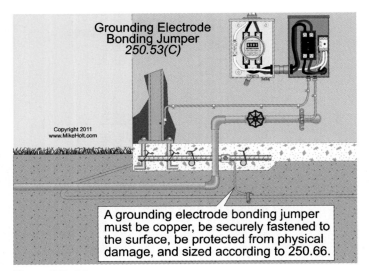

Figure 250–96

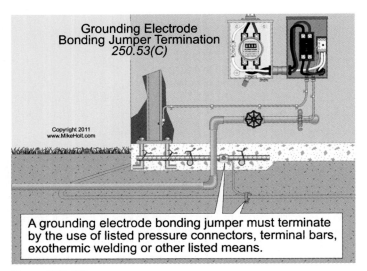

Figure 250–97

(D) Underground Metal Water Pipe Electrode.

(1) Continuity. The bonding connection to the interior metal water piping system, as required by 250.104(A), must not be dependent on water meters, filtering devices, or similar equipment likely to be disconnected for repairs or replacement. When necessary, a bonding jumper must be installed around insulated joints and equipment likely to be disconnected for repairs or replacement to assist in clearing and removing dangerous voltage on metal parts due to a ground fault [250.68(B)]. **Figure 250–98**

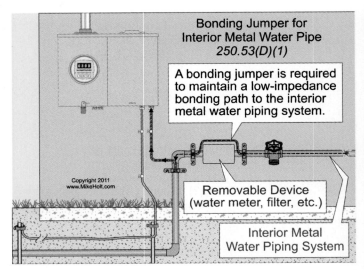

Figure 250–98

(2) Underground Metal Water Pipe Supplemental Electrode Required. When an underground metal water pipe grounding electrode is present [250.52(A)(1)], it must be supplemented by one of the following electrodes:

- Metal frame of the building/structure electrode [250.52(A)(2)]
- Concrete-encased electrode [250.52(A)(3)] **Figure 250–99**
- Ground ring electrode [250.52(A)(4)]
- Ground rod electrode meeting the requirements of 250.52(A)(5)
- Other listed electrodes [250.52(A)(6)]
- Metal underground systems, piping systems, or underground tanks [250.52(A)(8)]

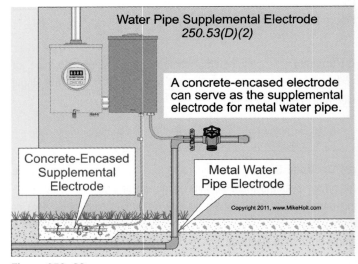

Figure 250–99

The termination of the supplemental grounding electrode conductor must be to one of the following locations: **Figure 250–100**

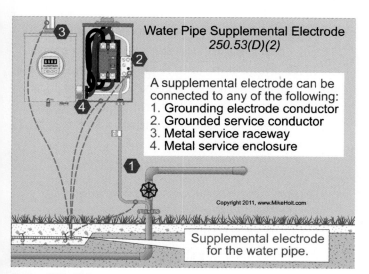

Water Pipe Supplemental Electrode
250.53(D)(2)

A supplemental electrode can be connected to any of the following:
1. Grounding electrode conductor
2. Grounded service conductor
3. Metal service raceway
4. Metal service enclosure

Copyright 2011, www.MikeHolt.com

Supplemental electrode for the water pipe.

Figure 250–100

(1) Grounding electrode conductor

(2) Service neutral conductor

(3) Metal service raceway

(4) Service equipment enclosure

Ex: The supplemental electrode is permitted to be bonded to interior metal water piping located not more than 5 ft from the point of entrance to the building/structure [250.68(C)(1)].

(E) Supplemental Ground Rod Electrode. The grounding electrode conductor to a ground rod that serves as a supplemental electrode isn't required to be larger than 6 AWG copper.

(F) Ground Ring. A ground ring encircling the building/structure, consisting of at least 20 ft of bare copper conductor not smaller than 2 AWG, must be buried not less than 30 in. [250.52(A)(4)]. **Figure 250–101**

(G) Ground Rod Electrodes. Ground rod electrodes must be installed so that not less than 8 ft of length is in contact with the soil. If rock bottom is encountered, the ground rod must be driven at an angle not to exceed 45 degrees from vertical. If rock bottom is encountered at an angle up to 45 degrees from vertical, the ground rod can be buried in a minimum 30 in. deep trench. **Figure 250–102**

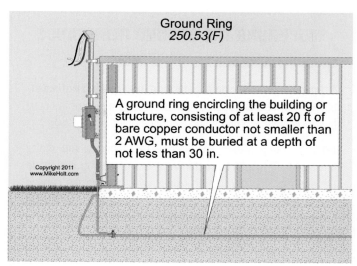

Ground Ring
250.53(F)

A ground ring encircling the building or structure, consisting of at least 20 ft of bare copper conductor not smaller than 2 AWG, must be buried at a depth of not less than 30 in.

Copyright 2011
www.MikeHolt.com

Figure 250–101

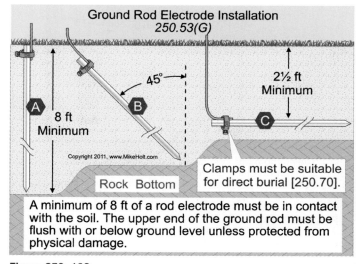

Ground Rod Electrode Installation
250.53(G)

45°

A
8 ft
Minimum

B

2½ ft
Minimum

C

Copyright 2011, www.MikeHolt.com

Rock Bottom

Clamps must be suitable for direct burial [250.70].

A minimum of 8 ft of a rod electrode must be in contact with the soil. The upper end of the ground rod must be flush with or below ground level unless protected from physical damage.

Figure 250–102

The upper end of the ground rod must be flush with or underground unless the grounding electrode conductor attachment is protected against physical damage as specified in 250.10.

Author's Comment: When the grounding electrode attachment fitting is located underground, it must be listed for direct soil burial [250.68(A) Ex 1 and 250.70].

MEASURING THE GROUND RESISTANCE

Measuring the Ground Resistance

A ground resistance clamp meter, or a three-point fall of potential ground resistance meter, can be used to measure the contact resistance of a grounding electrode to the earth.

Ground Clamp Meter. The ground resistance clamp meter measures the contact resistance of the grounding system to the earth by injecting a high-frequency signal via the service neutral conductor to the utility ground, and then measuring the strength of the return signal through the earth to the grounding electrode being measured. **Figure 250–103**

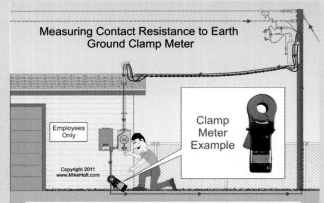

Measuring Contact Resistance to Earth
Ground Clamp Meter

Clamp Meter Example

Employees Only

Copyright 2011
www.MikeHolt.com

The clamp meter measures the contact resistance to the earth of the grounding electrode system by injecting a high-frequency signal to the utility ground, then measuring the strength of the return signal.

Figure 250–103

Fall of Potential Ground Resistance Meter. The three-point fall of potential ground resistance meter determines the contact resistance of a single grounding electrode to the earth by using Ohm's Law: R=E/I.

This meter divides the voltage difference between the electrode to be measured and a driven potential test stake (P) by the current flowing between the electrode to be measured and a driven current test stake (C). The test stakes are typically made of ¼ in. diameter steel rods, 24 in. long, driven two-thirds of their length into the earth.

The distance and alignment between the potential and current test stakes, and the electrode, is extremely important to the validity of the earth contact resistance measurements. For an 8

ft ground rod, the accepted practice is to space the current test stake (C) 80 ft from the electrode to be measured.

The potential test stake (P) is positioned in a straight line between the electrode to be measured and the current test stake (C). The potential test stake should be located at approximately 62 percent of the distance the current test stake is located from the electrode. Since the current test stake (C) for an 8 ft ground rod is located 80 ft from the grounding electrode, the potential test stake (P) will be about 50 ft from the electrode to be measured.

> *Question: If the voltage between the ground rod and the potential test stake (P) is 3V and the current between the ground rod and the current test stake (C) is 0.20A, then the earth contact resistance of the electrode to the earth will be _____.* **Figure 250–104**
>
> *(a) 5 ohms   (b) 10 ohms   (c) 15 ohms   (d) 25 ohms*
>
> **Answer:** *(c) 15 ohms*
>
> *Resistance = Voltage/Current*
> *E (Voltage) = 3V*
> *I (Current) = 0.20A*
> *R = E/I*
> *Resistance = 3V/0.20A*
> *Resistance = 15 ohms*

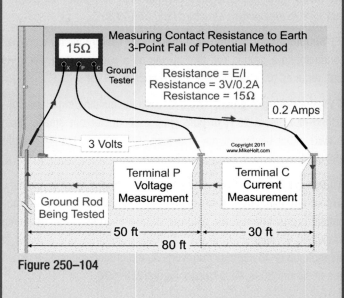

Measuring Contact Resistance to Earth
3-Point Fall of Potential Method

15Ω

Ground Tester

Resistance = E/I
Resistance = 3V/0.2A
Resistance = 15Ω

0.2 Amps

3 Volts

Copyright 2011
www.MikeHolt.com

Terminal P
Voltage
Measurement

Terminal C
Current
Measurement

Ground Rod
Being Tested

50 ft

30 ft

80 ft

Figure 250–104

Essential Rule 37   250.64

250.64 Grounding Electrode Conductor Installation.
Grounding electrode conductors must be installed as specified in (A) through (F).

(A) Aluminum Conductors. Aluminum grounding electrode conductors must not be in contact with masonry, subject to corrosive conditions, or within 18 in. of the earth.

(B) Conductor Protection. Where installed exposed, grounding electrode conductors must be protected where subject to physical damage and are permitted to be installed on or through framing members. Grounding electrode conductors 6 AWG copper and larger can be installed exposed along the surface of the building if securely fastened and not subject to physical damage.

Grounding electrode conductors sized 8 AWG must be protected by installing them in rigid metal conduit, intermediate metal conduit, PVC conduit, electrical metallic tubing, or reinforced thermosetting resin conduit.

Author's Comment: A ferrous metal raceway containing a grounding electrode conductor must be made electrically continuous by bonding each end of that type of raceway to the grounding electrode conductor [250.64(E)], so it's best to use PVC conduit.

(C) Continuous. Grounding electrode conductor(s) must be installed without a splice or joint except: **Figures 250–105 and 250–106**

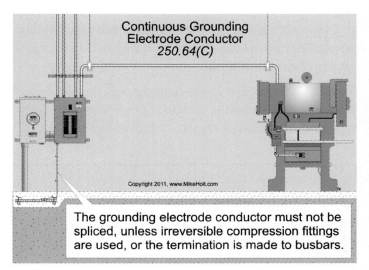

Continuous Grounding
Electrode Conductor
250.64(C)

Copyright 2011, www.MikeHolt.com

The grounding electrode conductor must not be spliced, unless irreversible compression fittings are used, or the termination is made to busbars.

Figure 250–105

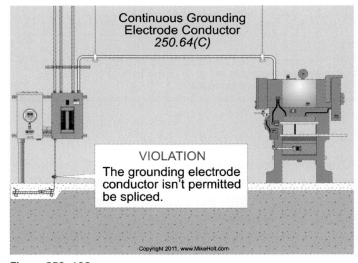

Continuous Grounding
Electrode Conductor
250.64(C)

VIOLATION
The grounding electrode conductor isn't permitted be spliced.

Copyright 2011, www.MikeHolt.com

Figure 250–106

(1) By irreversible compression-type connectors or exothermic welding.

(2) Sections of busbars connected together to form a grounding electrode conductor.

(3) Bolted, riveted, or welded connections of structural metal frames of buildings or structures.

(4) Threaded, welded, brazed, soldered or bolted-flange connections of metal water piping.

(D) Grounding Electrode Conductor for Multiple Service Disconnects. If a service consists of more than a single enclosure, grounding electrode connections must be made in one of the following methods:

(1) Common Grounding Electrode Conductor and Taps. A grounding electrode conductor tap must extend to the inside of each service disconnecting means enclosure.

The common grounding electrode conductor must be sized in accordance with 250.66, based on the sum of the circular mil area of the largest ungrounded service-entrance conductors. **Figure 250–107**

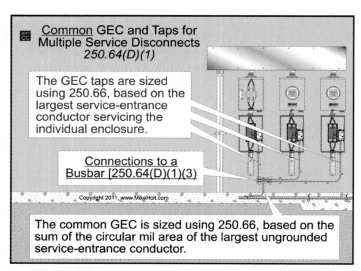

Figure 250–107

A grounding electrode conductor must extend from each service disconnecting means, sized not smaller than specified in Table 250.66, based on the area of the largest ungrounded conductor for each service disconnecting means.

The grounding electrode tap conductors must be connected to the common grounding electrode conductor, without splicing the common grounding electrode conductor, by one of the following methods:

(1) Exothermic welding.

(2) Connectors listed as grounding and bonding equipment.

(3) Connections to a busbar not less than ¼ in. × 2 in. that's securely fastened and installed in an accessible location.

(2) Individual Grounding Electrode Conductors. A grounding electrode conductor must be connected between the grounded conductor in each service equipment disconnecting means enclosure and the grounding electrode system, each sized in accordance with 250.66 based on the ungrounded service-entrance conductor(s) supplying the individual service disconnecting means. **Figure 250–108**

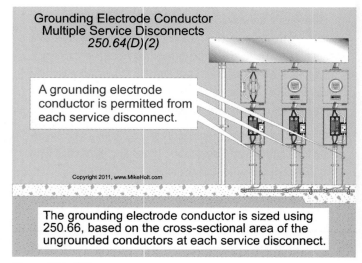

Figure 250–108

(3) Common Location. A single grounding electrode conductor is permitted from a common location, sized not smaller than specified in Table 250.66, based on the area of the ungrounded conductor at the location where the connection is made. **Figure 250–109**

(E) Ferrous Metal Enclosures Containing Grounding Electrode Conductors. To prevent inductive choking of grounding electrode conductors, ferrous raceways and enclosures containing grounding electrode conductors must have each end of the raceway or enclosure bonded to the grounding electrode conductor in accordance with 250.92(B) for installations at service equipment. **Figure 250–110**

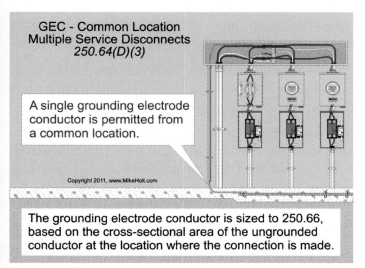

GEC - Common Location
Multiple Service Disconnects
250.64(D)(3)

A single grounding electrode conductor is permitted from a common location.

Copyright 2011, www.MikeHolt.com

The grounding electrode conductor is sized to 250.66, based on the cross-sectional area of the ungrounded conductor at the location where the connection is made.

Figure 250–109

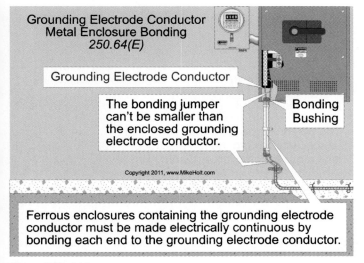

Grounding Electrode Conductor
Metal Enclosure Bonding
250.64(E)

Grounding Electrode Conductor

The bonding jumper can't be smaller than the enclosed grounding electrode conductor.

Bonding Bushing

Copyright 2011, www.MikeHolt.com

Ferrous enclosures containing the grounding electrode conductor must be made electrically continuous by bonding each end to the grounding electrode conductor.

Figure 250–110

For other than service equipment locations, ferrous raceways and enclosures containing grounding electrode conductors must have each end of the raceway or enclosure bonded to the grounding electrode conductor in accordance with 250.92(B)(2) through (B)(4).

Author's Comment: Nonferrous metal raceways, such as aluminum rigid metal conduit, enclosing the grounding electrode conductor aren't required to meet the "bonding each end of the raceway to the grounding electrode conductor" provisions of this section.

⚠ **CAUTION:** *The effectiveness of a grounding electrode is significantly reduced if a ferrous metal raceway containing a grounding electrode conductor isn't bonded to the ferrous metal raceway at both ends. This is because a single conductor carrying high-frequency induced lightning current in a ferrous raceway causes the raceway to act as an inductor, which severely limits (chokes) the current flow through the grounding electrode conductor. ANSI/IEEE 142—Recommended Practice for Grounding of Industrial and Commercial Power Systems (Green Book) states: "An inductive choke can reduce the current flow by 97 percent."*

Author's Comment: To save a lot of time and effort, install the grounding electrode conductor exposed if it's not subject to physical damage [250.64(B)], or enclose it in PVC conduit suitable for the application [352.10(F)].

(F) Termination to Grounding Electrode.

(1) Single Grounding Electrode Conductor. A single grounding electrode conductor is permitted to terminate to any grounding electrode of the grounding electrode system. **Figure 250–111**

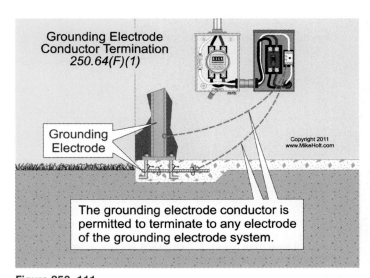

Grounding Electrode
Conductor Termination
250.64(F)(1)

Grounding Electrode

Copyright 2011
www.MikeHolt.com

The grounding electrode conductor is permitted to terminate to any electrode of the grounding electrode system.

Figure 250–111

(2) Multiple Grounding Electrode Conductors. When multiple grounding electrode conductors are installed [250.64(D)(2)], each grounding electrode conductor is permitted to terminate to any grounding electrode of the grounding electrode system. **Figure 250–112**

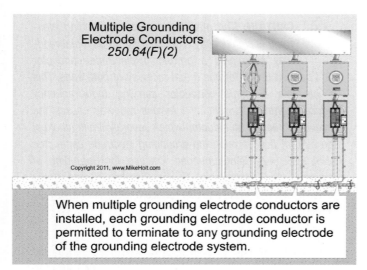

When multiple grounding electrode conductors are installed, each grounding electrode conductor is permitted to terminate to any grounding electrode of the grounding electrode system.

Figure 250–112

(3) Termination to Busbar. A grounding electrode conductor and grounding electrode bonding jumpers are permitted to terminate to a busbar sized not less than ¼ in. × 2 in. that's securely fastened at an accessible location. The terminations to the busbar must be made by a listed connector or by exothermic welding. **Figure 250–113**

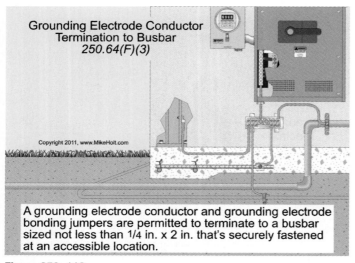

A grounding electrode conductor and grounding electrode bonding jumpers are permitted to terminate to a busbar sized not less than 1/4 in. x 2 in. that's securely fastened at an accessible location.

Figure 250–113

Essential Rule 38   **250.66**

250.66 Sizing Grounding Electrode Conductor. Except as permitted in (A) through (C), a grounding electrode conductor must be sized in accordance with Table 250.66.

(A) Ground Rod. If the grounding electrode conductor is connected to a ground rod as permitted in 250.52(A)(5), that portion of the grounding electrode conductor that's the sole connection to the ground rod isn't required to be larger than 6 AWG copper. **Figure 250–114**

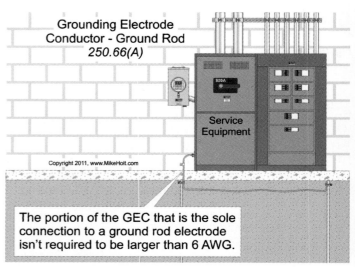

The portion of the GEC that is the sole connection to a ground rod electrode isn't required to be larger than 6 AWG.

Figure 250–114

(B) Concrete-Encased Grounding Electrode. If the grounding electrode conductor is connected to a concrete-encased electrode, the portion of the grounding electrode conductor that's the sole connection to the concrete-encased electrode isn't required to be larger than 4 AWG copper. **Figure 250–115**

(C) Ground Ring. If the grounding electrode conductor is connected to a ground ring, the portion of the conductor that's the sole connection to the ground ring isn't required to be larger than the conductor used for the ground ring.

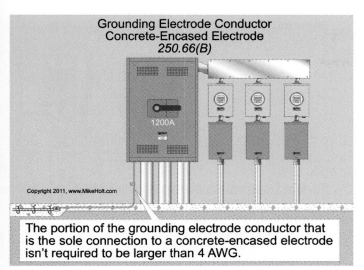

Grounding Electrode Conductor
Concrete-Encased Electrode
250.66(B)

The portion of the grounding electrode conductor that is the sole connection to a concrete-encased electrode isn't required to be larger than 4 AWG.

Figure 250–115

Author's Comments:

- A ground ring encircling the building/structure in direct contact with the earth must consist of at least 20 ft of bare copper conductor not smaller than 2 AWG [250.52(A)(4)]. See 250.53(F) for the installation requirements for a ground ring.

- Table 250.66 is used to size the grounding electrode conductor when the conditions of 250.66(A), (B), or (C) don't apply. **Figure 250–116**

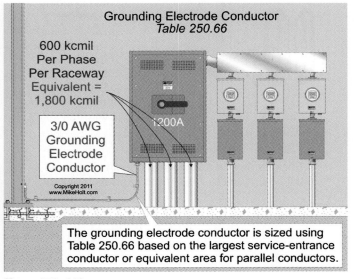

Grounding Electrode Conductor
Table 250.66

600 kcmil Per Phase Per Raceway Equivalent = 1,800 kcmil

3/0 AWG Grounding Electrode Conductor

The grounding electrode conductor is sized using Table 250.66 based on the largest service-entrance conductor or equivalent area for parallel conductors.

Figure 250–116

Table 250.66 Sizing Grounding Electrode Conductor	
Conductor or Area of Parallel Conductors	Copper Grounding Electrode Conductor
12 through 2 AWG	8 AWG
1 or 1/0 AWG	6 AWG
2/0 or 3/0 AWG	4 AWG
4/0 through 350 kcmil	2 AWG
400 through 600 kcmil	1/0 AWG
700 through 1,100 kcmil	2/0 AWG
1,200 kcmil and larger	3/0 AWG

Essential Rule 39   **250.92**

PART V. BONDING

250.92 Bonding Equipment for Services.

(A) Bonding Requirements for Equipment for Services. The metal parts of equipment indicated below must be bonded together in accordance with 250.92(B). **Figure 250–117**

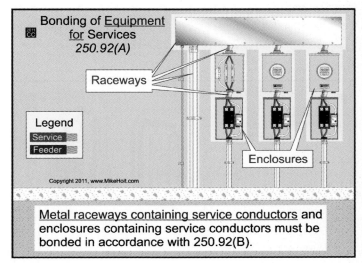

Bonding of Equipment
for Services
250.92(A)

Raceways

Legend
Service
Feeder

Enclosures

Metal raceways containing service conductors and enclosures containing service conductors must be bonded in accordance with 250.92(B).

Figure 250–117

(1) Metal raceways containing, enclosing, or supporting service conductors.

(2) Metal enclosures containing service conductors.

Author's Comment: Metal raceways or metal enclosures containing feeder and branch-circuit conductors are required to be connected to the circuit equipment grounding conductor in accordance with 250.86. **Figure 250–118**

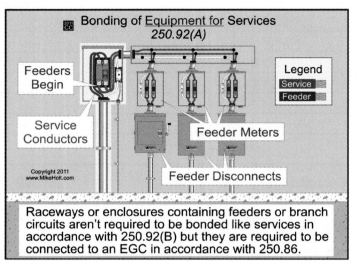

Figure 250–118

(B) Methods of Bonding. Bonding jumpers around reducing washers or oversized, concentric, or eccentric knockouts are required. Standard locknuts are permitted to make a mechanical connection of the raceway(s), but they can't serve as the bonding means required by this section. **Figures 250–119 and 250–120**

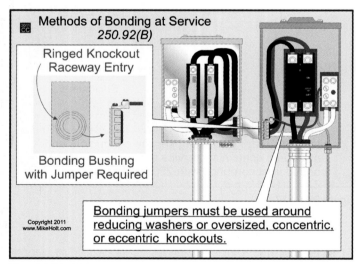

Figure 250–119

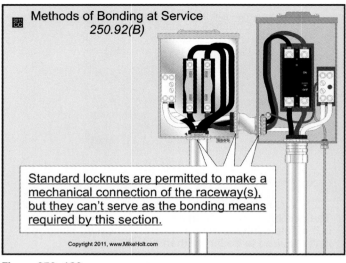

Figure 250–120

Electrical continuity at service equipment, service raceways, and service conductor enclosures must be ensured by one of the following methods:

(1) Neutral Conductor. By bonding the metal parts to the service neutral conductor. **Figure 250–121**

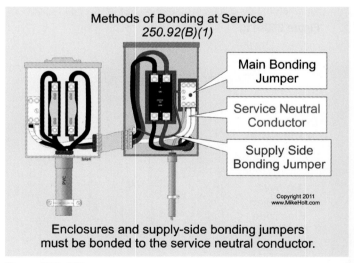

Figure 250–121

Author's Comments:

- A main bonding jumper is required to bond the service disconnect to the service neutral conductor [250.24(B) and 250.28].

- At service equipment, the service neutral conductor provides the effective ground-fault current path to the power supply [250.24(C)]; therefore, an equipment grounding conductor isn't required to be installed within PVC conduit containing service-entrance conductors [250.142(A)(1) and 352.60 Ex 2]. **Figure 250–122**

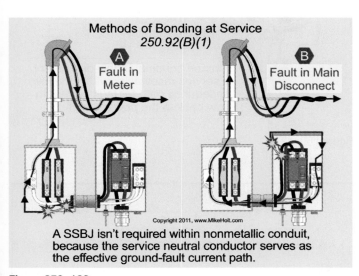

A SSBJ isn't required within nonmetallic conduit, because the service neutral conductor serves as the effective ground-fault current path.

Figure 250–122

(2) Threaded Fittings. By terminating metal raceways to metal enclosures by threaded <u>hubs</u> on enclosures if made up wrenchtight. **Figure 250–123**

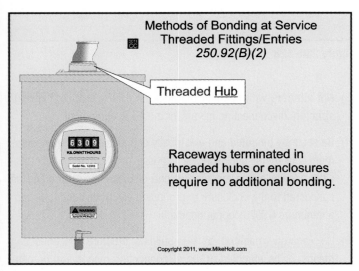

Raceways terminated in threaded hubs or enclosures require no additional bonding.

Figure 250–123

(3) Threadless Fittings. By terminating metal raceways to metal enclosures by threadless fittings <u>if</u> made up tight. **Figure 250–124**

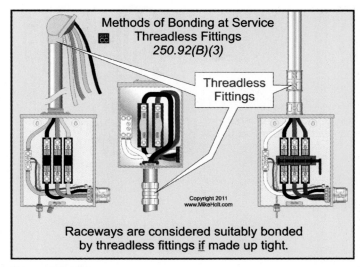

Raceways are considered suitably bonded by threadless fittings <u>if</u> made up tight.

Figure 250–124

(4) Other listed devices, such as bonding-type locknuts, bushings, wedges, or bushings with bonding jumpers.

Author's Comments:

- A listed bonding wedge or bushing with a bonding jumper must be used to bond one end of the service raceway to the service neutral conductor. The bonding jumper used for this purpose must be sized in accordance with Table 250.66, based on the area of the largest ungrounded service conductors within the raceway [250.102(C)]. **Figure 250–125**

- When a metal raceway containing service conductors terminates to an enclosure without a ringed knockout, a bonding-type locknut can be used. **Figure 250–126**

- A bonding locknut differs from a standard locknut in that it's a bonding screw with a sharp point that drives into the metal enclosure to ensure a solid connection.

- Bonding one end of a service raceway to the service neutral provides the low-impedance fault current path to the source. **Figure 250–127**

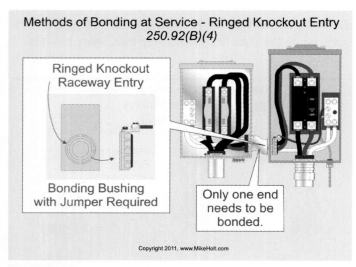

Methods of Bonding at Service - Ringed Knockout Entry
250.92(B)(4)

Ringed Knockout Raceway Entry

Bonding Bushing with Jumper Required

Only one end needs to be bonded.

Copyright 2011, www.MikeHolt.com

Figure 250–125

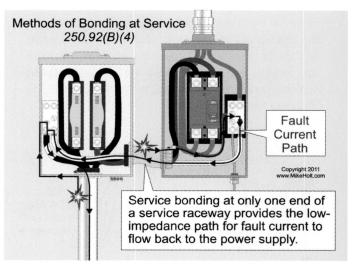

Methods of Bonding at Service
250.92(B)(4)

Fault Current Path

Copyright 2011 www.MikeHolt.com

Service bonding at only one end of a service raceway provides the low-impedance path for fault current to flow back to the power supply.

Figure 250–127

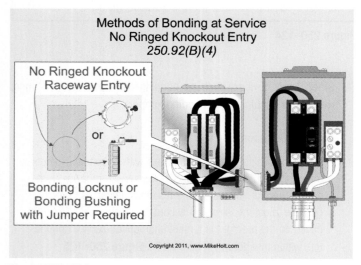

Methods of Bonding at Service
No Ringed Knockout Entry
250.92(B)(4)

No Ringed Knockout Raceway Entry

or

Bonding Locknut or Bonding Bushing with Jumper Required

Copyright 2011, www.MikeHolt.com

Figure 250–126

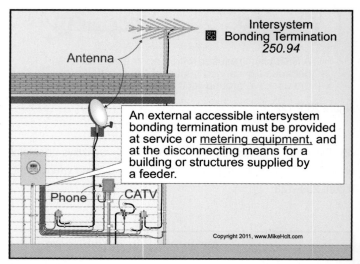

Antenna

Intersystem Bonding Termination
250.94

An external accessible intersystem bonding termination must be provided at service or metering equipment, and at the disconnecting means for a building or structures supplied by a feeder.

Phone   CATV

Copyright 2011, www.MikeHolt.com

Figure 250–128

Essential Rule 40   250.94

250.94 Intersystem Bonding Termination. An external accessible intersystem bonding termination for the connection of communications systems bonding conductors must be provided at service equipment or metering equipment enclosure and disconnecting means for buildings or structures supplied by a feeder. **Figure 250–128**. The intersystem bonding termination must:

(1) Be accessible for connection and inspection. **Figure 250–129**

(2) Consist of a set of terminals with the capacity for connection of not less than three intersystem bonding conductors.

(3) Not interfere with opening the enclosure for a service, building/structure disconnecting means, or metering equipment.

(4) Be securely mounted and electrically connected to service equipment, the meter enclosure, or exposed nonflexible metallic service raceway, or be mounted at one of these enclosures and be connected to the enclosure or grounding electrode conductor with a minimum 6 AWG copper conductor.

(5) Be securely mounted to the building/structure disconnecting means, or be mounted at the disconnecting means and be connected to the metallic enclosure or grounding electrode conductor with a minimum 6 AWG copper conductor. **Figure 250–130**

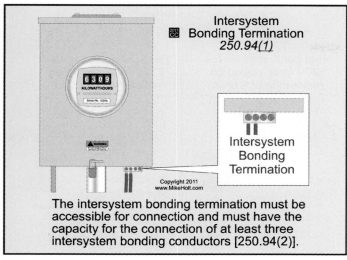

Intersystem Bonding Termination 250.94(1)

The intersystem bonding termination must be accessible for connection and must have the capacity for the connection of at least three intersystem bonding conductors [250.94(2)].

Figure 250–129

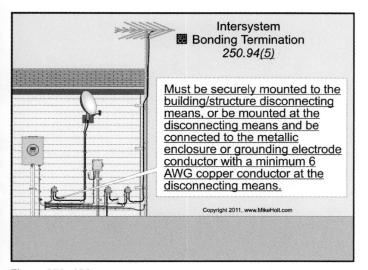

Intersystem Bonding Termination 250.94(5)

Must be securely mounted to the building/structure disconnecting means, or be mounted at the disconnecting means and be connected to the metallic enclosure or grounding electrode conductor with a minimum 6 AWG copper conductor at the disconnecting means.

Figure 250–130

(6) The terminals must be listed as grounding and bonding equipment.

Author's Comment: According to Article 100, an intersystem bonding termination is a device that provides a means to connect communications systems grounding and bonding conductors to the building grounding electrode system.

Ex: At existing buildings or structures, an external accessible means for bonding communications systems together can be by the use of a:

(1) *Nonflexible metallic raceway,*

(2) *Grounding electrode conductor, or*

(3) *Connection approved by the authority having jurisdiction.*

Note 2: Communications systems must be bonded to the intersystem bonding termination in accordance with the following *Code* requirements: **Figure 250–131**

- Antennas/Satellite Dishes, 810.15 and 810.21
- CATV, 820.100
- Telephone Circuits, 800.100

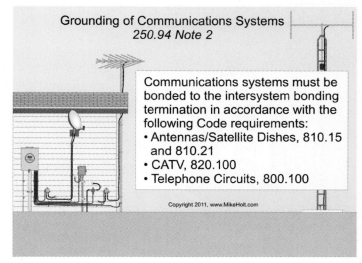

Grounding of Communications Systems 250.94 Note 2

Communications systems must be bonded to the intersystem bonding termination in accordance with the following Code requirements:
- Antennas/Satellite Dishes, 810.15 and 810.21
- CATV, 820.100
- Telephone Circuits, 800.100

Figure 250–131

Author's Comment: All external communications systems must be connected to the intersystem bonding termination to minimize the damage to them from induced potential (voltage) differences between the systems from a lightning event. **Figure 250–132**

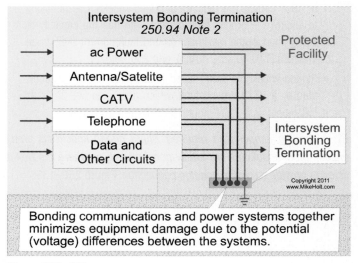

Intersystem Bonding Termination 250.94 Note 2

Bonding communications and power systems together minimizes equipment damage due to the potential (voltage) differences between the systems.

Figure 250–132

Essential Rule 41   250.97

250.97 Bonding Metal Parts Containing 277V and 480V Circuits. Metal raceways or cables containing 277V and/or 480V feeder or branch circuits terminating at ringed knockouts must be bonded to the metal enclosure with a bonding jumper sized in accordance with 250.122, based on the rating of the circuit overcurrent device [250.102(D)]. **Figure 250–133**

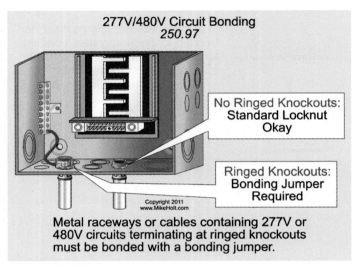

277V/480V Circuit Bonding
250.97

No Ringed Knockouts: **Standard Locknut Okay**

Ringed Knockouts: **Bonding Jumper Required**

Copyright 2011
www.MikeHolt.com

Metal raceways or cables containing 277V or 480V circuits terminating at ringed knockouts must be bonded with a bonding jumper.

Figure 250–133

Author's Comments:

- Bonding jumpers for raceways and cables containing 277V or 480V circuits are required at ringed knockout terminations to ensure the ground-fault current path has the capacity to safely conduct the maximum ground-fault current likely to be imposed [110.10, 250.4(A)(5), and 250.96(A)].

- Ringed knockouts aren't listed to withstand the heat generated by a 277V ground fault, which generates five times as much heat as a 120V ground fault. **Figure 250–134**

Ex: A bonding jumper isn't required where ringed knockouts aren't encountered, knockouts are totally punched out, or where the box is listed to provide a reliable bonding connection. **Figure 250–135**

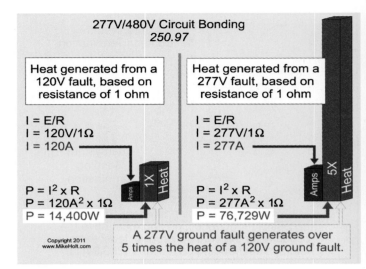

277V/480V Circuit Bonding
250.97

Heat generated from a 120V fault, based on resistance of 1 ohm

$I = E/R$
$I = 120V/1\Omega$
$I = 120A$

$P = I^2 \times R$
$P = 120A^2 \times 1\Omega$
$P = 14,400W$

Heat generated from a 277V fault, based on resistance of 1 ohm

$I = E/R$
$I = 277V/1\Omega$
$I = 277A$

$P = I^2 \times R$
$P = 277A^2 \times 1\Omega$
$P = 76,729W$

Copyright 2011
www.MikeHolt.com

A 277V ground fault generates over 5 times the heat of a 120V ground fault.

Figure 250–134

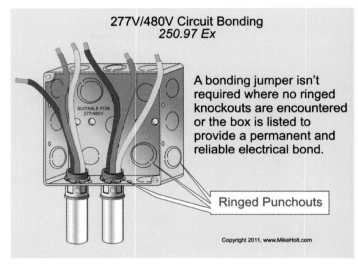

277V/480V Circuit Bonding
250.97 Ex

SUITABLE FOR 277/480V

A bonding jumper isn't required where no ringed knockouts are encountered or the box is listed to provide a permanent and reliable electrical bond.

Ringed Punchouts

Copyright 2011, www.MikeHolt.com

Figure 250–135

Essential Rule 42   250.102

250.102 Bonding Conductors and Jumpers.

(A) Material. Equipment bonding jumpers must be copper.

(B) Termination. Equipment bonding jumpers must terminate by listed pressure connectors, terminal bars, exothermic welding, or other listed means [250.8(A)].

(C) Size for Supply-Side Bonding Jumper.

(1) Single Raceway Installations. The supply-side bonding jumper is sized to Table 250.66, based on the largest ungrounded conductor within the raceway. If the ungrounded supply conductors are larger than 1,100 kcmil copper or 1,750 kcmil aluminum, the supply-side bonding jumper must be sized not less than 12½ percent of the area of the largest set of ungrounded supply conductors.

(2) Parallel Conductor Installations. If the ungrounded supply conductors are paralleled in two or more raceways or cables, the size of the supply-side bonding jumper for each raceway or cable is sized in accordance with Table 250.66, based on the size of the largest ungrounded conductors in each raceway or cable. A single supply-side bonding jumper for bonding two or more raceways or cables must be sized in accordance with (C)(1).

Question 1: What size supply-side bonding jumper is required for a metal raceway containing 700 kcmil service conductors? **Figure 250–136**

(a) 1 AWG   (b) 1/0 AWG   (c) 2/0 AWG   (d) 3/0 AWG

Answer: (c) 2/0 AWG [Table 250.66]

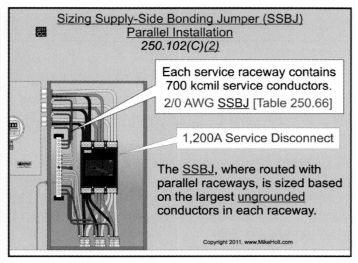

Sizing Supply-Side Bonding Jumper (SSBJ)
Parallel Installation
250.102(C)(2)

Each service raceway contains 700 kcmil service conductors. 2/0 AWG SSBJ [Table 250.66]

1,200A Service Disconnect

The SSBJ, where routed with parallel raceways, is sized based on the largest ungrounded conductors in each raceway.

Copyright 2011, www.MikeHolt.com

Figure 250–136

Question 2: What size single supply-side bonding jumper is required for three metal raceways containing 700 kcmil service conductors? **Figure 250–137**

(a) 1 AWG   (b) 1/0 AWG   (c) 2/0 AWG   (d) 300 AWG

Answer: (d) 300 kcmil [250.102(C)(1)]

700 kcmil x 3 = 2,100 kcmil
2,100 kcmil x 0.125 = 263 kcmil
Chapter 9, Table 8, use 300 kcmil

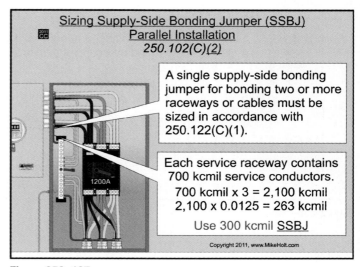

Sizing Supply-Side Bonding Jumper (SSBJ)
Parallel Installation
250.102(C)(2)

A single supply-side bonding jumper for bonding two or more raceways or cables must be sized in accordance with 250.122(C)(1).

Each service raceway contains 700 kcmil service conductors.
700 kcmil x 3 = 2,100 kcmil
2,100 x 0.0125 = 263 kcmil
Use 300 kcmil SSBJ

Copyright 2011, www.MikeHolt.com

Figure 250–137

(3) Different Materials. If the ungrounded supply conductors and the supply-side bonding jumper are of different materials (copper or aluminum), the supply-side bonding jumper is sized on the assumed use of the same material.

(D) Load Side Equipment Bonding Jumper Sizing. Bonding jumpers on the load side of feeder and branch-circuit overcurrent devices are sized in accordance with 250.122, based on the rating of the circuit overcurrent device.

Author's Comment: The equipment bonding jumper isn't required to be larger than the largest ungrounded circuit conductors [250.122(A)].

Question: What size equipment bonding jumper is required for a metal raceway where the circuit conductors are protected by a 1,200A overcurrent device? **Figure 250–138**

(a) 1 AWG (b) 1/0 AWG (c) 2/0 AWG (d) 3/0 AWG

Answer: (d) 3/0 AWG [Table 250.122]

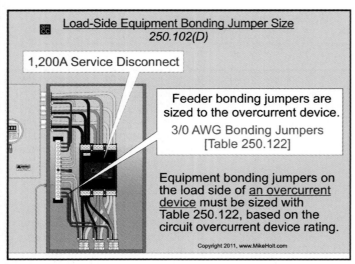

Figure 250–138

If a single equipment bonding jumper is used to bond two or more raceways, it must be sized in accordance with 250.122, based on the rating of the largest circuit overcurrent device. **Figure 250–139**

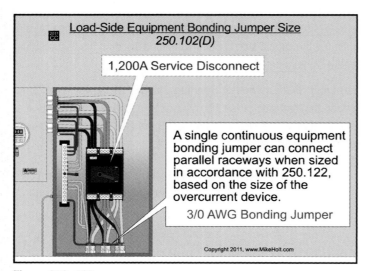

Figure 250–139

(E) Installation. Equipment bonding jumpers, as well as bonding jumpers or conductors can be installed inside or outside of a raceway.

(1) Inside a Raceway or Enclosure. If installed inside a raceway, the conductors must be identified in accordance with 250.119 and if circuit conductors are spliced or terminated on equipment within a metal box, the equipment grounding conductor associated with those circuits must be connected to the box in accordance with 250.148.

(2) Outside a Raceway. If the equipment bonding jumper is installed outside of a raceway, its length must not exceed 6 ft and it must be routed with the raceway. **Figure 250–140**

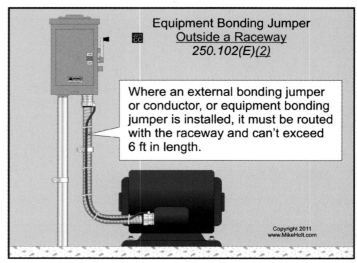

Figure 250–140

Ex: An equipment bonding jumper or supply-side bonding jumper of any length can be used to bond isolated sections of metal raceways at outside pole locations.

(3) Protection. Aluminum bonding jumpers or conductors and equipment bonding jumpers must not be in contact with masonry, subject to corrosive conditions, or within 18 in. of the earth [250.64(A)] and conductors must be protected where subject to physical damage in accordance with 250.64(B).

Essential Rule 43   250.104

250.104 Bonding of Piping Systems and Exposed Structural Metal.

Author's Comment: To remove dangerous voltage on metal parts from a ground fault, electrically conductive metal water piping systems, metal sprinkler piping, metal gas piping, as well as exposed structural steel members likely to become energized, must be connected to an effective ground-fault current path [250.4(A)(4)].

(A) Metal Water Piping System. The metal water piping system must be bonded as required in (A)(1), (A)(2), or (A)(3). The bonding jumper must be copper where within 18 in. of the earth [250.64(A)], securely fastened to the surface on which it's mounted [250.64(B)], and adequately protected if exposed to physical damage [250.64(B)]. In addition, all points of attachment must be accessible.

Author's Comment: Bonding isn't required for isolated sections of metal water piping connected to a nonmetallic water piping system. **Figure 250–141**

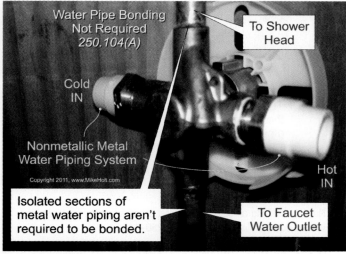

Figure 250–141

(1) Building/Structure Supplied by a Service. The metal water piping system, including the metal sprinkler water piping system of a building/structure supplied with service conductors must be bonded to the: **Figure 250–142**

- Service equipment enclosure,
- Service neutral conductor,
- Grounding electrode conductor of sufficient size, or
- Grounding electrode system.

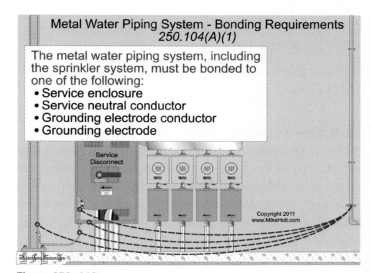

Figure 250–142

The metal water piping system bonding jumper must be sized in accordance with Table 250.66, based on the cross-sectional area of the ungrounded service conductors.

Question: *What size bonding jumper is required for the metal water piping system if the 300 kcmil service conductors are paralleled in two raceways?* **Figure 250–143**

(a) 6 AWG   (b) 4 AWG   (c) 2 AWG   (d) 1/0 AWG

Answer: *(d) 1/0 AWG, based on 600 kcmil conductors, in accordance with Table 250.66*

Author's Comment: If hot and cold metal water pipes are electrically connected, only one bonding jumper is required, either to the cold or hot water pipe.

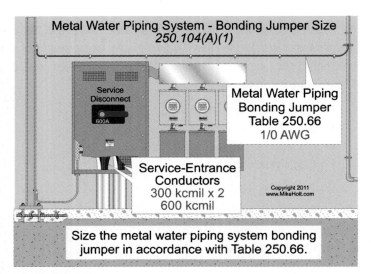

Figure 250–143

(2) Multiple Occupancy Building. When the metal water piping system in an individual occupancy is metallically isolated from other occupancies, the metal water piping system for that occupancy can be bonded to the equipment grounding terminal of the occupancy's panelboard. The bonding jumper must be sized in accordance with Table 250.122, based on the ampere rating of the occupancy's feeder overcurrent device. **Figure 250–144**

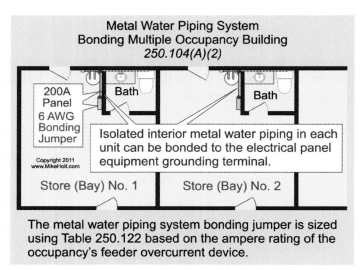

The metal water piping system bonding jumper is sized using Table 250.122 based on the ampere rating of the occupancy's feeder overcurrent device.

Figure 250–144

(3) Building/Structure Supplied by a Feeder. The metal water piping system of a building/structure supplied by a feeder must be bonded to:

- The equipment grounding terminal of the building disconnect enclosure,
- The feeder equipment grounding conductor, or
- The grounding electrode system.

The bonding jumper is sized to Table 250.66, based on the cross-sectional area of the ungrounded feeder conductor.

(B) Other Metal-Piping Systems. Metal-piping systems such as sprinkler, gas, or air that are likely to become energized must be bonded. The equipment grounding conductor for the circuit that's likely to energize the piping can serve as the bonding means. **Figure 250–145**

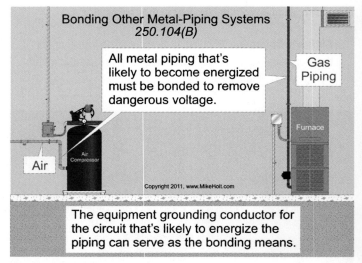

Figure 250–145

Note 1: Bonding all piping and metal air ducts within the premises will provide additional safety. **Figure 250–146**

Note 2: *The National Fuel Gas Code, NFPA 54, Section 7.13 contains further information about bonding gas piping.*

Author's Comment: Informational Notes in the *NEC* are for information purposes only and aren't enforceable as a requirement of the *Code* [90.5(C)].

Bonding Other Metal Piping and Air Ducts
250.104(B) Note 1

Bonding all piping and metal air ducts within the premises will provide additional safety.

Copyright 2011, www.MikeHolt.com

Figure 250–146

(C) Structural Metal. Exposed structural metal that forms a metal building frame that's likely to become energized must be bonded to the: **Figure 250–147**

- Service equipment enclosure,
- Service neutral conductor,
- Building/structure disconnecting means for buildings or structures supplied by a feeder or branch circuit,
- Grounding electrode conductor if of sufficient size, or
- Grounding electrode system.

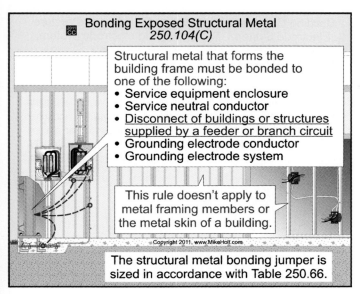

Bonding Exposed Structural Metal
250.104(C)

Structural metal that forms the building frame must be bonded to one of the following:
• Service equipment enclosure
• Service neutral conductor
• Disconnect of buildings or structures supplied by a feeder or branch circuit
• Grounding electrode conductor
• Grounding electrode system

This rule doesn't apply to metal framing members or the metal skin of a building.

Copyright 2011, www.MikeHolt.com

The structural metal bonding jumper is sized in accordance with Table 250.66.

Figure 250–147

Author's Comment: This rule doesn't require the bonding of sheet metal framing members (studs) or the metal skin of a wood frame building.

The bonding jumper must be sized in accordance with Table 250.66, based on the area of the ungrounded supply conductors. The bonding jumper must be copper where within 18 in. of the earth [250.64(A)], securely fastened to the surface on which it's carried [250.64(B)], and adequately protected if exposed to physical damage [250.64(B)]. In addition, all points of attachment must be accessible, except as permitted in 250.68(A).

(D) Separately Derived Systems. Metal water piping systems and structural metal that forms a building frame must be bonded as required in (D)(1) through (D)(3).

(1) Metal Water Pipe. The nearest available point of the metal water piping system in the area served by a separately derived system must be bonded to the neutral point of the separately derived system where the grounding electrode conductor is connected. **Figure 250–148**

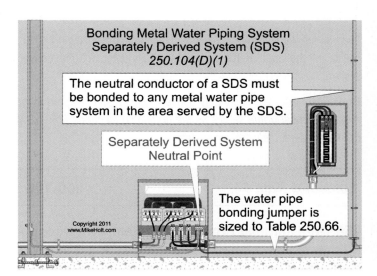

Bonding Metal Water Piping System
Separately Derived System (SDS)
250.104(D)(1)

The neutral conductor of a SDS must be bonded to any metal water pipe system in the area served by the SDS.

Separately Derived System Neutral Point

Copyright 2011 www.MikeHolt.com

The water pipe bonding jumper is sized to Table 250.66.

Figure 250–148

The bonding jumper must be sized in accordance with Table 250.66, based on the area of the ungrounded conductor of the derived system.

Ex 2: The metal water piping system is permitted to be bonded to the structural metal building frame if it serves as the grounding electrode [250.52(A)(1)] for the separately derived system. **Figure 250–149**

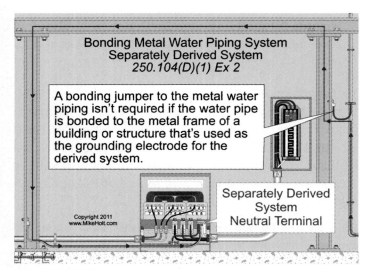

Figure 250–149

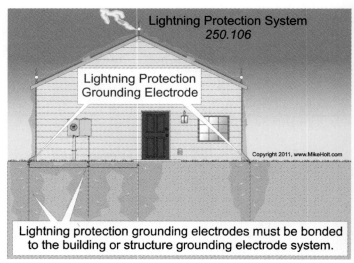

Figure 250–150

(2) Structural Metal. Exposed structural metal interconnected to form the building frame must be bonded to the neutral point of each separately derived system where the grounding electrode conductor is connected.

The bonding jumper must be sized in accordance with Table 250.66, based on the area of the ungrounded conductors of the derived system.

Ex 1: Bonding to the separately derived system isn't required if the metal structural frame serves as the grounding electrode [250.52(A)(2)] for the separately derived system.

Essential Rule 44	250.106

250.106 Lightning Protection System. If a lightning protection system is installed on a building/structure, it must be bonded to the building/structure grounding electrode system. **Figure 250–150**

Author's Comment: The grounding electrode for a lightning protection system must not be used as the required grounding electrode system for the buildings or structures [250.60]. **Figure 250–151**

Note 1: See NFPA 780—*Standard for the Installation of Lightning Protection Systems,* which contains detailed information on grounding, bonding, and side-flash distance from lightning protection systems.

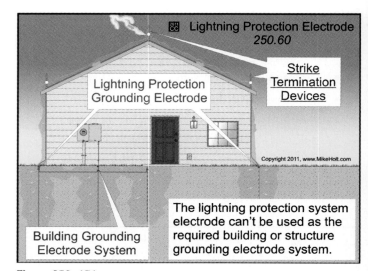

Figure 250–151

Note 2: To minimize the likelihood of arcing between metal parts because of induced voltage, metal raceways, enclosures, and other metal parts of electrical equipment may require bonding or spacing from the lightning protection conductors in accordance with NFPA 780—*Standard for the Installation of Lightning Protection Systems.* **Figure 250–152**

Figure 250–152

Note: The equipment grounding conductor is intended to serve as the effective ground-fault current path. See 250.2. **Figure 250–154**

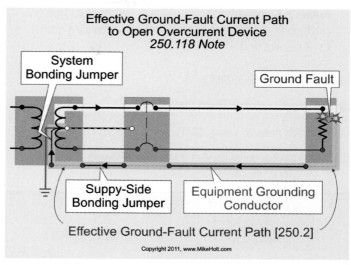

Figure 250–154

Essential Rule 45   250.118

PART VI. EQUIPMENT GROUNDING AND EQUIPMENT GROUNDING CONDUCTORS

250.118 Types of Equipment Grounding Conductors.

An equipment grounding conductor can be any one or a combination of the following: **Figure 250–153**

Author's Comment: The effective ground-fault path is an intentionally constructed low-impedance conductive path designed to carry fault current from the point of a ground fault on a wiring system to the electrical supply source. Its purpose is to quickly remove dangerous voltage from a ground fault by opening the circuit overcurrent device [250.2]. **Figure 250–155**

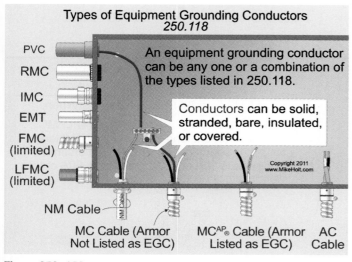

Figure 250–153

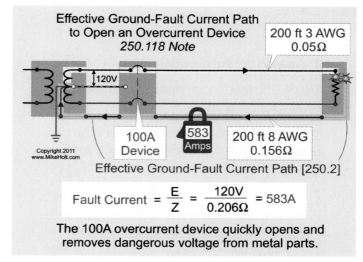

Figure 250–155

(1) A bare or insulated copper or aluminum conductor sized in accordance with 250.122.

Author's Comment: Examples include PVC conduit, Type NM cable, and Type MC cable with an equipment grounding conductor of the wire type.

(2) Rigid metal conduit (RMC).

(3) Intermediate metal conduit (IMC).

(4) Electrical metallic tubing (EMT).

(5) Listed flexible metal conduit (FMC) where: **Figure 250–156**

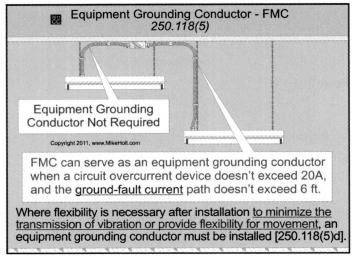

Figure 250–156

a. The raceway terminates in listed fittings.

b. The circuit conductors are protected by an overcurrent device rated 20A or less.

c. The combined length of the flexible conduit in the same ground-fault current path doesn't exceed 6 ft. **Figure 250–157**

d. If flexibility is required to minimize the transmission of vibration from equipment or to provide flexibility for equipment that requires movement after installation, an equipment grounding conductor of the wire type must be installed with the circuit conductors in accordance with 250.102(E), and it must be sized in accordance with 250.122, based on the rating of the circuit overcurrent device.

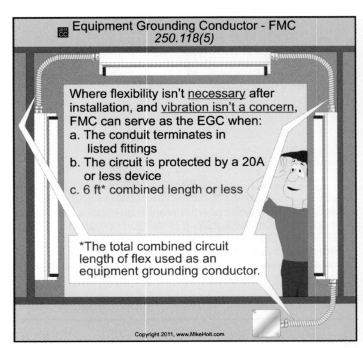

Figure 250–157

(6) Listed liquidtight flexible metal conduit (LFMC) where: **Figure 250–158**

a. The raceway terminates in listed fittings.

b. For ⅜ in. through ½ in., the circuit conductors are protected by an overcurrent device rated 20A or less.

c. For ¾ in. through 1¼ in., the circuit conductors are protected by an overcurrent device rated 60A or less.

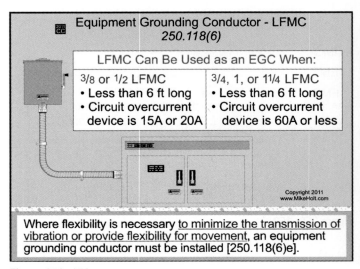

Figure 250–158

d. The combined length of the flexible conduit in the same ground-fault current path doesn't exceed 6 ft.

e. If flexibility is required to minimize the transmission of vibration from equipment or to provide flexibility for equipment that requires movement after installation, an equipment grounding conductor of the wire type must be installed with the circuit conductors in accordance with 250.102(E), and it must be sized in accordance with 250.122, based on the rating of the circuit overcurrent device.

(8) The sheath of Type AC cable containing an aluminum bonding strip. **Figure 250–159**

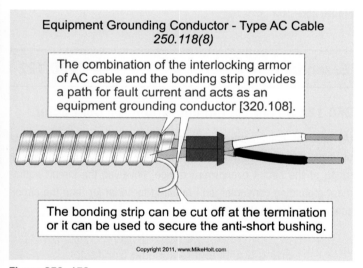

Figure 250–159

Author's Comments:

• The internal aluminum bonding strip isn't an equipment grounding conductor, but it allows the interlocked armor to serve as an equipment grounding conductor because it reduces the impedance of the armored spirals to ensure that a ground fault will be cleared. It's the aluminum bonding strip in combination with the cable armor that creates the circuit equipment grounding conductor. Once the bonding strip exits the cable, it can be cut off because it no longer serves any purpose.

• The effective ground-fault current path must be maintained by the use of fittings specifically listed for Type AC cable [320.40]. See 300.12, 300.15, and 320.100.

(9) The copper sheath of Type MI cable.

(10) Type MC cable that provides an effective ground-fault current path in accordance with one or more of the following:

(a) It contains an insulated or uninsulated equipment grounding conductor in compliance with 250.118(1). **Figure 250–160**

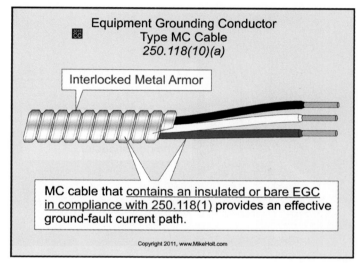

Figure 250–160

(b) The combined metallic sheath and uninsulated equipment grounding/bonding conductor of interlocked metal tape-type MC cable that's listed and identified as an equipment grounding conductor. **Figure 250–161**

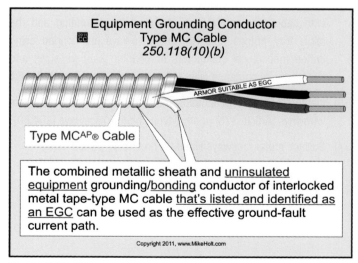

Figure 250–161

Author's Comment: Once the bare aluminum grounding/bonding conductor exits the cable, it can be cut off because it no longer serves any purpose. The effective ground-fault current path must be maintained by the use of fittings specifically listed for Type MCAP® cable [330.40]. See 300.12, 300.15, and 330.100. **Figure 250–162**

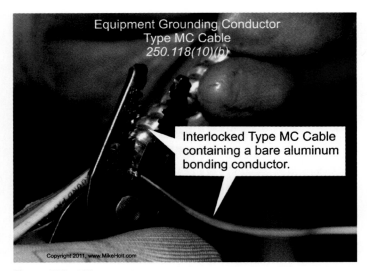

Figure 250–162

(c)   The metallic sheath or the combined metallic sheath and equipment grounding conductors of the smooth or corrugated tubetype MC cable that's listed and identified as an equipment grounding conductor.

(11) Metallic cable trays where continuous maintenance and supervision ensure only qualified persons will service the cable tray, with cable tray and fittings identified for grounding and the cable tray, fittings [392.10], and raceways are bonded using bolted mechanical connectors or bonding jumpers sized and installed in accordance with 250.102 [392.60]. **Figure 250–163**

(13) Listed electrically continuous metal raceways, such as metal wireways [Article 376] or strut-type channel raceways [384.60].

(14) Surface metal raceways listed for grounding [Article 386].

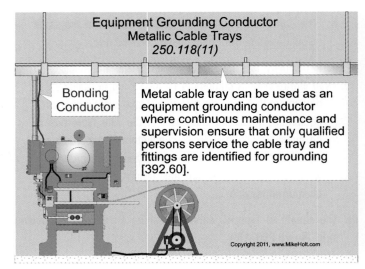

Figure 250–163

Essential Rule 46   **250.122**

250.122 Sizing Equipment Grounding Conductor.

(A) General. Equipment grounding conductors of the wire type must be sized not smaller than shown in Table 250.122, based on the rating of the circuit overcurrent device; however, the circuit equipment grounding conductor isn't required to be larger than the circuit conductors. **Figure 250–164**

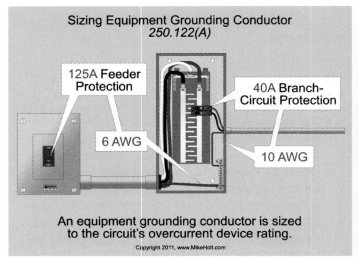

Figure 250–164

Equipment grounding conductors can be sectioned within a multiconductor cable, provided the combined circular mil area complies with Table 250.122.

Table 250.122 Sizing Equipment Grounding Conductor	
Overcurrent Device Rating	**Copper Conductor**
15A	14 AWG
20A	12 AWG
30A—60A	10 AWG
70A—100A	8 AWG
110A—200A	6 AWG
225A—300A	4 AWG
350A—400A	3 AWG
450A—500A	2 AWG
600A	1 AWG
700A—800A	1/0 AWG
1,000A	2/0 AWG
1,200A	3/0 AWG

(B) Increased in Size. If ungrounded conductors are increased in size from the minimum size, equipment grounding conductors must be proportionately increased in size according to the circular mil area of the ungrounded conductors.

> **Author's Comment:** Ungrounded conductors are sometimes increased in size to accommodate conductor voltage drop, harmonic current heating, short-circuit rating, or simply for future capacity.

Question: If the ungrounded conductors for a 40A circuit are increased in size from 8 AWG to 6 AWG, the circuit equipment grounding conductor must be increased in size from 10 AWG to _____. Figure 250–165

(a) 10 AWG   (b) 8 AWG   (c) 6 AWG   (d) 4 AWG

Answer: (b) 8 AWG

The circular mil area of 6 AWG is 59 percent more than 8 AWG (26,240 Cmil/16,510 Cmil) [Chapter 9, Table 8].

According to Table 250.122, the circuit equipment grounding conductor for a 40A overcurrent device will be 10 AWG (10,380 Cmil), but the circuit equipment grounding conductor for this circuit must be increased in size by a multiplier of 1.59.

Conductor Size = 10,380 Cmil x 1.59
Conductor Size = 16,504 Cmil
Conductor Size = 8 AWG, Chapter 9, Table 8

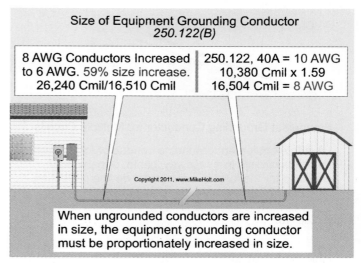

Size of Equipment Grounding Conductor 250.122(B)

8 AWG Conductors Increased to 6 AWG. 59% size increase. 26,240 Cmil/16,510 Cmil	250.122, 40A = 10 AWG 10,380 Cmil x 1.59 16,504 Cmil = 8 AWG

Copyright 2011, www.MikeHolt.com

When ungrounded conductors are increased in size, the equipment grounding conductor must be proportionately increased in size.

Figure 250–165

(C) Multiple Circuits. When multiple circuits are installed in the same raceway, cable, or cable tray, only one equipment grounding conductor is required for the multiple circuits, sized in accordance with 250.122, based on the rating of the largest circuit overcurrent device. **Figures 250–166 and 250–167**

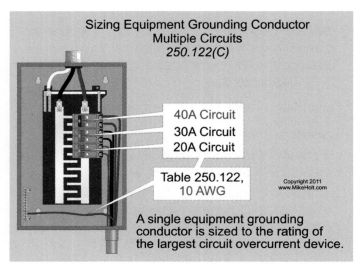

Figure 250–166

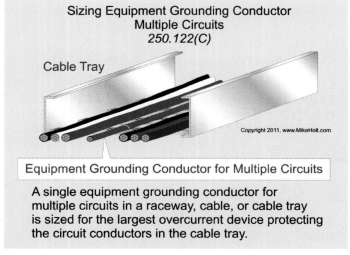

Figure 250–167

Author's Comment: Single conductors used as equipment grounding conductors in cable trays must be sized 4 AWG and larger [392.10(B)(1)(c)].

(D) Motor Branch Circuits.

(1) General. The equipment grounding conductor of the wire type must be sized in accordance with Table 250.122, based on the rating of the motor circuit branch-circuit short-circuit and ground-fault overcurrent device, but this conductor isn't required to be larger than the circuit conductors [250.122(A)].

Question: What size equipment grounding conductor is required for a 2 hp, 230V, single-phase motor? **Figure 250–168**

(a) 14 AWG (b) 12 AWG (c) 10 AWG (d) 8 AWG

Answer: (a) 14 AWG

Step 1: Determine the branch-circuit conductor size [430.22(A) and Table 310.15(B)(16)]
2 hp, 230V Motor FLC = 12A [Table 430.248]
12A x 1.25 = 15A, 14 AWG, rated 20A at 75°C [Table 310.15(B)(16)]

Step 2: Determine the branch-circuit protection [240.6(A), 430.52(C)(1), and Table 430.248]
12A x 2.50 = 30A

Step 3: The circuit equipment grounding conductor must be sized to the 30A overcurrent device—10 AWG [Table 250.122], but it's not required to be sized larger than the circuit conductors—14 AWG.

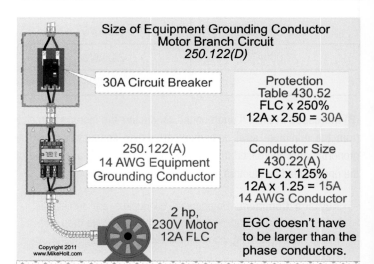

Figure 250–168

(F) Parallel Runs. If circuit conductors are installed in parallel in separate raceways as permitted by 310.10(H), an equipment grounding conductor must be installed for each parallel conductor set. **Figure 250–169.** Where conductors are installed in parallel in the same raceway or cable tray, a single equipment grounding conductor is permitted. **Figure 250–170**

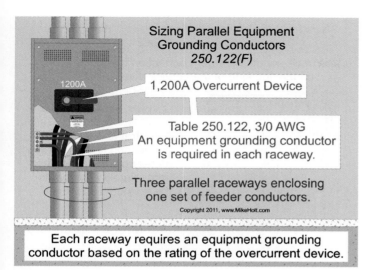

Figure 250–169

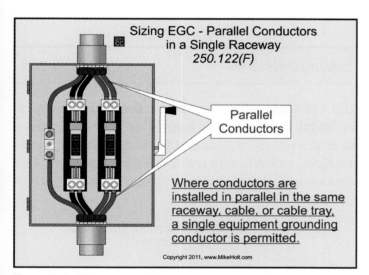

Figure 250–170

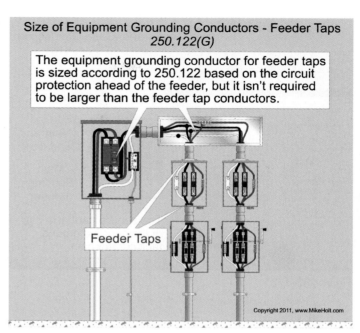

Figure 250–171

Each equipment grounding conductor must be sized in accordance with Table 250.122, based on the rating of the circuit overcurrent device, but it's not required to be larger than the circuit conductors [250.122(A)].

Author's Comment: In cable trays, single-conductor equipment grounding conductors can be insulated, covered, or bare, but must be sized 4 AWG and larger [392.10(B)(1)(c)].

(G) Feeder Tap Conductors. Equipment grounding conductors for feeder taps must be sized in accordance with Table 250.122, based on the ampere rating of the overcurrent device ahead of the feeder, but in no case is it required to be larger than the feeder tap conductors. **Figure 250–171**

Essential Rule 47   **250.142**

PART VII. METHODS OF EQUIPMENT GROUNDING

250.142 Use of Neutral Conductor for Equipment Grounding.

Author's Comment: To remove dangerous voltage on metal parts from a ground fault, the metal parts of electrical raceways, cables, enclosures, and equipment must be connected to an equipment grounding conductor of a type recognized in 250.118 in accordance with 250.4(A)(3).

(A) Supply-Side Equipment. The neutral conductor can be used as the circuit equipment grounding conductor for metal parts of equipment, raceways, and enclosures at the following locations:

(1) Service Equipment. On the supply side or within the enclosure of the service disconnect in accordance with 250.24(B). **Figure 250–172**

(3) Separately Derived Systems. At the source of a separately derived system or within the enclosure of the system disconnecting means in accordance with 250.30(A)(1).

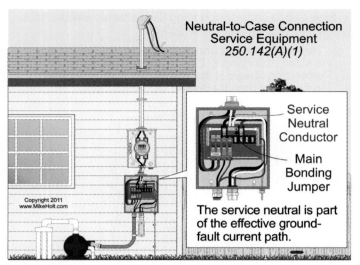

Figure 250–172

DANGER: *Failure to install the system bonding jumper as required by 250.30(A)(1) creates a condition where dangerous touch voltage from a ground fault won't be removed.*

(B) Load-Side Equipment. Except as permitted in 250.30(A)(1) for separately derived systems and 250.32(B) Ex, for separate buildings/structures, the neutral conductor isn't permitted to serve as an equipment grounding conductor on the load side of service equipment.

Ex 1: In existing installations, the frames of ranges, wall-mounted ovens, counter-mounted cooking units, and clothes dryers can be connected to the neutral conductor in accordance with 250.140 Ex.

Ex 2: The neutral conductor can be connected to meter socket enclosures on the load side of the service disconnecting means if: **Figure 250–173**

(1) Ground-fault protection isn't provided on service equipment,

(2) Meter socket enclosures are immediately adjacent to the service disconnecting means, and

(3) The neutral conductor is sized in accordance with 250.122, based on the ampere rating of the occupancy's feeder overcurrent device.

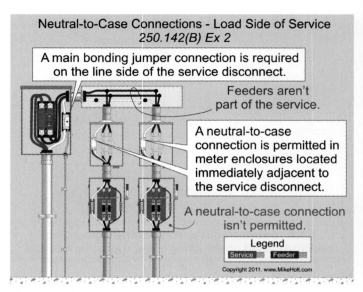

Figure 250–173

Essential Rule 48 | **250.146**

250.146 Connecting Receptacle Grounding Terminal to Metal Enclosure. An equipment bonding jumper sized in accordance with 250.122, based on the rating of the circuit overcurrent device, must connect the grounding terminal of a receptacle to a metal box, except as permitted for (A) through (D). **Figure 250–174**

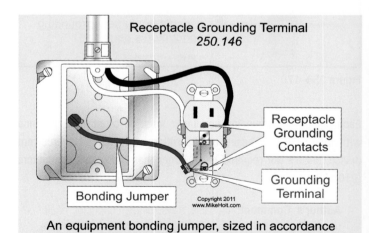

An equipment bonding jumper, sized in accordance with 250.122, must connect the grounding terminal of the receptacle to the metal box.

Figure 250–174

Author's Comment: The *NEC* doesn't restrict the position of the receptacle grounding terminal; it can be up, down, or sideways. *Code* proposals to specify the mounting position of receptacles have always been rejected. **Figure 250–175**

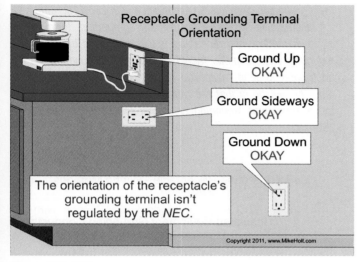

Figure 250–175

(A) Surface-Mounted Box. An equipment bonding jumper from a receptacle to a metal box that's surface mounted isn't required if there's direct metal-to-metal contact between the device yoke and the metal box. To ensure a suitable bonding path between the device yoke and a metal box, at least one of the insulating retaining washers on the yoke screw must be removed. **Figure 250–176**

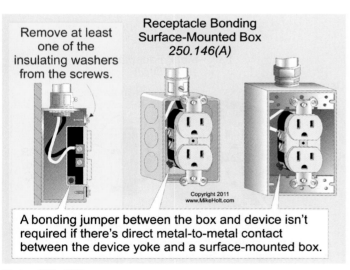

Figure 250–176

An equipment bonding jumper isn't required for receptacles attached to listed exposed work covers when the receptacle is attached to the cover with at least two fasteners that have a thread locking or screw or nut locking means, and the cover mounting holes are located on a flat non-raised portion of the cover. **Figure 250–177**

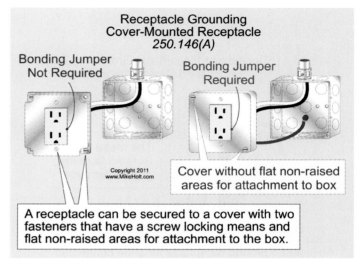

Figure 250–177

(B) Self-Grounding Receptacles. Receptacle yokes listed as self-grounding are designed to establish the bonding path between the device yoke and a metal box via the two metal mounting screws. **Figure 250–178**

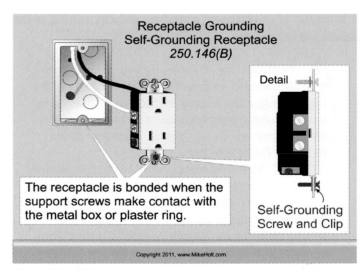

Figure 250–178

(C) Floor Boxes. Listed floor boxes are designed to establish the bonding path between the device yoke and a metal box.

(D) Isolated Ground Receptacles. If installed for the reduction of electrical noise, the grounding terminal of an isolated ground receptacle must be connected to an insulated equipment grounding conductor run with the circuit conductors. **Figure 250–179**

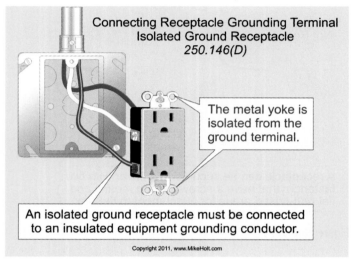

Figure 250–179

The circuit equipment grounding conductor is permitted to pass through panelboards [408.40 Ex], boxes, wireways, or other enclosures [250.148 Ex] without a connection to the enclosure as long as it terminates at an equipment grounding conductor terminal of the derived system or service.

⚠ **CAUTION:** *Type AC Cable—Type AC cable containing an insulated equipment grounding conductor of the wire type can be used to supply receptacles having insulated grounding terminals because the metal armor of the cable is listed as an equipment grounding conductor [250.118(8)].* **Figure 250–180**

Type MC Cable—The metal armor sheath of interlocked Type MC cable containing an insulated equipment grounding conductor isn't listed as an equipment grounding conductor. Therefore, this wiring method with a single equipment grounding conductor can't supply an isolated ground receptacle installed in a metal box (because the box isn't connected to an equipment grounding conductor). However, Type MC cable with two insulated equipment grounding conductors is acceptable, since one equipment grounding conductor

connects to the metal box and the other to the isolated ground receptacle. See **Figure 250–180**

The armor assembly of interlocked Type MCAP® cable with a 10 AWG bare aluminum grounding/bonding conductor running just below the metal armor is listed to serve as an equipment grounding conductor in accordance with 250.118(10)(b).

Nonmetallic Boxes—Because the grounding terminal of an isolated ground receptacle is insulated from the metal mounting yoke, a metal faceplate must not be used when an isolated ground receptacle is installed in a nonmetallic box. The reason is that the metal faceplate isn't connected to an equipment grounding conductor [406.3(D)(2)]. **Figure 250–181**

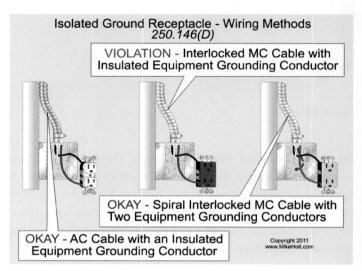

Figure 250–180

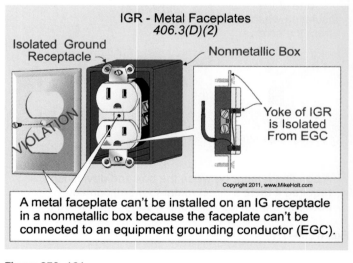

Figure 250–181

Author's Comment: When should an isolated ground receptacle be installed and how should the isolated ground system be designed? These questions are design issues and must not be answered based on the *NEC* alone [90.1(C)]. In most cases, using isolated ground receptacles is a waste of money. For example, IEEE 1100—*Powering and Grounding Electronic Equipment* (Emerald Book) states: "The results from the use of the isolated ground method range from no observable effects, the desired effects, or worse noise conditions than when standard equipment bonding configurations are used to serve electronic load equipment [8.5.3.2]."

In reality, few electrical installations truly require an isolated ground system. For those systems that can benefit from an isolated ground system, engineering opinions differ as to what's a proper design. Making matters worse—of those properly designed, few are correctly installed and even fewer are properly maintained. For more information on how to properly ground electronic equipment, go to: www.MikeHolt.com, click on the "Technical" link, and then visit the "Power Quality" page.

Essential Rule 49   250.148

250.148 Continuity and Attachment of Equipment Grounding Conductors in Boxes.
If circuit conductors are spliced or terminated on equipment within a metal box, the equipment grounding conductor associated with those circuits must be connected to the box in accordance with the following: **Figure 250–182**

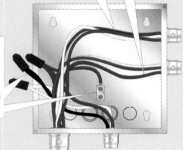

Continuity and Attachment of Equipment Grounding Conductors to Metal Boxes
250.148

Where circuit conductors aren't spliced or terminated in the box, equipment grounding conductors can pass through without terminating to the box.

Where circuit conductors are spliced or terminated on equipment in the box, equipment grounding conductors must terminate to the box.

Copyright 2011, www.MikeHolt.com

Figure 250–182

Ex: The circuit equipment grounding conductor for an isolated ground receptacle installed in accordance with 250.146(D) isn't required to terminate to a metal box. **Figure 250–183**

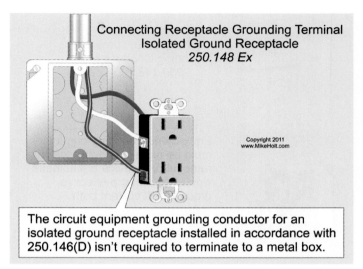

Connecting Receptacle Grounding Terminal Isolated Ground Receptacle
250.148 Ex

Copyright 2011
www.MikeHolt.com

The circuit equipment grounding conductor for an isolated ground receptacle installed in accordance with 250.146(D) isn't required to terminate to a metal box.

Figure 250–183

(A) Splicing. Equipment grounding conductors must be spliced together with a device listed for the purpose [110.14(B)]. **Figure 250–184**

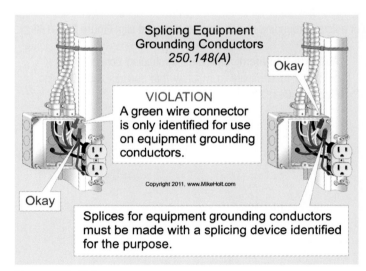

Splicing Equipment Grounding Conductors
250.148(A)

Okay

VIOLATION
A green wire connector is only identified for use on equipment grounding conductors.

Okay

Copyright 2011, www.MikeHolt.com

Splices for equipment grounding conductors must be made with a splicing device identified for the purpose.

Figure 250–184

Author's Comment: Wire connectors of any color can be used with equipment grounding conductor splices, but green wire connectors can only be used with equipment grounding conductors.

(B) Equipment Grounding Continuity. Equipment grounding conductors must terminate in a manner such that the disconnection or the removal of a receptacle, luminaire, or other device won't interrupt the grounding continuity. **Figure 250–185**

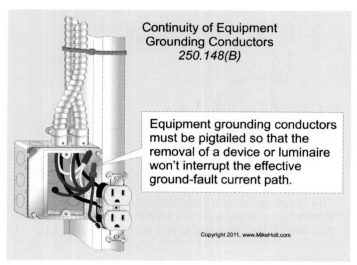

Figure 250–185

(C) Metal Boxes. Equipment grounding conductors within metal boxes must be connected to the metal box with a grounding screw that's not used for any other purpose, an equipment fitting listed for grounding, or a listed grounding device such as a ground clip. **Figure 250–186**

Author's Comment: Equipment grounding conductors aren't permitted to terminate to a screw that secures a plaster ring. **Figure 250–187**

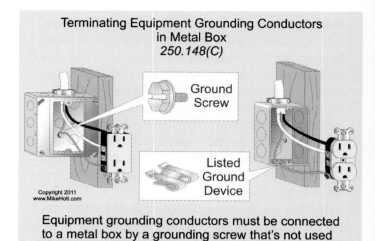

Figure 250–186

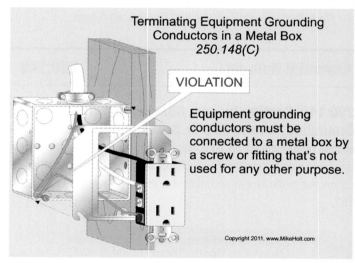

Figure 250–187

Wiring Methods

INTRODUCTION TO ARTICLE 300—WIRING METHODS

Article 300 contains the general requirements for all wiring methods included in the *NEC*. However, the article doesn't apply to communications systems, which are covered in Chapter 8, except when Article 300 is specifically referenced in Chapter 8.

This article is primarily concerned with how to install, route, splice, protect, and secure conductors and raceways. How well you conform to the requirements of Article 300 will generally be evident in the finished work, because many of the requirements tend to determine the appearance of the installation.

Because of this, it's often easy to spot Article 300 problems if you're looking for *Code* violations. For example, you can easily see when someone runs an equipment grounding conductor outside a raceway instead of grouping all conductors of a circuit together, as required by 300.3(B).

A good understanding of Article 300 will start you on the path to correctly installing the wiring methods included in Chapter 3. Be sure to carefully consider the accompanying illustrations, and refer to the definitions in Article 100 as needed.

Essential Rule 50	300.3

PART I. GENERAL

300.3 Conductors.

(A) Conductors. Single conductors must be installed within a Chapter 3 wiring method, such as a raceway, cable, or enclosure.

Ex: Overhead conductors can be installed in accordance with 225.6.

(B) Circuit Conductors Grouped Together. All conductors of a circuit must be installed in the same raceway, cable, trench, cord, or cable tray, except as permitted by (1) through (4). **Figure 300–1**

(1) Paralleled Installations. Conductors installed in parallel in accordance with 310.10(H) must have all circuit conductors within the same raceway, cable tray, trench, or cable. **Figure 300–2**

Ex: Parallel conductors run underground can be installed in different raceways (Phase A in raceway 1, Phase B in raceway 2, and so forth) if, in order to reduce or eliminate inductive heating, if the raceway is nonmetallic or nonmagnetic and the installation complies with 300.20(B). See 300.5(I) Ex 2.

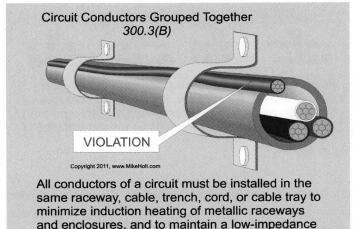

Circuit Conductors Grouped Together
300.3(B)

VIOLATION

Copyright 2011. www.MikeHolt.com

All conductors of a circuit must be installed in the same raceway, cable, trench, cord, or cable tray to minimize induction heating of metallic raceways and enclosures, and to maintain a low-impedance ground-fault current path.

Figure 300–1

Author's Comment: All conductors of a circuit must be installed in the same raceway, cable, trench, cord, or cable tray to minimize induction of the heating of ferrous metal raceways and enclosures, and to maintain a low-impedance ground-fault current path [250.4(A)(3)]. **Figure 300–3**

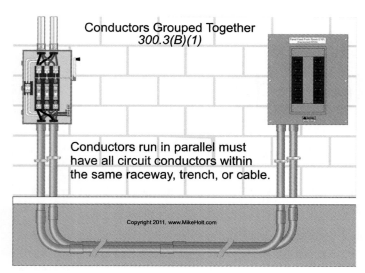

Figure 300-2

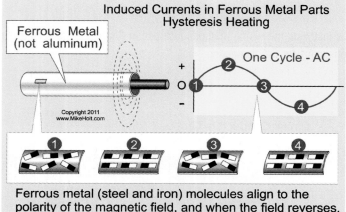

Figure 300-3

(2) Grounding and Bonding Conductors. Equipment grounding jumpers can be located outside of a flexible raceway if the bonding jumper is installed in accordance with 250.102(E)(2). **Figure 300-4**

(3) Nonferrous Wiring Methods. Circuit conductors can be installed in different raceways (Phase A in raceway 1, Phase B in raceway 2, and so on) if, in order to reduce or eliminate inductive heating, the raceway is nonmetallic or nonmagnetic and the installation complies with 300.20(B). See 300.3(B)(1) and 300.5(I) Ex 2.

(C) Conductors of Different Systems.

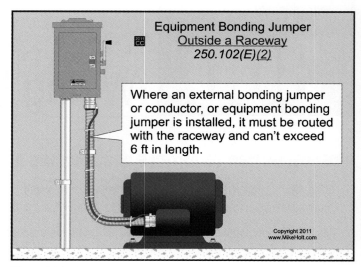

Figure 300-4

(1) Mixing. Power conductors of alternating-current and direct-current systems rated 600V or less can occupy the same raceway, cable, or enclosure if all conductors have an insulation voltage rating not less than the maximum circuit voltage. **Figure 300-5**

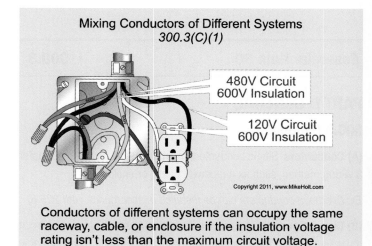

Figure 300-5

Author's Comments:

- Control, signal, and communications wiring must be separated from power and lighting circuits so the higher-voltage conductors don't accidentally energize the control, signal, or communications wiring: **Figure 300–6**

  - CATV Coaxial Cable, 820.133(A)
  - Class 1, Class 2, and Class 3 Control Circuits, 725.48 and 725.136(A)
  - Communications Circuits, 800.133(A)(1)(c)
  - Fire Alarm Circuits, 760.136(A)
  - Instrumentation Tray Cable, 727.5
  - Sound Circuits, 640.9(C)

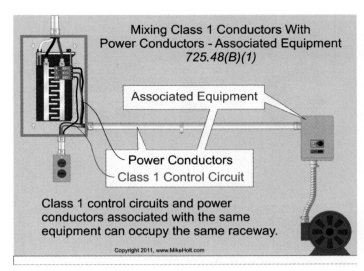

Figure 300–7

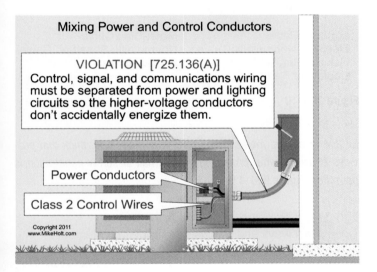

Figure 300–6

- Class circuit conductors can be installed with associated power conductors [725.48(B)(1)] if all conductors have an insulation voltage rating not less than the maximum circuit voltage [300.3(C)(1)]. **Figure 300–7**

- A Class 2 circuit that's been reclassified as a Class 1 circuit [725.130(A) Ex 2] can be installed with associated power conductors [725.48(B)(1)] if all conductors have an insulation voltage rating not less than the maximum circuit voltage [300.3(C)(1)]. **Figure 300–8**

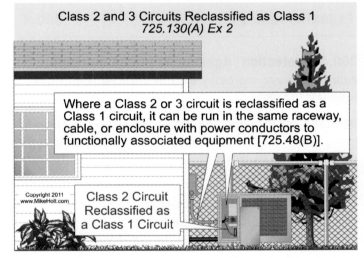

Figure 300–8

Note 2: PV system conductors, both direct current and alternating current, are permitted to be installed in the same raceways, outlet and junction boxes, or similar fittings with each other, but they must be kept entirely independent of all other non-PV system wiring [690.4(B)]. **Figure 300–9**

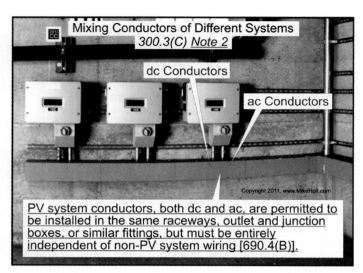

Figure 300–9

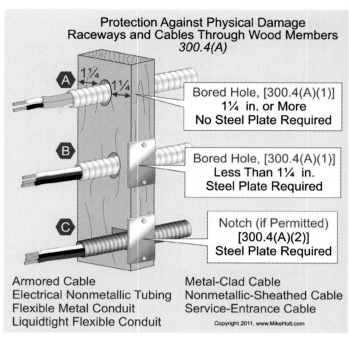

Figure 300–10

Essential Rule 51   300.4

300.4 Protection Against Physical Damage. Conductors, raceways, and cables must be protected against physical damage [110.27(B)].

(A) Cables and Raceways Through Wood Members. When the following wiring methods are installed through wood members, they must comply with (1) and (2). **Figure 300–10**

- Armored Cable, Article 320
- Electrical Nonmetallic Tubing, Article 362
- Flexible Metal Conduit, Article 348
- Liquidtight Flexible Metal Conduit, Article 350
- Liquidtight Flexible Nonmetallic Conduit, Article 356
- Metal-Clad Cable, Article 330
- Nonmetallic-Sheathed Cable, Article 334
- Service-Entrance Cable, Article 338
- Underground Feeder and Branch-Circuit Cable, Article 340

(1) Holes in Wood Members. Holes through wood framing members for the above cables or raceways must be not less than 1¼ in. from the edge of the wood member. If the edge of the hole is less than 1¼ in. from the edge, a ⅟₁₆ in. thick steel plate of sufficient length and width must be installed to protect the wiring method from screws and nails.

Ex 1: A steel plate isn't required to protect rigid metal conduit, intermediate metal conduit, PVC conduit, or electrical metallic tubing.

Ex 2: A listed and marked steel plate less than ⅟₁₆ in. thick that provides equal or better protection against nail or screw penetration is permitted. **Figure 300–11**

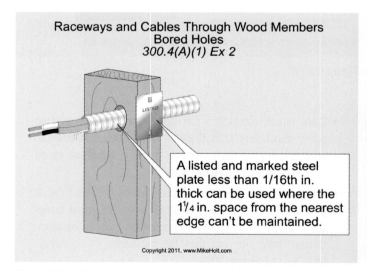

Figure 300–11

Author's Comment: Hardened steel plates thinner than ⅟₁₆ in. have been tested and found to provide better protection from screw and nail penetration than the thicker plates.

(2) Notches in Wood Members. If notching of wood framing members for cables and raceways are permitted by the building code, a 1/16 in. thick steel plate of sufficient length and width must be installed to protect the wiring method laid in these wood notches from screws and nails.

⚠️ **CAUTION:** *When drilling or notching wood members, be sure to check with the building inspector to ensure you don't damage or weaken the structure and violate the building code.*

Ex 1: A steel plate isn't required to protect rigid metal conduit, intermediate metal conduit, PVC conduit, or electrical metallic tubing.

Ex 2: A listed and marked steel plate less than 1/16 in. thick that provides equal or better protection against nail or screw penetration is permitted. **Figure 300–12**

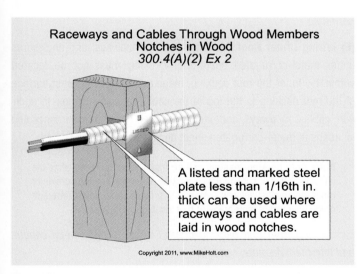

Raceways and Cables Through Wood Members
Notches in Wood
300.4(A)(2) Ex 2

A listed and marked steel plate less than 1/16th in. thick can be used where raceways and cables are laid in wood notches.

Figure 300–12

(B) Nonmetallic-Sheathed Cable and Electrical Nonmetallic Tubing Through Metal Framing Members.

(1) Nonmetallic-Sheathed Cable (NM). If Type NM cables pass through factory or field openings in metal framing members, the cable must be protected by listed bushings or listed grommets that cover all metal edges. The protection fitting must be securely fastened in the opening before the installation of the cable. **Figure 300–13**

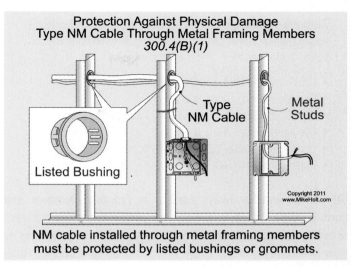

Protection Against Physical Damage
Type NM Cable Through Metal Framing Members
300.4(B)(1)

Type NM Cable

Metal Studs

Listed Bushing

NM cable installed through metal framing members must be protected by listed bushings or grommets.

Figure 300–13

(2) Type NM Cable and Electrical Nonmetallic Tubing. If nails or screws are likely to penetrate Type NM cable or electrical nonmetallic tubing, a steel sleeve, steel plate, or steel clip not less than 1/16 in. in thickness must be installed to protect the cable or tubing.

Ex: A listed and marked steel plate less than 1/16 in. thick that provides equal or better protection against nail or screw penetration is permitted.

(C) Behind Suspended Ceilings. Wiring methods, such as cables or raceways, installed behind panels designed to allow access must be supported in accordance with its applicable article. **Figure 300–14**

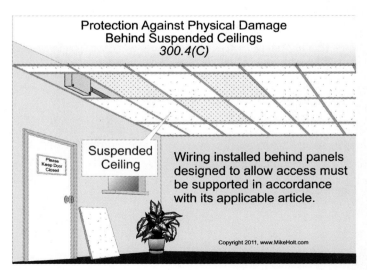

Protection Against Physical Damage
Behind Suspended Ceilings
300.4(C)

Suspended Ceiling

Wiring installed behind panels designed to allow access must be supported in accordance with its applicable article.

Figure 300–14

Author's Comment: This rule doesn't apply to control, signal, and communications cables, but similar requirements are contained in Chapters 6, 7, and 8 as follows:

- CATV Coaxial Cable, 820.21 and 820.24
- Communications Cable, 800.21
- Control and Signaling Cable, 725.21 and 725.24
- Fire Alarm Cable, 760.7 and 760.8
- Optical Fiber Cable, 770.21 and 770.24
- Audio Cable, 640.6(B)

(D) Cables and Raceways Parallel to Framing Members and Furring Strips. Cables or raceways run parallel to framing members or furring strips must be protected if they're likely to be penetrated by nails or screws, by installing the wiring method so it isn't less than 1¼ in. from the nearest edge of the framing member or furring strip. If the edge of the framing member or furring strip is less than 1¼ in. away, a ¹⁄₁₆ in. thick steel plate of sufficient length and width must be installed to protect the wiring method from screws and nails. **Figure 300–15**

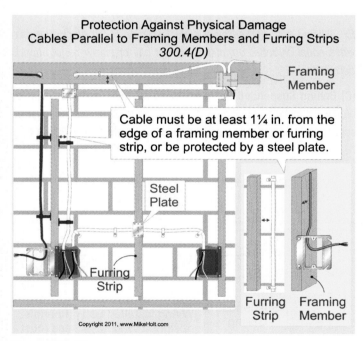

Figure 300–15

Author's Comment: This rule doesn't apply to control, signaling, and communications cables, but similar requirements are contained in Chapters 6, 7, and 8 as follows:

- CATV Coaxial Cable, 820.24
- Communications Cable, 800.24
- Control and Signaling Cable, 725.24
- Optical Fiber Cable, 770.24
- Fire Alarm Cable, 760.8
- Audio Cable, 640.6(B)

Ex 1: Protection isn't required for rigid metal conduit, intermediate metal conduit, PVC conduit, or electrical metallic tubing.

Ex 2: For concealed work in finished buildings, or finished panels for prefabricated buildings if such supporting is impracticable, the cables can be fished between access points.

Ex 3: A listed and marked steel plate less than ¹⁄₁₆ in. thick that provides equal or better protection against nail or screw penetration is permitted.

(E) Wiring Under Roof Decking. Cables, raceways, <u>and enclosures</u> under metal-corrugated sheet roof decking must not be located within 1½ in. of the roof decking, measured from the <u>lowest surface of the roof decking to the top</u> of the cable, raceway, <u>or box. In addition, cables, raceways, and enclosures aren't permitted in concealed locations of metal-corrugated sheet decking type roofing.</u>

> **Note:** Roof decking material will be installed or replaced after the initial raceway or cabling which may be penetrated by the screws or other mechanical devices designed to provide "hold down" strength of the waterproof membrane or roof insulating material.

Ex: Spacing from roof decking doesn't apply to rigid metal conduit and intermediate metal conduit.

(F) Cables and Raceways Installed in Grooves. Cables and raceways installed in a groove must be protected by a ¹⁄₁₆ in. thick steel plate or sleeve, or by 1¼ in. of free space.

> **Author's Comment:** An example is Type NM cable installed in a groove cut into the Styrofoam-type insulation building block structure and then covered with wallboard.

Ex 1: Protection isn't required if the cable is installed in rigid metal conduit, intermediate metal conduit, PVC conduit, or electrical metallic tubing.

Ex 2: A listed and marked steel plate less than ¹⁄₁₆ in. thick that provides equal or better protection against nail or screw penetration is permitted.

(G) Insulating Fittings. If raceways contain insulated circuit conductors 4 AWG and larger that enter an enclosure, the conductors must be protected from abrasion during and after installation by a fitting identified to provide a smooth, rounded insulating surface, such as an insulating bushing. **Figure 300–16**

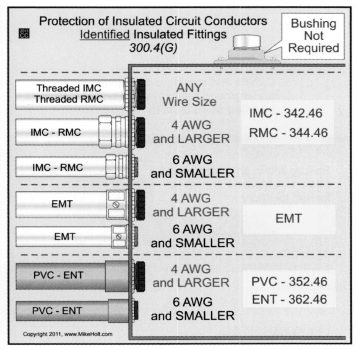

Figure 300–16

Author's Comments:

- If IMC or RMC conduit enters an enclosure without a connector, a bushing must be provided, regardless of the conductor size [342.46 and 344.46].
- An insulated fitting isn't required for a grounding electrode. **Figure 300–17**

Ex: Insulating bushings aren't required if a raceway terminates in a threaded raceway entry that provides a smooth, rounded, or flared surface for the conductors. An example would be a meter hub fitting or a Meyer's hub-type fitting.

(H) Structural Joints. A listed expansion/deflection fitting or other means approved by the authority having jurisdiction must be used where a raceway crosses a structural joint intended for expansion, contraction or deflection.

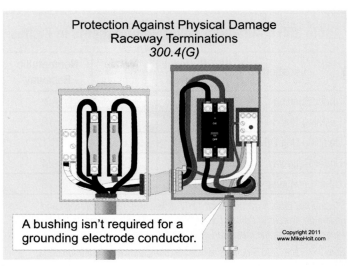

Figure 300–17

Essential Rule 52   **300.5**

300.5 Underground Installations.

(A) Minimum Burial Depths. When cables or raceways are installed underground, they must have a minimum "cover" in accordance with Table 300.5. **Figure 300–18**

Underground Installations - Minimum Cover Depths
Table 300.5

	UF or USE Cables or Conductors	RMC or IMC	PVC not Encased in Concrete	Residential 15A & 20A GFCI 120V Branch Ckts
Street Driveway Parking Lot	24 in.	24 in.	24 in.	24 in.
Driveways One - Two Family	18 in.	18 in.	18 in.	12 in.
Solid Rock With not Less than 2 in. of Concrete	Raceway Only			Raceway Only
All Other Applications	24 in.	6 in.	18 in.	12 in.

Figure 300–18

Table 300.5 Minimum Cover Requirements in Inches			
Location	Buried Cables	Metal Raceway	Nonmetallic Raceway
Under Building	0	0	0
Dwelling Unit	24/12*	6	18
Dwelling Unit Driveway	18/12*	6	18/12*
Under Roadway	24	24	24
Other Locations	24	6	18

*Residential branch circuits rated 120V or less with GFCI protection and maximum overcurrent protection of 20A. Note: This is a summary of the NEC's Table 300.5. See the table in the NEC for full details.

Note 1 to Table 300.5 defines "Cover" as the distance from the top of the underground cable or raceway to the top surface of finished grade. Figure 300–05 02 N1

Author's Comment: The cover requirements contained in 300.5 don't apply to the following signaling, communications, and other power-limited wiring systems: **Figure 300–19**

- CATV, 90.3
- Class 2 and 3 Circuits, 725.3
- Communications Cables and Raceways, 90.3
- Fire Alarm Circuits, 760.3
- Optical Fiber Cables and Raceways, 770.3

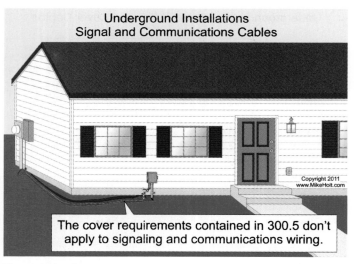

Underground Installations Signal and Communications Cables

The cover requirements contained in 300.5 don't apply to signaling and communications wiring.

Figure 300–19

(B) Wet Locations. The interior of enclosures or raceways installed in an underground installation are considered to be a wet location. Cables and insulated conductors installed in underground enclosures or raceways must be listed for use in wet locations according to 310.10(C). Splices within an underground enclosure must be listed as suitable for wet locations [110.14(B)]. **Figure 300–20**

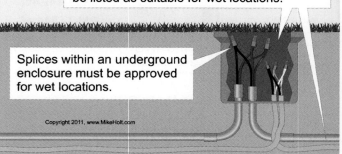

Underground Installations Wet Locations 300.5(B)

Cables and insulated conductors installed in underground raceways and enclosures must be listed as suitable for wet locations.

Splices within an underground enclosure must be approved for wet locations.

Figure 300–20

Author's Comment: The definition of a "Wet Location" as contained in Article 100, includes installations underground, in concrete slabs in direct contact with the earth, locations subject to saturation with water, and unprotected locations exposed to weather. If raceways are installed in wet locations above grade, the interior of these raceways is also considered to be a wet location [300.9].

(C) Cables Under Buildings. Cables installed under a building must be installed in a raceway that extends past the outside walls of the building.

Ex 2: Type MC Cable listed for direct burial is permitted under a building without installation in a raceway [330.10(A)(5)]. **Figure 300–21**

(D) Protecting Underground Cables and Conductors. Direct-buried conductors and cables such as Types MC, UF, and USE must be protected from damage in accordance with (1) through (4).

(1) Emerging from Grade. Direct-buried cables or conductors that emerge from grade must be installed in an enclosure or raceway to protect against physical damage. Protection isn't required to extend more than 18 in. below grade, and protection above ground must extend to a height of not less than 8 ft. **Figure 300–22**

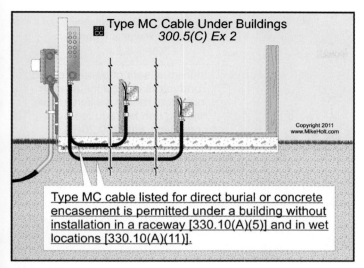

Figure 300–21

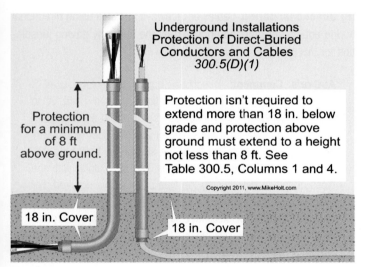

Figure 300–22

(2) Conductors Entering Buildings. Conductors that enter a building must be protected to the point of entrance.

(4) Enclosure or Raceway Damage. If direct-buried cables, enclosures, or raceways are subject to physical damage, the conductors must be installed in rigid metal conduit, intermediate metal conduit, or Schedule 80 PVC conduit.

(E) Underground Splices and Taps. Direct-buried conductors or cables can be spliced or tapped underground without a splice box [300.15(G)], if the splice or tap is made in accordance with 110.14(B). Figure 300–23

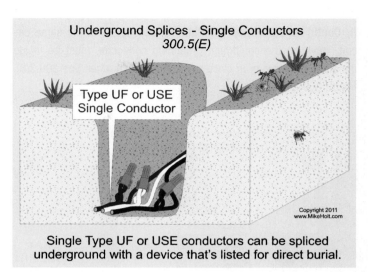

Figure 300–23

(F) Backfill. Backfill material for underground wiring must not damage the underground cable or raceway, or contribute to the corrosion of the metal raceway.

> **Author's Comment:** Large rocks, chunks of concrete, steel rods, mesh, and other sharp-edged objects must not be used for backfill material, because they can damage the underground conductors, cables, or raceways.

(G) Raceway Seals. If moisture could enter a raceway and contact energized live parts, a seal must be installed at one or both ends of the raceway.

> **Author's Comment:** This is a common problem for equipment located downhill from the supply, or in underground equipment rooms. See 230.8 for service raceway seals and 300.7(A) for different temperature area seals.

> **Note:** Hazardous explosive gases or vapors make it necessary to seal underground raceways that enter the building in accordance with 501.15.

> **Author's Comment:** It isn't the intent of this Note to imply that sealing fittings of the types required in hazardous locations be installed in unclassified locations, except as required in Chapter 5. This also doesn't imply that the sealing material provides a watertight seal, but only that it prevents moisture from entering the raceways.

(H) Bushing. Raceways that terminate underground must have a bushing or fitting at the end of the raceway to protect emerging cables or conductors.

(I) Conductors Grouped Together. All conductors of the same circuit, including the equipment grounding conductor, must be inside the same raceway, or in close proximity to each other. See 300.3(B). Figure 300–24

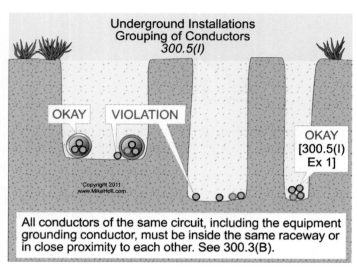

Figure 300–24

Ex 1: *Conductors can be installed in parallel in raceways, multiconductor cables, or direct-buried single-conductor cables. Each raceway or multiconductor cable must contain all conductors of the same circuit including the equipment grounding conductor. Each direct-buried single-conductor cable must be located in close proximity in the trench to the other single conductor cables in the same parallel set of conductors, including equipment grounding conductors.*

Ex 2: *Parallel circuit conductors installed in accordance with 310.10(H) of the same phase or neutral can be installed in underground PVC conduits, if inductive heating at raceway terminations is reduced by the use of aluminum locknuts and cutting a slot between the individual holes through which the conductors pass as required by 300.20(B).* **Figure 300–25**

> **Author's Comment:** Installing ungrounded and neutral conductors in different PVC conduits makes it easier to terminate larger parallel sets of conductors, but it will result in higher levels of electromagnetic fields (EMF).

(J) Earth Movement. Direct-buried conductors, cables, or raceways that are subject to movement by settlement or frost must be arranged to prevent damage to conductors or equipment connected to the wiring.

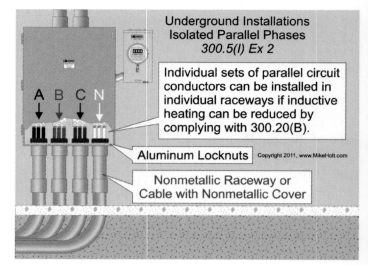

Figure 300–25

(K) Directional Boring. Cables or raceways installed using directional boring equipment must be approved by the authority having jurisdiction for this purpose.

> **Author's Comment:** Directional boring technology uses a directional drill, which is steered continuously from point "A" to point "B." When the drill head comes out of the earth at point "B," it's replaced with a back-reamer and the duct or raceway being installed is attached to it. The size of the boring rig (hp, torque, and pull-back power) comes into play, along with the types of soil, in determining the type of raceways required. For telecommunications work, multiple poly innerducts are pulled in at one time. At major crossings, such as expressways, railroads, or rivers, outerduct may be installed to create a permanent sleeve for the innerducts.
>
> "Innerduct" and "outerduct" are terms usually associated with optical fiber cable installations, while "unitduct" comes with factory installed conductors. All of these come in various sizes. Galvanized rigid metal conduit, Schedule 40 and Schedule 80 PVC, HDPE conduit and nonmetallic underground conduit with conductors (NUCC) are common wiring methods used with directional boring installations.

Essential Rule 53   300.10

300.10 Electrical Continuity. Metal raceways, cables, boxes, fittings, cabinets, and enclosures for conductors must be metallically joined together to form a continuous, low-impedance fault current path capable of carrying any fault current likely to be imposed on it [110.10, 250.4(A)(3), and 250.122]. **Figure 300–26**

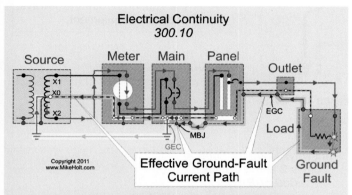

Figure 300–26

Metal raceways and cable assemblies must be mechanically secured to boxes, fittings, cabinets, and other enclosures.

Ex 1: Short lengths of metal raceways used for the support or protection of cables aren't required to be electrically continuous, nor are they required to be connected to an equipment grounding conductor of a type recognized in 250.118 [250.86 Ex 2 and 300.12 Ex]. **Figure 300–27**

Essential Rule 54   300.11

300.11 Securing and Supporting.

(A) Secured in Place. Raceways, cable assemblies, boxes, cabinets, and fittings must be securely fastened in place. The ceiling-support wires or ceiling grid must not be used to support raceways and cables (power, signaling, or communications). However, independent support wires that are secured at both ends and provide secure support are permitted. **Figure 300–28**

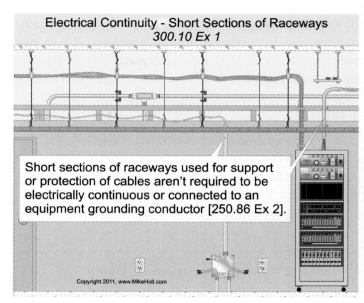

Figure 300–27

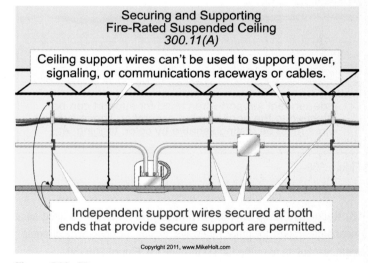

Figure 300–28

Author's Comment: Outlet boxes [314.23(D)] and luminaires can be secured to the suspended-ceiling grid if securely fastened to the ceiling-framing members by mechanical means such as bolts, screws, or rivets, or by the use of clips or other securing means identified for use with the type of ceiling-framing member(s) used [410.36(B)].

(1) Fire-Rated Ceiling Assembly. Electrical wiring within the cavity of a fire-rated floor-ceiling or roof-ceiling assembly can be supported by independent support wires attached to the ceiling assembly. The independent support wires must be distinguishable from the suspended-ceiling support wires by color, tagging, or other effective means.

(2) Nonfire-Rated Ceiling Assembly. Wiring in a nonfire-rated floor-ceiling or roof-ceiling assembly can be supported by independent support wires attached to the ceiling assembly. The independent support wires must be distinguishable from the suspended-ceiling support wires by color, tagging, or other effective means. **Figure 300–29**

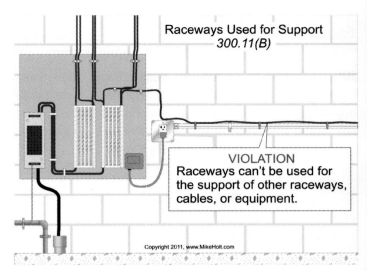

Figure 300–30

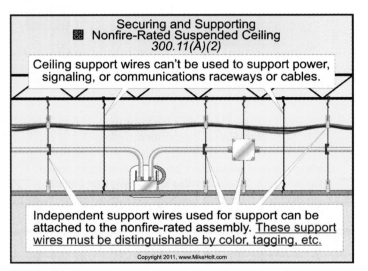

Figure 300–29

(B) Raceways Used for Support. Raceways must not be used as a means of support for other raceways, cables, or nonelectrical equipment, except as permitted in (1) through (3). **Figure 300–30**

(1) Identified. If the raceway or means of support is identified for the purpose.

(2) Class 2 and 3 Circuits. Class 2 and 3 cable can be supported by the raceway that supplies power to the equipment controlled by the Class 2 or 3 circuit. **Figure 300–31**

(3) Boxes Supported by Raceways. Raceways are permitted as a means of support for threaded boxes and conduit bodies in accordance with 314.23(E) and (F), or to support luminaires in accordance with 410.36(E).

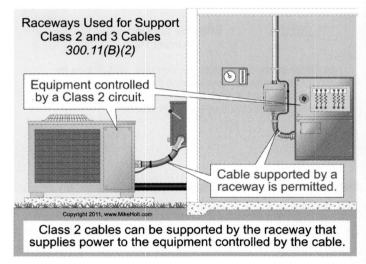

Figure 300–31

(C) Cables Not Used as Means of Support. Cables must not be used to support other cables, raceways, or nonelectrical equipment. **Figure 300–32**

Essential Rule 55	300.12

300.12 Mechanical Continuity. Raceways and cable sheaths must be mechanically continuous between boxes, cabinets, and fittings. **Figure 300–33**

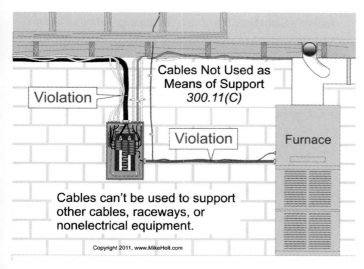

Figure 300–32

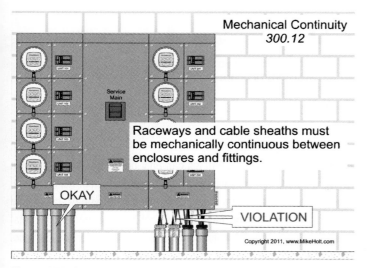

Figure 300–33

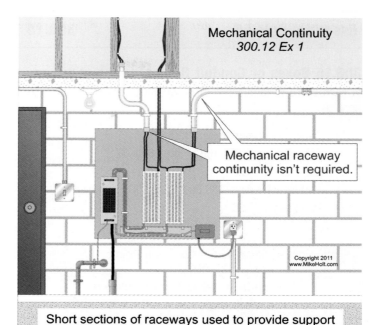

Figure 300–34

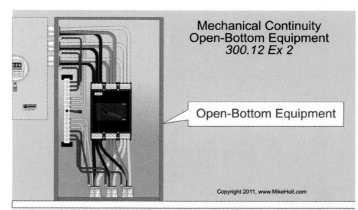

Figure 300–35

Ex 1: Short sections of raceways used to provide support or protection of cable from physical damage aren't required to be mechanically continuous [250.86 Ex 2 and 300.10 Ex 1]. **Figure 300–34**

Ex 2: Raceways at the bottom of open-bottom equipment, such as switchboards, motor control centers, and transformers, aren't required to be mechanically secured to the equipment. **Figure 300–35**

> **Author's Comment:** When raceways are stubbed into an open-bottom switchboard, the raceway, including the end fitting, can't rise more than 3 in. above the bottom of the switchboard enclosure [408.5].

Essential Rule 56   300.15

300.15 Boxes or Conduit Bodies. A box must be installed at each splice or termination point, except as permitted for: **Figure 300–36**

- Cabinet or Cutout Boxes, 312.8
- Conduit Bodies, 314.16(C) **Figure 300–37**
- Luminaires, 410.64
- Surface Raceways, 386.56 and 388.56
- Wireways, 376.56

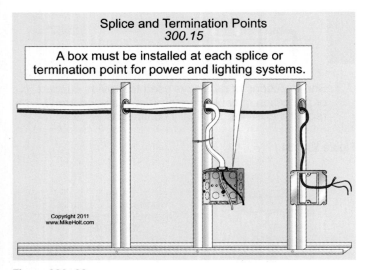

Splice and Termination Points
300.15

A box must be installed at each splice or termination point for power and lighting systems.

Copyright 2011
www.MikeHolt.com

Figure 300–36

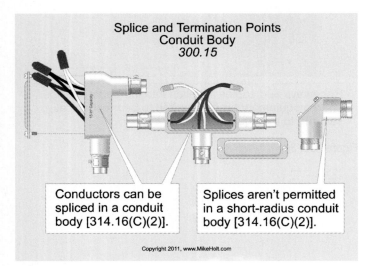

Splice and Termination Points
Conduit Body
300.15

Conductors can be spliced in a conduit body [314.16(C)(2)].

Splices aren't permitted in a short-radius conduit body [314.16(C)(2)].

Copyright 2011, www.MikeHolt.com

Figure 300–37

Author's Comment: Boxes aren't required for the following signaling and communications cables or raceways: **Figure 300–38**

- CATV, 90.3
- Class 2 and 3 Control and Signaling, 725.3
- Communications, 90.3
- Optical Fiber, 770.3

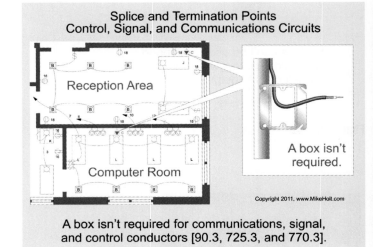

Splice and Termination Points
Control, Signal, and Communications Circuits

Reception Area

Computer Room

A box isn't required.

Copyright 2011, www.MikeHolt.com

A box isn't required for communications, signal, and control conductors [90.3, 725.3, and 770.3].

Figure 300–38

Fittings and Connectors. Fittings can only be used with the specific wiring methods for which they're listed and designed. For example, Type NM cable connectors must not be used with Type AC cable, and electrical metallic tubing fittings must not be used with rigid metal conduit or intermediate metal conduit, unless listed for the purpose. **Figure 300–39**

> **Author's Comment:** PVC conduit couplings and connectors are permitted with electrical nonmetallic tubing if the proper glue is used in accordance with manufacturer's instructions [110.3(B)]. See 362.48.

(C) Raceways for Support or Protection. When a raceway is used for the support or protection of cables, a fitting to reduce the potential for abrasion must be placed at the location the cables enter the raceway. **Figure 300–40**

(F) Fitting. A fitting is permitted in lieu of a box or conduit body where conductors aren't spliced or terminated within the fitting if it's accessible after installation. **Figure 300–41**

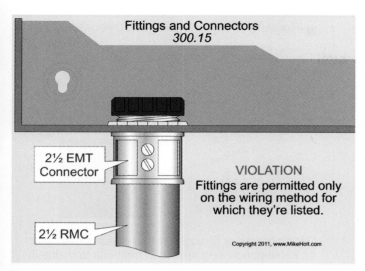

Figure 300–39

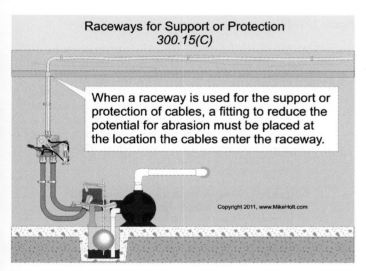

Figure 300–40

(G) Underground Splices. A box or conduit body isn't required where a splice is made underground if the conductors are spliced with a splicing device listed for direct burial. See 110.14(B) and 300.5(E).

> **Author's Comment:** See the definition of "Conduit Body" in Article 100.

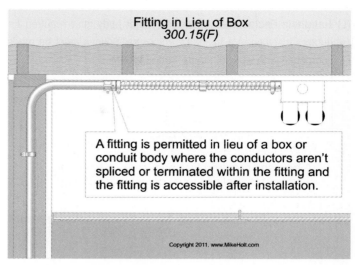

Figure 300–41

(I) Enclosures. A box or conduit body isn't required where a splice is made in a cabinet or in cutout boxes containing switches or over-current devices if the splices or taps don't fill the wiring space at any cross section to more than 75 percent, and the wiring at any cross section doesn't exceed 40 percent. See 312.8 and 404.3(B). **Figure 300–42**

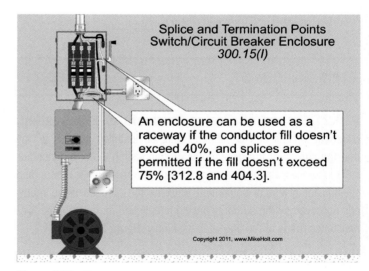

Figure 300–42

> **Author's Comment:** See the definitions of "Cabinet" and "Cutout Box" in Article 100.

(L) Handhole Enclosures. A box or conduit body isn't required for conductors installed in a handhole enclosure. Splices must be made in accordance with 314.30. **Figure 300–43**

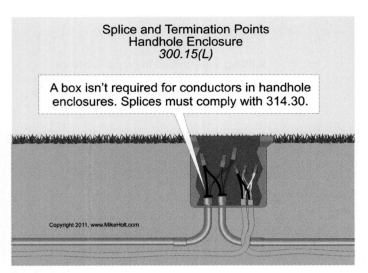

Figure 300–43

> **Author's Comment:** Splices or terminations within a handhole must be accomplished by the use of fittings listed as suitable for wet locations [110.14(B) and 314.30(C)].

Essential Rule 57	300.21

300.21 Spread of Fire or Products of Combustion.

Electrical circuits and equipment must be installed in such a way that the spread of fire or products of combustion won't be substantially increased. Openings <u>into or</u> through fire-rated walls, floors, and ceilings for electrical equipment must be fire-stopped using methods approved by the authority having jurisdiction to maintain the fire-resistance rating of the fire-rated assembly. **Figure 300–44**

> **Author's Comment:** Fire-stopping materials are listed for the specific types of wiring methods and the construction of the assembly that they penetrate.

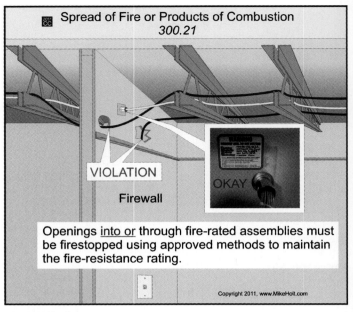

Figure 300–44

Note: Directories of electrical construction materials published by qualified testing laboratories contain listing and installation restrictions necessary to maintain the fire-resistive rating of assemblies. Outlet boxes must have a horizontal separation not less than 24 in. when installed in a fire-rated assembly, unless an outlet box is listed for closer spacing or protected by fire-resistant "putty pads" in accordance with manufacturer's instructions. **Figure 300–45**

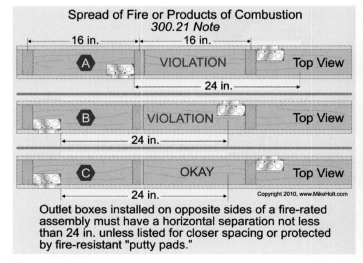

Figure 300–45

Author's Comments:

- Boxes installed in fire-resistance-rated assemblies must be listed for the purpose. If steel boxes are used, they must be secured to the framing member, so cut-in type boxes aren't permitted (UL White Book, *Guide Information for Electrical Equipment,* www.ul.com/regulators/2008_WhiteBook.pdf).

- This rule also applies to control, signaling, and communications cables or raceways.

  – CATV, 820.26
  – Communications, 800.26
  – Control and Signaling, 725.25
  – Fire Alarm, 760.3(A)
  – Optical Fiber, 770.26
  – Sound Systems, 640.3(A)

Essential Rule 58   300.22

300.22 Wiring in Ducts Not for Air Handling, <u>Fabricated</u> Ducts for Environmental Air, and Other Spaces For Environmental Air <u>(Plenums).</u> The provisions of this section apply to the installation and uses of electrical wiring and equipment in ducts <u>used for dust, loose stock, or vapor removal; ducts specifically fabricated for environmental air, and spaces used for environmental air (plenums).</u>

(A) Ducts Used for Dust, Loose Stock, or Vapor. Ducts that transport dust, loose stock, or vapors must not have any wiring method installed within them. **Figure 300–46**

Ducts Used for Dust, Loose Stock, or Vapor
300.22(A)

Ducts that transport dust, loose stock, or vapors must not have any wiring method installed within them.

Copyright 2011, www.MikeHolt.com

Figure 300–46

(B) Ducts <u>Specifically Fabricated</u> for Environmental Air. If necessary for direct action upon, or sensing of, the contained air, Type MC cable that has a smooth or corrugated impervious metal sheath without an overall nonmetallic covering, electrical metallic tubing, flexible metallic tubing, intermediate metal conduit, or rigid metal conduit without an overall nonmetallic covering can be installed in ducts <u>specifically fabricated to transport environmental air.</u> Flexible metal conduit in lengths not exceeding 4 ft can be used to connect physically adjustable equipment and devices within the <u>fabricated duct.</u>

Equipment is only permitted within the duct <u>specifically fabricated to transport environmental air</u> if necessary for the direct action upon, or sensing of, the contained air. Equipment, devices, and/or illumination are only permitted to be installed in the duct if necessary to facilitate maintenance and repair. **Figure 300–47**

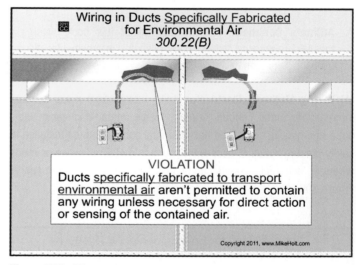

Wiring in Ducts <u>Specifically Fabricated</u>
for Environmental Air
300.22(B)

VIOLATION
Ducts <u>specifically fabricated to transport environmental air</u> aren't permitted to contain any wiring unless necessary for direct action or sensing of the contained air.

Copyright 2011, www.MikeHolt.com

Figure 300–47

(C) Other Spaces Used for Environmental Air <u>(Plenums).</u> This section applies to spaces used for air-handling purposes, but not fabricated for environmental air-handling purposes. This requirement doesn't apply to habitable rooms or areas of buildings, the prime purpose of which isn't air handling.

Note 1: The spaces above a suspended ceiling or below a raised floor used for environmental air are examples of the type of space to which this section applies. **Figure 300–48**

Note 2: The phrase "other space used for environmental air (plenum) " correlates with the term "plenum" in NFPA 90A, Standard for the Installation of Air-Conditioning and Ventilating Systems, and other mechanical codes where the ceiling cavity plenum is used for return air purposes, as well as some other air-handling spaces.

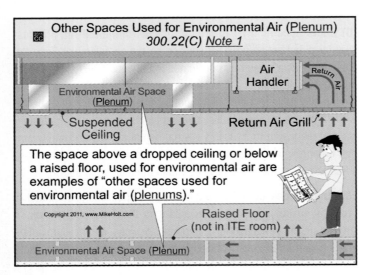

Figure 300—48

Author's Comment: For the purpose of this book, when the *NEC* references "other space used for environmental air (plenum)," the term cavity plenum space' will be used.

(1) Wiring Methods. Electrical metallic tubing, rigid metal conduit, intermediate metal conduit, armored cable, metal-clad cable without a nonmetallic cover, and flexible metal conduit can be installed in cavity plenum space. If accessible, surface metal raceways or metal wireways with metal <u>covers</u> can be installed in cavity plenum space. **Figure 300—49**

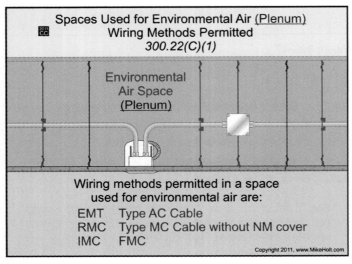

Figure 300—49

Author's Comments:

- PVC conduit [Article 352], electrical nonmetallic tubing [Article 362], liquidtight flexible conduit, and nonmetallic cables aren't permitted to be installed in spaces used for environmental air because they give off deadly toxic fumes when burned or superheated.

- Plenum-rated control, signaling, and communications cables and raceways are permitted in cavity plenum space: **Figure 300—50**

  – CATV, 820.179(A)
  – Communications, 800.21
  – Control and Signaling, 725.154(A)
  – Fire Alarm, 760.7
  – Optical Fiber Cables and Raceways, 770.113(C)
  – Sound Systems, 640.9(C) and 725.154(A)

- Any wiring method suitable for the condition can be used in a space not used for environmental air-handling purposes. **Figure 300—51**

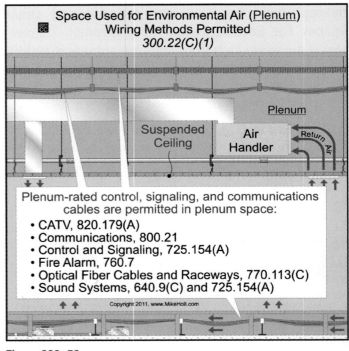

Figure 300—50

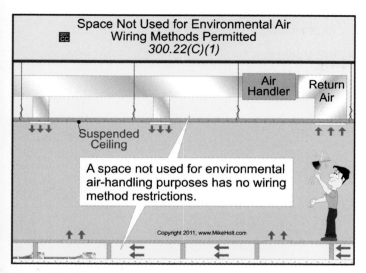

Figure 300–51

(2) Cable Tray Systems.

(a) Metal Cable Tray Systems. Metal cable tray systems can be installed to support the wiring methods and equipment permitted by this section. **Figure 300–52**

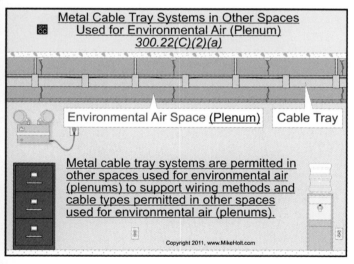

Figure 300–52

(3) Equipment. Electrical equipment with metal enclosures is permitted to be installed in cavity plenum space.

Author's Comment: Examples of electrical equipment permitted in cavity plenum space would be air-handlers, junction boxes, dry-type transformers; however transformers must not be rated over 50 kVA when located in hollow spaces [450.13(B)]. **Figure 300–53**

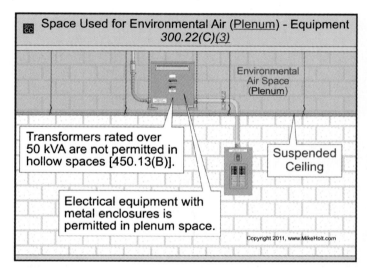

Figure 300–53

Notes

Mike Holt's Illustrated Guide to Essential Rules of the National Electrical Code, Based on the 2011 NEC

Conductors for General Wiring

INTRODUCTION TO ARTICLE 310—CONDUCTORS FOR GENERAL WIRING

This article contains the general requirements for conductors, such as insulation markings, ampacity ratings, and conditions of use. Article 310 doesn't apply to conductors that are part of flexible cords, fixture wires, or to conductors that are an integral part of equipment [90.7 and 300.1(B)].

People often make errors in applying the ampacity tables contained in Article 310. If you study the explanations carefully, you'll avoid common errors such as applying Table 310.15(B)(17) when you should be applying Table 310.15(B)(16).

Why so many tables? Why does Table 310.15(B)(17) list the ampacity of 6 THHN as 105 amperes, yet Table 310.15(B)(16) lists the same conductor as having an ampacity of only 75 amperes? To answer that, go back to Article 100 and review the definition of ampacity. Notice the phrase "conditions of use." These tables set a maximum current value at which premature failure of the conductor insulation shouldn't occur during normal use, under the conditions described in the tables.

The designations THHN, THHW, RHH, and so on, are insulation types. Every type of insulation has a limit to how much heat it can withstand. When current flows through a conductor, it creates heat. How well the insulation around a conductor can dissipate that heat depends on factors such as whether that conductor is in free air or not. Think about what happens when you put on a sweater, a jacket, and then a coat—all at the same time. You heat up. Your skin can't dissipate heat with all that clothing on nearly as well as it dissipates heat in free air. The same principal applies to conductors.

Conductor insulation also fails with age. That's why we conduct cable testing and take other measures to predict failure and replace certain conductors (for example, feeders or critical equipment conductors) while they're still within design specifications. But conductor insulation failure takes decades under normal use—and it's a maintenance issue. However, if a conductor is forced to exceed the ampacity listed in the appropriate table, and as a result its design temperature is exceeded, insulation failure happens much more rapidly—often catastrophically. Consequently, exceeding the allowable ampacity of a conductor is a serious safety issue.

Essential Rule 59	310.15

PART II. INSTALLATION

310.15 Conductor Ampacity.

Author's Comment: According to Article 100, ampacity means the <u>maximum</u> current, in amperes, a conductor can carry continuously, where the temperature of the conductor won't be raised in excess of its insulation temperature rating. **Figure 310–1**

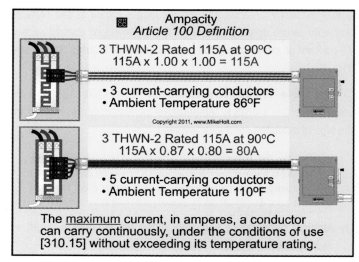

Figure 310–1

(A) General Requirements.

(1) Tables for Engineering Supervision. The ampacity of a conductor can be determined either by using the tables in accordance with 310.15(B), or under engineering supervision as provided in 310.15(C).

> **Note 1:** Ampacities provided by this section don't take voltage drop into consideration. See 210.19(A) Note 4, for branch circuits and 215.2(D) Note 2, for feeders.

(2) Conductor Ampacity—Lower Rating. Where more than <u>one ampacity applies</u> for a given circuit length, the lowest value must be used. **Figure 310–2**

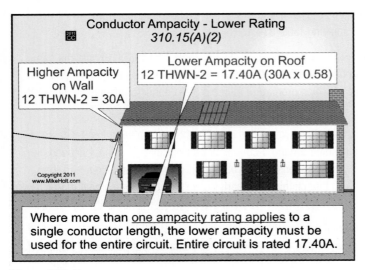

Figure 310–2

Ex: When different ampacities apply to a length of conductor, the higher ampacity is permitted for the entire circuit if the reduced ampacity length doesn't exceed 10 ft and its length doesn't exceed 10 percent of the length of the higher ampacity. **Figures 310–3 and 310–4**

(3) Insulation Temperature Limitation. Conductors must not be used where the operating temperature exceeds that designated for the type of insulated conductor involved.

> **Note 1:** The insulation temperature rating of a conductor [Table 310.104(A)] is the maximum temperature a conductor can withstand over a prolonged time period without serious degradation. The main factors to consider for conductor operating temperature include:

(1) Ambient temperature may vary along the conductor length as well as from time to time [Table 310.15(B)(2)(a)].

(2) Heat generated internally in the conductor—load current flow.

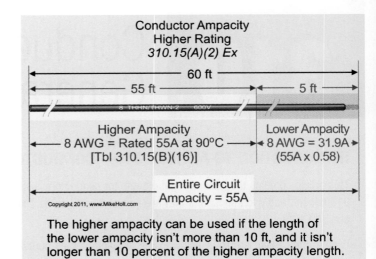

Figure 310–3

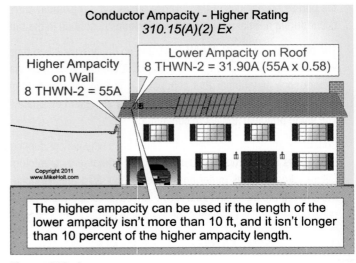

Figure 310–4

(3) The rate at which generated heat dissipates into the ambient medium.

(4) Adjacent load-carrying conductors have the effect of raising the ambient temperature and impeding heat dissipation [Table 310.15(B)(3)(a)].

> **Note 2:** See 110.14(C)(1) for the temperature limitation of terminations.

(B) Ampacity Table. The allowable conductor ampacities listed in Table 310.15(B)(16) are based on conditions where the ambient temperature isn't over 86°F, and no more than three current-carrying conductors are bundled together. **Figure 310–5**

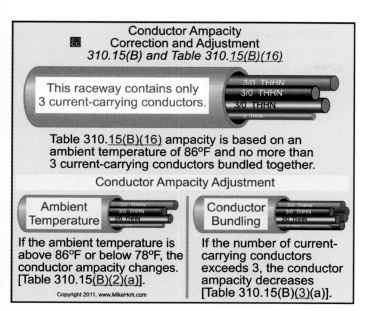

Figure 310–5

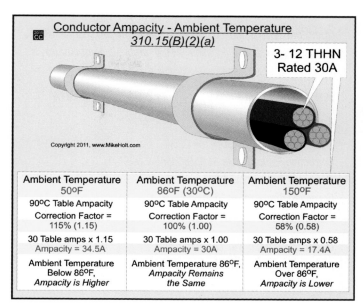

Figure 310–7

The temperature correction and adjustment factors apply to the conductor ampacity, based on the temperature rating of the conductor insulation in accordance with Table 310.15(B)(16). **Figure 310–6**

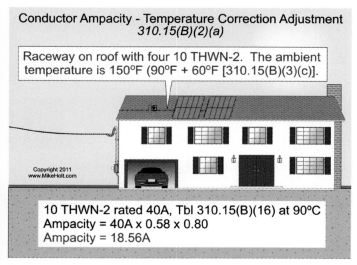

Figure 310–6

(2) Conductor Ampacity Ambient Temperature Correction. When conductors are installed in an ambient temperature other than 78°F to 86°F, the ampacities listed in Table 310.15(B)(16) must be corrected in accordance with the multipliers listed in Table 310.15(B)(2)(a). **Figure 310–7**

Table 310.15(B)(2)(a) Ambient Temperature Correction			
Ambient Temperature °F	Ambient Temperature °C	Correction Factor 75°C Conductors	Correction Factor 90°C Conductors
50 or less	10 or less	1.20	1.15
51–59°F	11–15°C	1.15	1.12
60–68°F	16–20°C	1.11	1.08
69–77°F	21–25°C	1.05	1.04
78–86°F	26–30°C	1.00	1.00
87–95°F	31–35°C	0.94	0.96
96–104°F	36–40°C	0.88	0.91
105–113°F	41–45°C	0.82	0.87
114–122°F	46–50°C	0.75	0.82
123–131°F	51–55°C	0.67	0.76
132–140°F	56–60°C	0.58	0.71
141–149°F	61–65°C	0.47	0.65
150–158°F	66–70°C	0.33	0.58
159–167°F	71–75°C	0.00	0.50
168–176°F	76–80°C	0.00	0.41
177–185°F	81–85°C	0.00	0.29

Question: *What's the corrected ampacity of 3/0 THHN/THWN conductors in a dry location if the ambient temperature is 108°F?*

(a) 173A   (b) 196A   (c) 213A   (d) 241A

Answer: *(b) 196A*

Conductor Ampacity [90°C] = 225A
Correction Factor [Table 310.(B)(2)(a)] = 0.87
Corrected Ampacity = 225A x 0.87
Corrected Ampacity = 196A

Question: *What's the corrected ampacity of 3/0 THHN/THWN conductors in a wet location if the ambient temperature is 108°F?*

(a) 164A   (b) 196A   (c) 213A   (d) 241A

Answer: *(a) 164A*

Conductor Ampacity [75°C] = 200A
Correction Factor [Table 310.(B)(2)(a)] = 0.82
Corrected Ampacity = 200A x 0.82
Corrected Ampacity = 164A

(3) Conductor Ampacity Adjustment.

(a) Four or More Current-Carrying Conductors in a Raceway or Cable. Where four or more current-carrying power conductors are in a raceway longer than 24 in. [310.15(B)(3)(a)(3)], or where cables are bundled for a length longer than 24 in., the ampacity of each conductor must be reduced in accordance with Table 310.15(B)(3)(a).

Table 310.15(B)(3)(a) Conductor Ampacity Adjustment for More Than Three Current-Carrying Conductors in a Raceway or Cable

Number of Conductors[1]	Adjustment
4–6	0.80 or 80%
7–9	0.70 or 70%
10–20	0.50 or 50%
21–30	0.45 or 50%
31–40	0.40 or 40%
41 and above	0.35 or 35%

[1]Number of conductors is the total number of conductors in the raceway or cable adjusted in accordance with 310.15(B)(5) and (6).

Author's Comment: Conductor ampacity reduction is required when four or more current-carrying conductors are bundled because heat generated by current flow is not able to dissipate as quickly as three or fewer current-carrying conductors. **Figures 310–8 and 310–9**

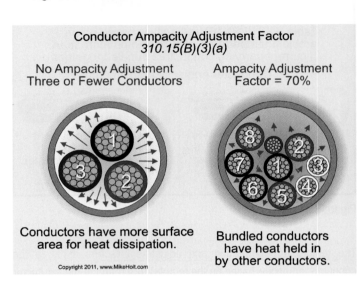

Figure 310–8

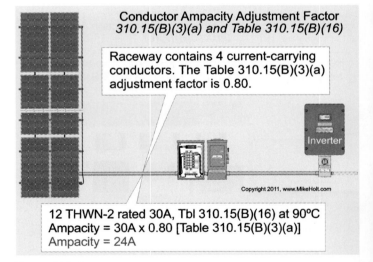

Figure 310–9

(1) Conductor ampacity adjustment of Table 310.15(B)(3)(a) does not apply to conductors installed in cable trays, 392.80 apply.

(2) Conductor ampacity adjustment of Table 310.15(B)(3)(a) does not apply to conductors in raceways having a length not exceeding 24 in. **Figure 310–10**

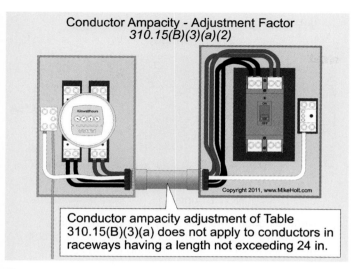

Conductor Ampacity - Adjustment Factor
310.15(B)(3)(a)(2)

Conductor ampacity adjustment of Table 310.15(B)(3)(a) does not apply to conductors in raceways having a length not exceeding 24 in.

Copyright 2011, www.MikeHolt.com

Figure 310–10

(4) Conductor ampacity adjustment of Table 310.15(B)(3)(a) does not apply to conductors within Type AC or Type MC cable under the following conditions: **Figure 310–11**

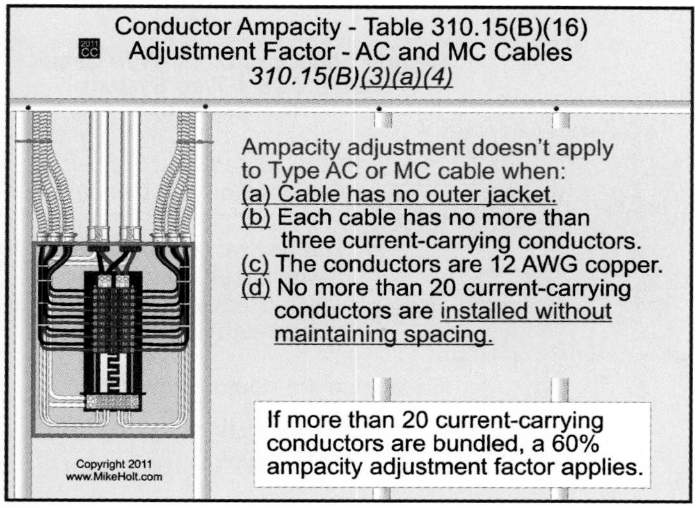

Conductor Ampacity - Table 310.15(B)(16)
Adjustment Factor - AC and MC Cables
310.15(B)(3)(a)(4)

Ampacity adjustment doesn't apply to Type AC or MC cable when:
(a) Cable has no outer jacket.
(b) Each cable has no more than three current-carrying conductors.
(c) The conductors are 12 AWG copper.
(d) No more than 20 current-carrying conductors are installed without maintaining spacing.

If more than 20 current-carrying conductors are bundled, a 60% ampacity adjustment factor applies.

Copyright 2011
www.MikeHolt.com

Figure 310–11

(a) The cables don't have an outer jacket,

(b) Each cable has no more than three current-carrying conductors,

(c) The conductors are 12 AWG copper, and

(d) No more than 20 current-carrying conductors (ten 2-wire cables or six 3-wire cables) are installed without maintaining spacing for a continuous length longer than 24 in.

(5) Ampacity adjustment of 60 percent applies to conductors within Type AC or Type MC cable without an overall outer jacket under the following conditions:

(b) The number of current-carrying conductors exceeds 20.

(c) The cables are stacked or bundled longer than 24 in. without spacing being maintained.

(c) Circular Raceways Exposed to Sunlight on Rooftops. When applying ampacity adjustment correction factors, the ambient temperature adjustment contained in Table 310.15(B)(3)(c) is added to the outdoor ambient temperature for conductors installed in circular raceways exposed to direct sunlight on or above rooftops to determine the applicable ambient temperature for ampacity correction factors in Table 310.15(B)(2)(a) or Table 310.15(B)(2)(b). **Figures 310–12 and 310–13**

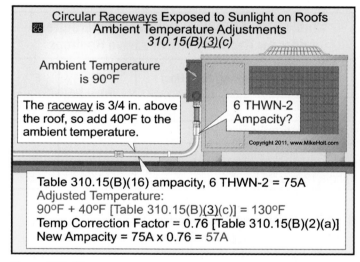

Circular Raceways Exposed to Sunlight on Roofs
Ambient Temperature Adjustments
310.15(B)(3)(c)

Ambient Temperature is 90°F

The raceway is 3/4 in. above the roof, so add 40°F to the ambient temperature.

6 THWN-2 Ampacity?

Copyright 2011, www.MikeHolt.com

Table 310.15(B)(16) ampacity, 6 THWN-2 = 75A
Adjusted Temperature:
90°F + 40°F [Table 310.15(B)(3)(c)] = 130°F
Temp Correction Factor = 0.76 [Table 310.15(B)(2)(a)]
New Ampacity = 75A x 0.76 = 57A

Figure 310–12

Note 1: See the ASHRAE *Handbook—Fundamentals* (www.ashrae.org) as a source for the average ambient temperatures in various locations.

Note 2: The temperature adders in Table 310.15(B)(3)(c) are based on the results of averaging the ambient temperatures.

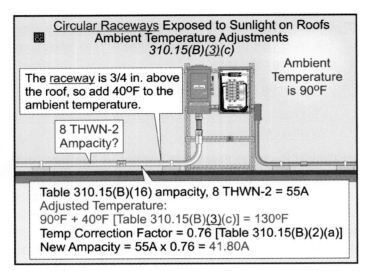

Figure 310–13

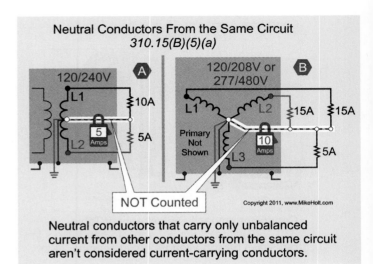

Figure 310–14

Table 310.15(B)(3)(c) Ambient Temperature Adder for Raceways On or Above Rooftops

Distance of Raceway Above Roof	C°	F°
0 to ½ in.	33	60
Above ½ in. to 3½ in.	22	40
Above 3½ in. to 12 in.	17	30
Above 12 in. to 36 in.	14	25

Author's Comment: This rule requires the ambient temperature used for ampacity correction to be adjusted where conductors or cables are installed in a circular raceway on or above a rooftop and the raceway is exposed to direct sunlight. The reasoning is that the air inside circular raceways in direct sunlight is significantly hotter than the surrounding air, and appropriate ampacity corrections must be made in order to comply with 310.10.

(5) Neutral Conductors.

(a) The neutral conductor of a 3-wire, single-phase, 120/240V system, or 4-wire, three-phase, 120/208V or 277/480V wye-connected system, isn't considered a current-carrying conductor for conductor ampacity adjustment of 310.15(B)(3)(a). **Figure 310–14**

(b) The neutral conductor of a 3-wire circuit from a 4-wire, three-phase, 120/208V or 277/480V wye-connected system is considered a current-carrying conductor for conductor ampacity adjustment of 310.15(B)(3)(a).

Author's Comment: When a 3-wire circuit is supplied from a 4-wire, three-phase, 120/208V or 277/480V wye-connected system, the neutral conductor carries approximately the same current as the ungrounded conductors. **Figure 310–15**

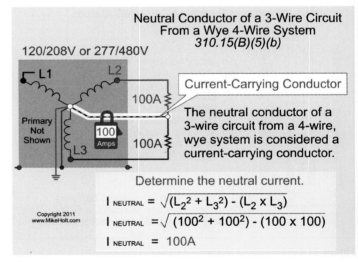

Figure 310–15

(c) The neutral conductor of a 4-wire, three-phase, 120/208V or 277/480V wye-connected system is considered a current-carrying conductor for conductor ampacity adjustment of 310.15(B)(3)(a) if more than 50 percent of the neutral load consists of nonlinear loads. **Figure 310–16**

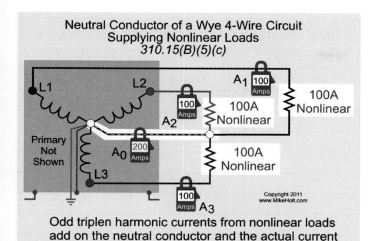

Neutral Conductor of a Wye 4-Wire Circuit
Supplying Nonlinear Loads
310.15(B)(5)(c)

Odd triplen harmonic currents from nonlinear loads add on the neutral conductor and the actual current can be twice the ungrounded conductor's current.

Figure 310–16

Author's Comment: Nonlinear loads supplied by a 4-wire, three-phase, 120/208V or 277/480V wye-connected system can produce unwanted and potentially hazardous odd triplen harmonic currents (3rd, 9th, 15th, and so on) that can add on the neutral conductor. To prevent fire or equipment damage from excessive harmonic neutral current, the designer should consider increasing the size of the neutral conductor or installing a separate neutral for each phase. For more information, visit www.MikeHolt.com, click on the "Technical" link, then the "Power Quality" link. Also see 210.4(A) Note, 220.61 Note 2, and 450.3 Note 2.

(6) Grounding Conductors. Grounding and bonding conductors aren't considered current carrying. Figure 310–17

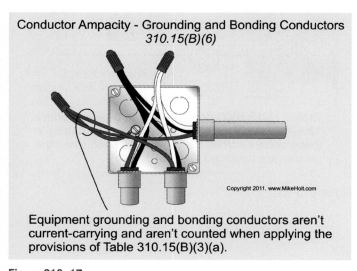

Conductor Ampacity - Grounding and Bonding Conductors
310.15(B)(6)

Equipment grounding and bonding conductors aren't current-carrying and aren't counted when applying the provisions of Table 310.15(B)(3)(a).

Figure 310–17

(7) Dwelling Unit Feeder/Service Conductors. For individual dwelling units of one-family, two-family, and multifamily dwellings, Table 310.15(B)(7) can be used to size 3-wire, single-phase, 120/240V service conductors. Figure 310–18

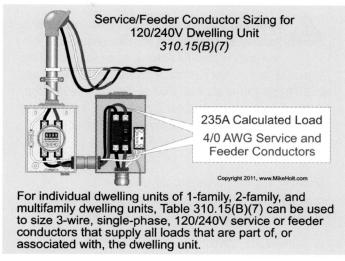

Service/Feeder Conductor Sizing for
120/240V Dwelling Unit
310.15(B)(7)

235A Calculated Load
4/0 AWG Service and
Feeder Conductors

For individual dwelling units of 1-family, 2-family, and multifamily dwelling units, Table 310.15(B)(7) can be used to size 3-wire, single-phase, 120/240V service or feeder conductors that supply all loads that are part of, or associated with, the dwelling unit.

Figure 310–18

Author's Comment: Table 310.15(B)(7) can't be used for service conductors for two-family or multifamily dwelling buildings. Figure 310–19

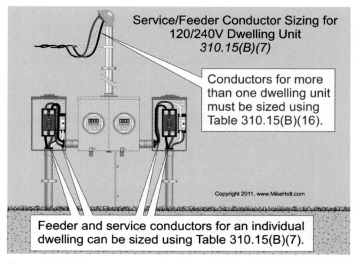

Service/Feeder Conductor Sizing for
120/240V Dwelling Unit
310.15(B)(7)

Conductors for more than one dwelling unit must be sized using Table 310.15(B)(16).

Feeder and service conductors for an individual dwelling can be sized using Table 310.15(B)(7).

Figure 310–19

Feeder conductors for individual dwelling units aren't required to be sized larger than service conductors sized to 310.15(B)(7) [215.2(A)(4)].

Neutral Conductor Sizing. For individual dwelling units of one-family, two-family, and multifamily dwellings, Table 310.15(B)(7) can be used to size the neutral conductor of a 3-wire, single-phase, 120/240V service or feeder that carries all loads associated with the dwelling unit, based on the calculated load in accordance with 220.61.

⚠️ **CAUTION:** *Because the service neutral conductor is required to serve as the effective ground-fault current path, it must be sized so it can safely carry the maximum fault current likely to be imposed on it [110.10 and 250.4(A)(5)]. This is accomplished by sizing the neutral conductor in accordance with Table 250.66, based on the area of the largest ungrounded service conductor [250.24(C)(1)].*

Question: *What size service conductors are required if the calculated load for a dwelling unit equals 195A, and the maximum unbalanced neutral load is 100A?* **Figure 310–20**

(a) 1/0 AWG and 6 AWG   (b) 2/0 AWG and 4 AWG
(c) 3/0 AWG and 2 AWG   (d) 4/0 AWG and 1 AWG

Answer: *(b) 2/0 AWG and 4 AWG*

Service Conductor: 2/0 AWG rated 200A [Table 310.15(B)(7)]

Neutral Conductor: 4 AWG is rated 100A in accordance with Table 310.15(B)(7). In addition, 250.24(C) requires the neutral conductor to be sized no smaller than 4 AWG based on 2/0 AWG service conductors in accordance with Table 250.66.

Table 310.15(B)(7) Conductor Sizes for 120/240V, 3-Wire, Single-Phase Dwelling Services and Feeders		
Amperes	Copper	Aluminum
100	4 AWG	2 AWG
110	3 AWG	1 AWG
125	2 AWG	1/0 AWG
150	1 AWG	2/0 AWG
175	1/0 AWG	3/0 AWG
200	2/0 AWG	4/0 AWG
225	3/0 AWG	250 kcmil
250	4/0 AWG	300 kcmil
300	250 kcmil	350 kcmil
350	350 kcmil	500 kcmil
400	400 kcmil	600 kcmil

⚠️ **WARNING:** *Table 310.15(B)(7) doesn't apply to 3-wire feeder/service conductors connected to a three-phase, 120/208V system, because the neutral conductor in these systems always carries neutral current, even when the load on the phases are balanced [310.15(B)(5)(b)]. For more information on this topic, see 220.61(C)(1).* **Figure 310–21**

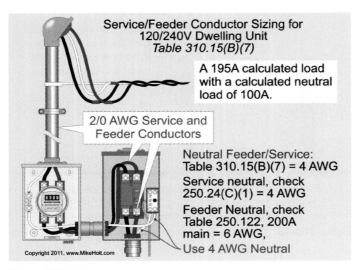

Service/Feeder Conductor Sizing for 120/240V Dwelling Unit
Table 310.15(B)(7)

A 195A calculated load with a calculated neutral load of 100A.

2/0 AWG Service and Feeder Conductors

Neutral Feeder/Service: Table 310.15(B)(7) = 4 AWG

Service neutral, check 250.24(C)(1) = 4 AWG

Feeder Neutral, check Table 250.122, 200A main = 6 AWG, Use 4 AWG Neutral

Copyright 2011, www.MikeHolt.com

Figure 310–20

Service/Feeder Conductor Sizing for Dwelling Unit
Table 310.15(B)(7)

120/208V

A   B

Amps 200

L1

L2

200 Amps

C   L3

200 Amps

200 Amps

N

A 3-wire feed from a 4-wire, three-phase wye system.

Copyright 2011 www.MikeHolt.com

Table 310.15(B)(7) doesn't apply to 3-wire, 1-phase, 120/208V circuits, because the neutral conductor in these circuits carries neutral current even when the phases are balanced [310.15(B)(5)(b)].

Figure 310–21

ARTICLE 312

Cabinets, Cutout Boxes, and Meter Socket Enclosures

INTRODUCTION TO ARTICLE 312—CABINETS, CUTOUT BOXES, AND METER SOCKET ENCLOSURES

This article addresses the installation and construction specifications for the items mentioned in its title. In Article 310, we observed that the conditions of use have an effect on the ampacity of a conductor. Likewise, the conditions of use have an effect on the selection and application of cabinets, cutout boxes, and meter socket enclosures. For example, you can't use just any enclosure in a wet location or in a hazardous location. The conditions of use impose special requirements for these situations.

For all such enclosures, certain requirements apply—regardless of the use. For example, you must cover any openings, protect conductors from abrasion, and allow sufficient bending room for conductors.

Notice that Article 408 covers switchboards and panelboards, with primary emphasis on the interior, or "guts" while the cabinet that would be used to enclose a panelboard is covered here in Article 312. Therefore you'll find that some important considerations such as wire-bending space at terminals of panelboards are included in this article.

Article 312 covers the installation and construction specifications for cabinets, cutout boxes, and meter socket enclosures. [312.1].

Author's Comment: A cabinet is an enclosure for either surface mounting or flush mounting and provided with a frame in which a door may be hung. A cutout box is designed for surface mounting with a swinging door [Article 100]. The industry name for a meter socket enclosure is "meter can."

Essential Rule 60	312.8

PART I. INSTALLATION

312.8 Enclosures With Splices, Taps, and Feed-Through Conductors.
Cabinets, cutout boxes, and meter socket enclosures can be used for conductors as feeding through, spliced, or tapping off to other enclosures, switches, or overcurrent devices where all of the following conditions are met:

(1) The total area of the conductors at any cross section doesn't exceed 40 percent of the cross-sectional area of the space. **Figure 312–1**

(2) The total area of conductors, splices, and taps installed at any cross section doesn't exceed 75 percent of the cross-sectional area of that space. **Figure 312–2**

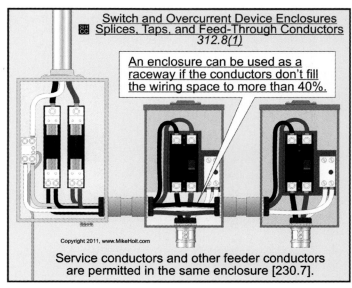

Switch and Overcurrent Device Enclosures
Splices, Taps, and Feed-Through Conductors
312.8(1)

An enclosure can be used as a raceway if the conductors don't fill the wiring space to more than 40%.

Copyright 2011, www.MikeHolt.com

Service conductors and other feeder conductors are permitted in the same enclosure [230.7].

Figure 312–1

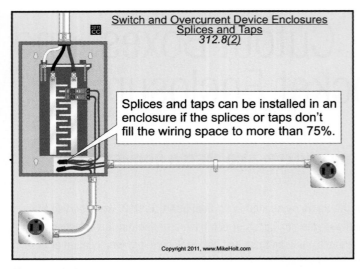

Figure 312–2

(3) A warning label on the enclosure identifies the disconnecting means for feed-through conductors. **Figure 312–3**

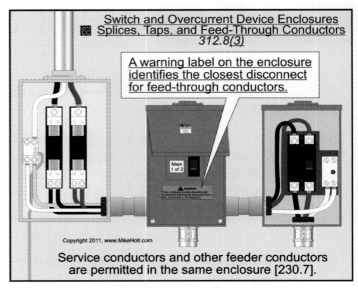

Figure 312–3

Outlet, Device, Pull and Junction Boxes; Conduit Bodies; and Handhole Enclosures

INTRODUCTION TO ARTICLE 314—OUTLET, DEVICE, PULL AND JUNCTION BOXES; CONDUIT BODIES; AND HANDHOLE ENCLOSURES

Article 314 contains installation requirements for outlet boxes, pull and junction boxes, conduit bodies, and handhole enclosures. As with Article 312, the conditions of use have a bearing on the type of material and equipment selected for a particular installation. If a raceway is installed in a wet location, for example, the correct fittings and the proper installation methods must be used.

Article 314 provides guidance for selecting and installing outlet and device boxes, pull and junction boxes, conduit bodies, and handhole enclosures. Information in this article will help you size an outlet box using the proper cubic-inch capacity as well as calculating the minimum dimensions for larger pull boxes. There are limits on the amount of weight that can be supported by an outlet box and rules on how to support a device or outlet box to various surfaces. This article will help you understand these type of rules so that your installation will be compliant with the *NEC*. As always, the clear illustrations in this unit will help you visualize the finished installation.

Essential Rule 61   **314.16**

PART II. INSTALLATION

314.16 Number of 6 AWG and Smaller Conductors in Boxes and Conduit Bodies.
Boxes containing 6 AWG and smaller conductors must be sized to provide sufficient free space for all conductors, devices, and fittings. In no case can the volume of the box, as calculated in 314.16(A), be less than the volume requirement as calculated in 314.16(B).

Conduit bodies must be sized in accordance with 314.16(C).

> **Author's Comment:** The requirements for sizing boxes and conduit bodies containing conductors 4 AWG and larger are contained in 314.28. The requirements for sizing handhole enclosures are contained in 314.30(A).

(A) Box Volume Calculations. The volume of a box includes the total volume of its assembled parts, including plaster rings, extension rings, and domed covers that are either marked with their volume in cubic inches (cu in.), or are made from boxes listed in Table 314.16(A). Figure 314–1

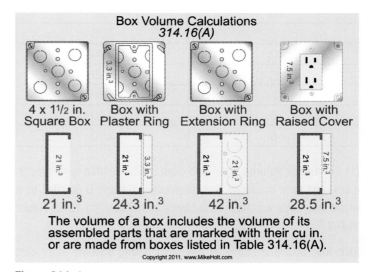

Box Volume Calculations
314.16(A)

4 x 1½ in. Square Box	Box with Plaster Ring	Box with Extension Ring	Box with Raised Cover
21 in.³	24.3 in.³	42 in.³	28.5 in.³

The volume of a box includes the volume of its assembled parts that are marked with their cu in. or are made from boxes listed in Table 314.16(A).

Copyright 2011, www.MikeHolt.com

Figure 314–1

(B) Box Fill Calculations. The calculated conductor volume determined by (1) through (5) and Table 314.16(B) are added together to determine the total volume of the conductors, devices, and fittings. Raceway and cable fittings, including locknuts and bushings, aren't counted for box fill calculations. **Figure 314–2**

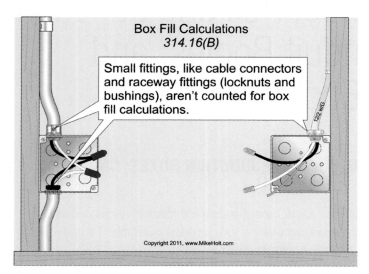

Box Fill Calculations
314.16(B)

Small fittings, like cable connectors and raceway fittings (locknuts and bushings), aren't counted for box fill calculations.

Figure 314–2

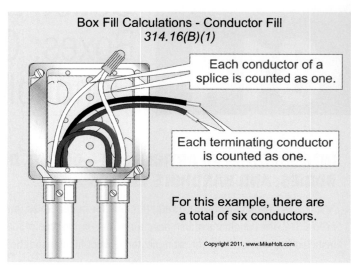

Box Fill Calculations - Conductor Fill
314.16(B)(1)

Each conductor of a splice is counted as one.

Each terminating conductor is counted as one.

For this example, there are a total of six conductors.

Figure 314–3

Table 314.16(B) Volume Allowance Required per Conductor	
Conductor AWG	Volume cu in.
18	1.50
16	1.75
14	2.00
12	2.25
10	2.50
8	3.00
6	5.00

(1) Conductor Volume. Each unbroken conductor that runs through a box, and each conductor that terminates in a box, is counted as a single conductor volume in accordance with Table 314.16(B). **Figure 314–3**

Each loop or coil of unbroken conductor having a length of at least twice the minimum length required for free conductors in 300.14 must be counted as two conductor volumes. Conductors that originate and terminate within the box, such as pigtails, aren't counted at all. **Figure 314–4**

> **Author's Comment:** According to 300.14, at least 6 in. of free conductor, measured from the point in the box where the conductors enter the enclosure, must be left at each outlet, junction, and switch point for splices or terminations of luminaires or devices.

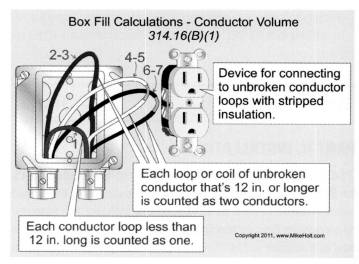

Box Fill Calculations - Conductor Volume
314.16(B)(1)

Device for connecting to unbroken conductor loops with stripped insulation.

Each loop or coil of unbroken conductor that's 12 in. or longer is counted as two conductors.

Each conductor loop less than 12 in. long is counted as one.

Figure 314–4

Ex: Equipment grounding conductors, and up to four 16 AWG and smaller fixture wires, can be omitted from box fill calculations if they enter the box from a domed luminaire or similar canopy, such as a ceiling paddle fan canopy. **Figure 314–5**

(2) Cable Clamp Volume. One or more internal cable clamps count as a single conductor volume in accordance with Table 314.16(B), based on the largest conductor that enters the box. Cable connectors that have their clamping mechanism outside of the box aren't counted. **Figure 314–6**

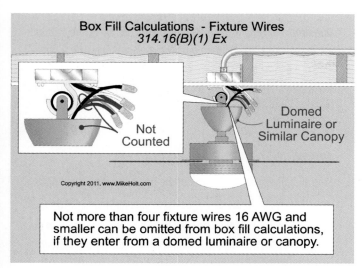

Box Fill Calculations - Fixture Wires
314.16(B)(1) Ex

Not Counted

Domed Luminaire or Similar Canopy

Copyright 2011, www.MikeHolt.com

Not more than four fixture wires 16 AWG and smaller can be omitted from box fill calculations, if they enter from a domed luminaire or canopy.

Figure 314–5

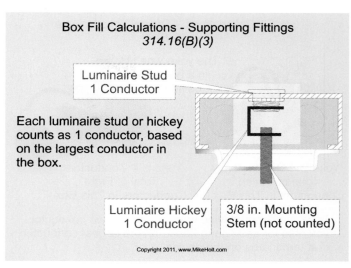

Box Fill Calculations - Supporting Fittings
314.16(B)(3)

Luminaire Stud 1 Conductor

Each luminaire stud or hickey counts as 1 conductor, based on the largest conductor in the box.

Luminaire Hickey 1 Conductor

3/8 in. Mounting Stem (not counted)

Copyright 2011, www.MikeHolt.com

Figure 314–7

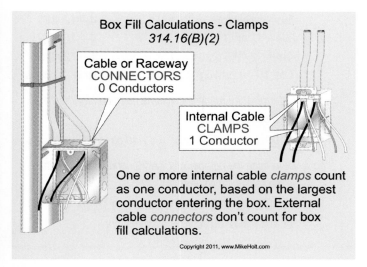

Box Fill Calculations - Clamps
314.16(B)(2)

Cable or Raceway CONNECTORS 0 Conductors

Internal Cable CLAMPS 1 Conductor

One or more internal cable *clamps* count as one conductor, based on the largest conductor entering the box. External cable *connectors* don't count for box fill calculations.

Copyright 2011, www.MikeHolt.com

Figure 314–6

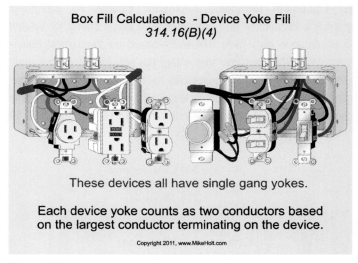

Box Fill Calculations - Device Yoke Fill
314.16(B)(4)

These devices all have single gang yokes.

Each device yoke counts as two conductors based on the largest conductor terminating on the device.

Copyright 2011, www.MikeHolt.com

Figure 314–8

(3) Support Fitting Volume. Each luminaire stud or luminaire hickey counts as a single conductor volume in accordance with Table 314.16(B), based on the largest conductor that enters the box. **Figure 314–7**

> **Author's Comment:** Luminaire stems don't need to be counted as a conductor volume.

(4) Device Yoke Volume. Each single-gang device yoke (regardless of the ampere rating of the device) counts as two conductor volumes, based on the largest conductor that terminates on the device in accordance with Table 314.16(B). **Figure 314–8**

Each multigang-device yoke counts as two conductor volumes for each gang, based on the largest conductor that terminates on the device in accordance with Table 314.16(B). **Figure 314–9**

> **Author's Comment:** A device that's too wide for mounting in a single-gang box, as described in Table 314.16(A), is counted based on the number of gangs required for the device.

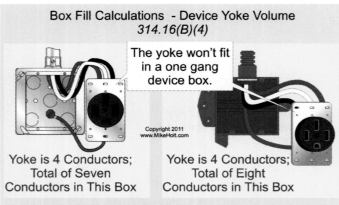

Box Fill Calculations - Device Yoke Volume
314.16(B)(4)

The yoke won't fit in a one gang device box.

Copyright 2011
www.MikeHolt.com

Yoke is 4 Conductors;
Total of Seven
Conductors in This Box

Yoke is 4 Conductors;
Total of Eight
Conductors in This Box

Each multigang device yoke counts as two conductor volumes for each gang based on the largest conductor that terminates on the device.

Figure 314–9

(5) Equipment Grounding Conductor Volume. All equipment grounding conductors in a box count as a single conductor volume in accordance with Table 314.16(B), based on the largest equipment grounding conductor that enters the box. Insulated equipment grounding conductors for receptacles having insulated grounding terminals (isolated ground receptacles) [250.146(D)], count as a single conductor volume in accordance with Table 314.16(B). **Figure 314–10**

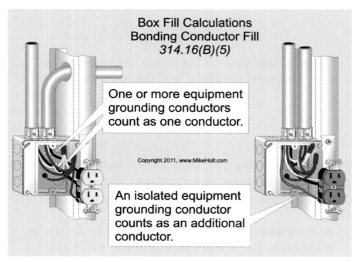

Box Fill Calculations
Bonding Conductor Fill
314.16(B)(5)

One or more equipment grounding conductors count as one conductor.

Copyright 2011, www.MikeHolt.com

An isolated equipment grounding conductor counts as an additional conductor.

Figure 314–10

Author's Comment: Conductor insulation isn't a factor that's considered when determining box volume calculations.

Question: How many 14 AWG conductors can be pulled through a 4 in. square x 2½ in. deep box with a plaster ring with a marking of 3.60 cu in.? The box contains two receptacles, five 12 AWG conductors, and two 12 AWG equipment grounding conductors. **Figure 314–11**

(a) 3   (b) 5   (c) 7   (d) 9

Answer: (b) 5

Step 1: Determine the volume of the box assembly [314.16(A)]:

Box 30.30 cu in. + 3.60 cu in. plaster ring = 33.90 cu in.

A 4 x 4 x 2⅛ in. box will have a gross volume of 34 cu in., but the interior volume is 30.30 cu in., as listed in Table 314.16(A).

Step 2: Determine the volume of the devices and conductors in the box:

Two—receptacles	4—12 AWG
Five—12 AWG	5—12 AWG
Two—12 AWG Grounds	1—12 AWG

Total 10—12 AWG x 2.25 cu in. = 22.50 cu in.

Step 3: Determine the remaining volume permitted for the 14 AWG conductors:

33.90 cu in. - 22.50 cu in. = 11.40 cu in.

Step 4: Determine the number of 14 AWG conductors permitted in the remaining volume:

14 AWG = 2.00 cu in. each [Table 314.16(B)]
11.40 cu in./2.00 cu in. = 5 conductors

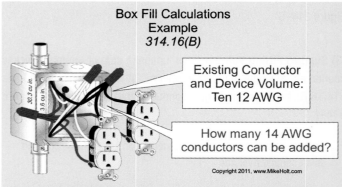

Box Fill Calculations
Example
314.16(B)

Existing Conductor and Device Volume:
Ten 12 AWG

How many 14 AWG conductors can be added?

Copyright 2011, www.MikeHolt.com

Step 1. Volume of box/ring: 30.3 + 3.6 cu in. = 33.9 cu in.
Step 2. Volume of existing conductors/devices = 22.5 cu in.
Step 3. Space remaining: 33.9 - 22.5 = 11.4 cu in.
Step 4. Number of 14 AWG added: 11.4/2.0 cu in. = 5

Figure 314–11

(C) Conduit Bodies.

(2) Splices. Splices are permitted in conduit bodies that are legibly marked by the manufacturer with their volume and the maximum number of conductors permitted in a conduit body is limited in accordance with 314.16(B).

Question: How many 12 AWG conductors can be spliced in a 15 cu in. conduit body? **Figure 314–12**

(a) 4   (b) 6   (c) 8   (d) 10

Answer: (b) 6 conductors (15 cu in./2.25 cu in.)

12 AWG = 2.25 cu in. [Table 314.16(B)]

15 cu in./2.25 cu in. = 6

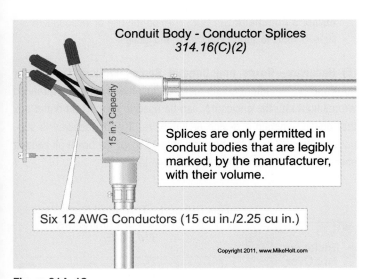

Figure 314–12

(3) Short-Radius Conduit Bodies. Capped elbows, handy ells, and service-entrance elbows aren't permitted to contain any splices. Figure 314–13

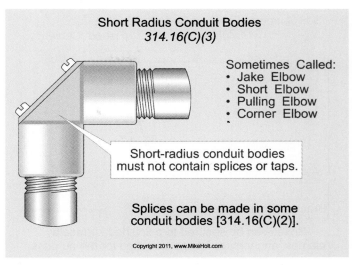

Figure 314–13

Essential Rule 62   314.23

314.23 Support of Boxes and Conduit Bodies. Boxes must be securely supported by one of the following methods:

(A) Surface. Boxes can be fastened to any surface that provides adequate support.

(B) Structural Mounting. Boxes can be supported from a structural member of a building or supported from grade by a metal, plastic, or wood brace.

(1) Nails and Screws. Nails or screws can be used to fasten boxes, provided the exposed threads of screws are protected to prevent abrasion of conductor insulation.

(2) Braces. Metal braces no less than 0.02 in. thick and wood braces not less than a nominal 1 in. x 2 in. can support a box.

(C) Finished Surface Support. Boxes can be secured to a finished surface (drywall or plaster walls or ceilings) by clamps, anchors, or fittings identified for the purpose. **Figure 314–14**

(D) Suspended-Ceiling Support. Outlet boxes can be supported to the structural or supporting elements of a suspended ceiling, if securely fastened by one of the following methods:

(1) Ceiling-Framing Members. An outlet box can be secured to suspended-ceiling framing members by bolts, screws, rivets, clips, or other means identified for the suspended-ceiling framing member(s). **Figure 314–15**

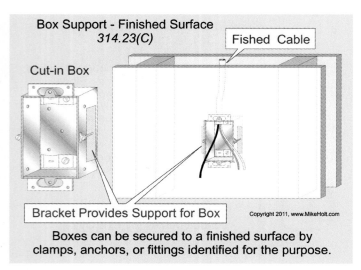

Figure 314–14

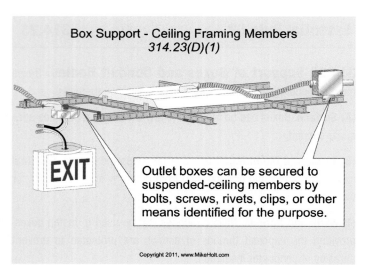

Figure 314–15

Author's Comment: If framing members of suspended-ceiling systems are used to support luminaires, they must be securely fastened to each other and must be securely attached to the building structure at appropriate intervals. In addition, luminaires must be attached to the suspended-ceiling framing members with screws, bolts, rivets, or clips listed and identified for such use [410.36(B)].

(2) Independent Support Wires. Outlet boxes can be secured, with fittings identified for the purpose, to the ceiling-support wires. If independent support wires are used for outlet box support, they must be taut and secured at both ends [300.11(A)]. **Figure 314–16**

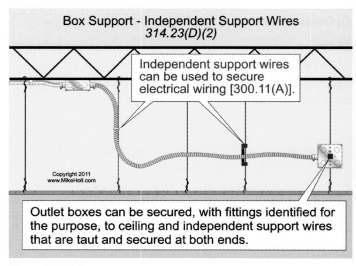

Figure 314–16

Author's Comment: See 300.11(A) on the use of independent support wires to support raceways and cables.

(E) Raceway—Boxes and Conduit Bodies Without Devices or Luminaires. Two intermediate metal or rigid metal conduits, threaded wrenchtight into the enclosure, can be used to support an outlet box that doesn't contain a device or luminaire, if each raceway is supported within 36 in. of the box or within 18 in. of the box if all conduit entries are on the same side. **Figure 314–17**

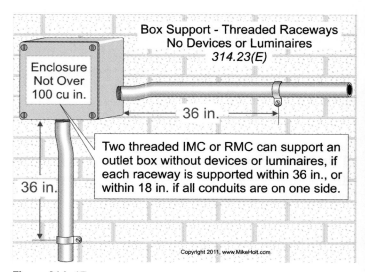

Figure 314–17

Ex: Conduit bodies are permitted to be supported by any of the following wiring methods:

   (1) Intermediate metal conduit, Type IMC

   (2) Rigid metal conduit, Type RMC

   (3) Rigid polyvinyl chloride conduit, Type PVC

   (4) Reinforced thermosetting resin conduit, Type RTRC

   (5) Electrical metallic tubing, Type EMT

(F) Raceway—Boxes and Conduit Bodies with Devices or Luminaires. Two intermediate metal or rigid metal conduits, threaded wrenchtight into the enclosure, can be used to support an outlet box containing devices or luminaires, if each raceway is supported within 18 in. of the box. **Figure 314–18**

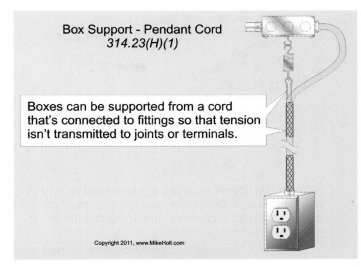

Figure 314–19

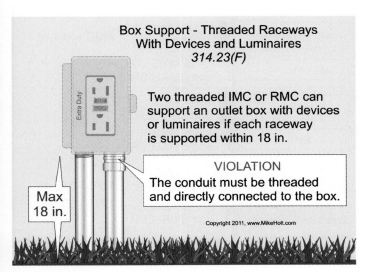

Figure 314–18

(H) Pendant Boxes.

(1) Flexible Cord. Boxes containing a hub can be supported from a cord connected to fittings that prevent tension from being transmitted to joints or terminals [400.10]. **Figure 314–19**

   Author's Comment: Only cords identified for use as pendants in Table 400.4 may be used for pendants. 314.25 Covers and Canopies. When the installation is complete, each outlet box must be provided with a cover or faceplate, unless covered by a fixture canopy, lampholder, or similar device. **Figure 314–20**

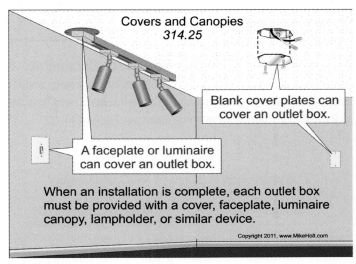

Figure 314–20

(A) Nonmetallic or Metallic. Nonmetallic covers are permitted on any box, but metal covers are only permitted if they can be connected to an equipment grounding conductor of a type recognized in 250.118, in accordance with 250.110 [250.4(A)(3)]. **Figure 314–21**

   Author's Comment: Metal switch faceplates [404.9(B)] and metal receptacle faceplates [406.6(A)] must be connected to an equipment grounding conductor.

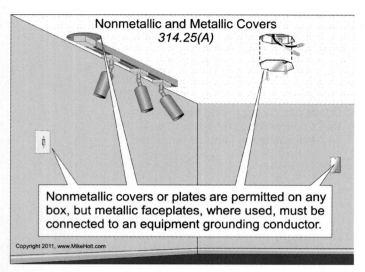

Nonmetallic and Metallic Covers
314.25(A)

Nonmetallic covers or plates are permitted on any box, but metallic faceplates, where used, must be connected to an equipment grounding conductor.

Copyright 2011, www.MikeHolt.com

Figure 314–21

Essential Rule 63   314.28

314.28 Boxes and Conduit Bodies for Conductors 4 AWG and Larger. Boxes and conduit bodies containing conductors 4 AWG and larger that are required to be insulated must be sized so the conductor insulation won't be damaged. **Figure 314–22**

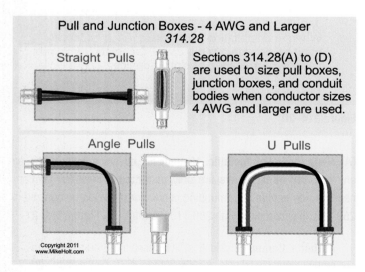

Pull and Junction Boxes - 4 AWG and Larger
314.28

Straight Pulls

Angle Pulls   U Pulls

Sections 314.28(A) to (D) are used to size pull boxes, junction boxes, and conduit bodies when conductor sizes 4 AWG and larger are used.

Copyright 2011
www.MikeHolt.com

Figure 314–22

Author's Comments:

- The requirements for sizing boxes and conduit bodies containing conductors 6 AWG and smaller are contained in 314.16.

- If conductors 4 AWG and larger enter a box or other enclosure, a fitting that provides a smooth, rounded, insulating surface, such as a bushing or adapter, is required to protect the conductors from abrasion during and after installation [300.4(G)]. **Figure 314–23**

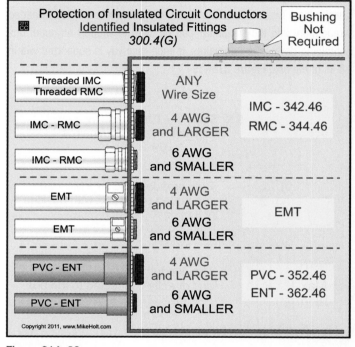

Protection of Insulated Circuit Conductors
<u>Identified</u> Insulated Fittings
300.4(G)

Bushing Not Required

Threaded IMC Threaded RMC	ANY Wire Size	IMC - 342.46 RMC - 344.46
IMC - RMC	4 AWG and LARGER	
IMC - RMC	6 AWG and SMALLER	
EMT	4 AWG and LARGER	EMT
EMT	6 AWG and SMALLER	
PVC - ENT	4 AWG and LARGER	PVC - 352.46 ENT - 362.46
PVC - ENT	6 AWG and SMALLER	

Copyright 2011, www.MikeHolt.com

Figure 314–23

(A) Minimum Size. For raceways containing conductors 4 AWG and larger, the minimum dimensions of boxes and conduit bodies must comply with the following:

(1) Straight Pulls. The minimum distance from where the conductors enter the box <u>or conduit body</u> to the opposite wall must not be less than eight times the trade size of the largest raceway. **Figure 314–24**

(2) Angle Pulls, U Pulls, or Splices.

- **Angle Pulls.** The distance from the raceway entry of the box <u>or conduit body</u> to the opposite wall must not be less than six times the trade size of the largest raceway, plus the sum of the trade sizes of the remaining raceways on the same wall and row. **Figure 314–25**

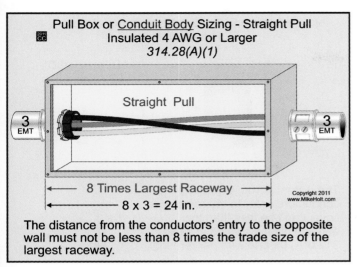

Pull Box or Conduit Body Sizing - Straight Pull
Insulated 4 AWG or Larger
314.28(A)(1)

Straight Pull

8 Times Largest Raceway
8 x 3 = 24 in.

The distance from the conductors' entry to the opposite wall must not be less than 8 times the trade size of the largest raceway.

Figure 314–24

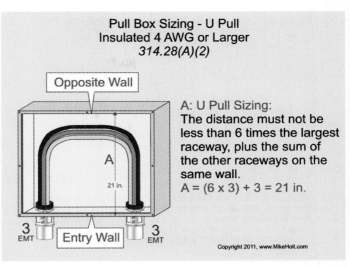

Pull Box Sizing - U Pull
Insulated 4 AWG or Larger
314.28(A)(2)

Opposite Wall

A: U Pull Sizing:
The distance must not be less than 6 times the largest raceway, plus the sum of the other raceways on the same wall.
A = (6 x 3) + 3 = 21 in.

21 in.

Entry Wall

Figure 314–26

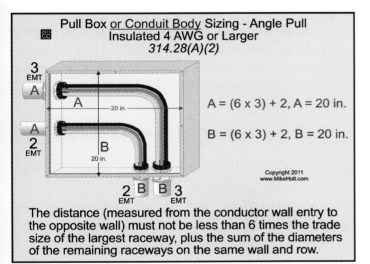

Pull Box or Conduit Body Sizing - Angle Pull
Insulated 4 AWG or Larger
314.28(A)(2)

A = (6 x 3) + 2, A = 20 in.

B = (6 x 3) + 2, B = 20 in.

The distance (measured from the conductor wall entry to the opposite wall) must not be less than 6 times the trade size of the largest raceway, plus the sum of the diameters of the remaining raceways on the same wall and row.

Figure 314–25

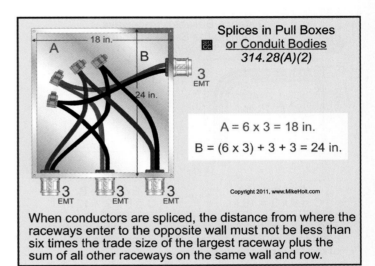

Splices in Pull Boxes or Conduit Bodies
314.28(A)(2)

18 in.

24 in.

A = 6 x 3 = 18 in.

B = (6 x 3) + 3 + 3 = 24 in.

When conductors are spliced, the distance from where the raceways enter to the opposite wall must not be less than six times the trade size of the largest raceway plus the sum of all other raceways on the same wall and row.

Figure 314–27

- **U Pulls.** When a conductor enters and leaves from the same wall of the box, the distance from where the raceways enter to the opposite wall must not be less than six times the trade size of the largest raceway, plus the sum of the trade sizes of the remaining raceways on the same wall and row. **Figure 314–26**

- **Splices.** When conductors are spliced, the distance from where the raceways enter to the opposite wall must not be less than six times the trade size of the largest raceway, plus the sum of the trade sizes of the remaining raceways on the same wall and row. **Figure 314–27**

- **Rows.** If there are multiple rows of raceway entries, each row is calculated individually and the row with the largest distance must be used. **Figure 314–28**

- **Distance Between Raceways.** The distance between raceways enclosing the same conductor must not be less than six times the trade size of the largest raceway, measured from the raceways' nearest edge-to-nearest edge. **Figure 314–29**

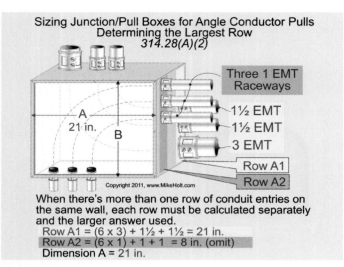

Figure 314–28

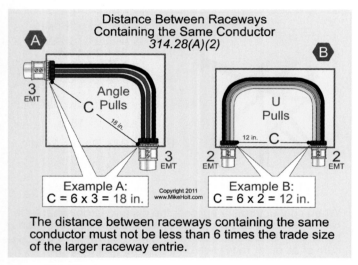

Figure 314–29

Ex: When conductors enter an enclosure with a removable cover, the distance from where the conductors enter to the removable cover must not be less than the bending distance as listed in Table 312.6(A) for one conductor per terminal. **Figure 314–30**

(3) Smaller Dimensions. Boxes or conduit bodies smaller than those required in 314.28(A)(1) and 314.28(A)(2) are permitted, if the enclosure is permanently marked with the maximum number and maximum size of conductors.

(B) Conductors in Pull or Junction Boxes. Pull boxes or junction boxes with any dimension over 6 ft must have all conductors cabled or racked in an approved manner.

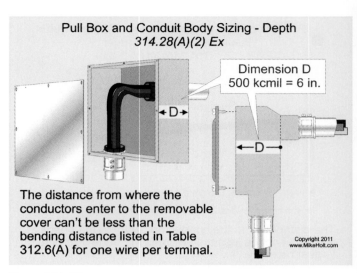

Figure 314–30

(C) Covers. Pull boxes, junction boxes, and conduit bodies must have a cover suitable for the conditions. Nonmetallic covers are permitted on any box, but metal covers are only permitted if they can be connected to an equipment grounding conductor of a type recognized in 250.118, in accordance with 250.110 [250.4(A)(3)]. **Figure 314–31**

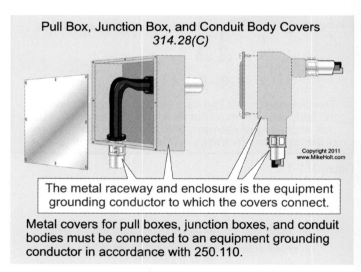

Figure 314–31

Metal covers for pull boxes, junction boxes, and conduit bodies must be connected to an equipment grounding conductor in accordance with 250.110.

(E) Power Distribution Block. Power distribution blocks installed in junction boxes over 100 cu in. must comply with the following: **Figure 314–32**

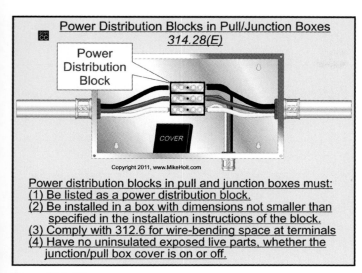

Power Distribution Blocks in Pull/Junction Boxes
314.28(E)

Power distribution blocks in pull and junction boxes must:
(1) Be listed as a power distribution block.
(2) Be installed in a box with dimensions not smaller than specified in the installation instructions of the block.
(3) Comply with 312.6 for wire-bending space at terminals
(4) Have no uninsulated exposed live parts, whether the junction/pull box cover is on or off.

Figure 314–32

(1) Installation. Be listed as a power distribution block.

(2) Size. Be installed in a box not smaller than required by the installation instructions of the power distribution block.

(3) Wire-Bending Space. The junction box is sized so that the wire-bending space requirements of 312.6 can be met.

(4) Live Parts. Exposed live parts on the power distribution block aren't present when the junction box cover is removed.

(5) Through Conductors. Where the junction box has conductors that don't terminate on the power distribution block(s), the through conductors must be arranged so the power distribution block terminals are unobstructed following installation.

314.29 Wiring to be Accessible. Boxes, conduit bodies, and handhole enclosures must be installed so that the wiring is accessible without removing any part of the building, sidewalks, paving, or earth. Figure 314–33

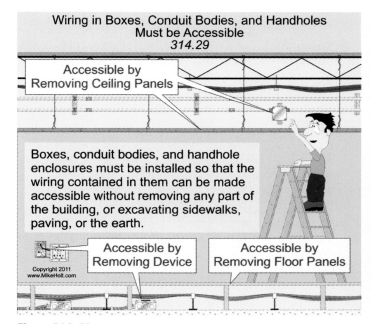

Wiring in Boxes, Conduit Bodies, and Handholes
Must be Accessible
314.29

Accessible by Removing Ceiling Panels

Boxes, conduit bodies, and handhole enclosures must be installed so that the wiring contained in them can be made accessible without removing any part of the building, or excavating sidewalks, paving, or the earth.

Accessible by Removing Device

Accessible by Removing Floor Panels

Figure 314–33

Ex: Listed boxes and handhole enclosures can be buried if covered by gravel, light aggregate, or noncohesive granulated soil, and their location is effectively identified and accessible for excavation.

Notes

ARTICLE
404

Switches

INTRODUCTION TO ARTICLE 404—SWITCHES

The requirements of Article 404 apply to switches of all types, including snap (toggle) switches, dimmer switches, fan switches, knife switches, circuit breakers used as switches, and automatic switches, such as time clocks and timers.

Essential Rule 65	404.2

404.2 Switch Connections.

(A) Three-Way and Four-Way Switches. Wiring for 3-way and 4-way switching must be done so that only the ungrounded conductors are switched. **Figure 404–1**

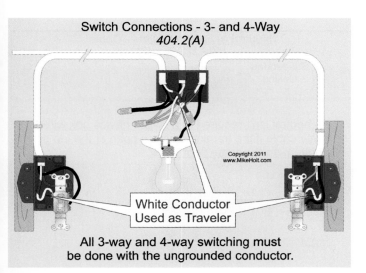

Switch Connections - 3- and 4-Way
404.2(A)

White Conductor Used as Traveler

All 3-way and 4-way switching must be done with the ungrounded conductor.

Figure 404–1

Author's Comment: In other words, the neutral conductor must not be switched. The white insulated conductor within a cable assembly can be used for single-pole, 3-way, or 4-way switch loops if it's permanently reidentified to indicate its use as an ungrounded conductor at each location where the conductor is visible and accessible [200.7(C)(2)].

If a metal raceway or metal-clad cable contains the ungrounded conductors for switches, the wiring must be arranged to avoid heating the surrounding metal by induction. This is accomplished by installing all circuit conductors in the same raceway in accordance with 300.3(B) and 300.20(A), or ensuring that they're all within the same cable.

Ex: A neutral conductor isn't required in the same raceway or cable with travelers and switch leg (switch loop) conductors. **Figure 404–2**

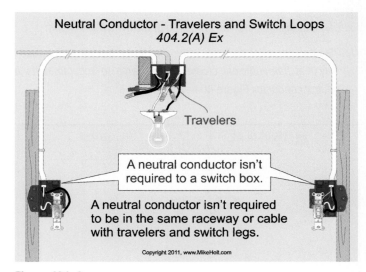

Neutral Conductor - Travelers and Switch Loops
404.2(A) Ex

Travelers

A neutral conductor isn't required to a switch box.

A neutral conductor isn't required to be in the same raceway or cable with travelers and switch legs.

Copyright 2011, www.MikeHolt.com

Figure 404–2

(B) Switching Neutral Conductors. Only the ungrounded conductor is permitted to be used for switching, and the grounded conductor must not be disconnected by switches or circuit breakers. **Figure 404–3**

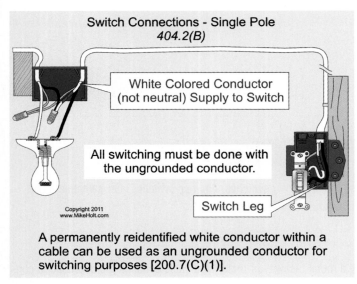

Figure 404-3

Ex: A switch or circuit breaker is permitted to disconnect a grounded circuit conductor where it disconnects all circuit conductors simultaneously.

(C) Switches Controlling Lighting Loads. Switches controlling line-to-neutral lighting loads must have a neutral provided at the switch location.

Ex: The neutral conductor isn't required at the switch location if:

(1) The conductors for switches enter the device box through a raceway that has sufficient cross-sectional area to accommodate a neutral conductor. **Figure 404-4**

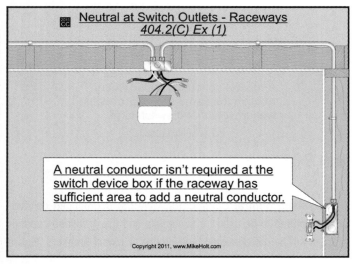

Figure 404-4

(2) Cable assemblies for switches enter the box through a framing cavity that's open at the top or bottom on the same floor level, or switches enter the box through a wall, floor, or ceiling that's unfinished on one side. **Figures 404-5 and 404-6**

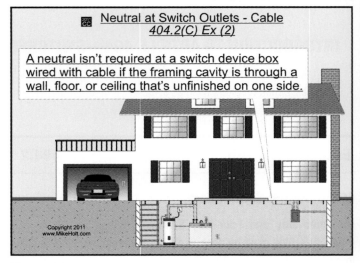

Figure 404-5

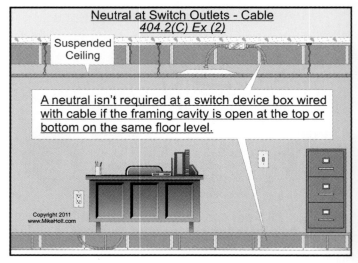

Figure 404-6

Note: The purpose of the neutral conductor is to complete a circuit path for electronic lighting control devices.

Essential Rule 66   404.9

404.9 Switch Faceplates.

(A) Mounting. Faceplates for switches must be installed so they completely cover the outlet box opening and, where flush mounted, the faceplate must seat against the wall surface.

(B) Grounding. The metal mounting yokes for switches, dimmers, and similar control switches must be connected to an equipment grounding conductor of a type recognized in 250.118, whether or not a metal faceplate is installed. The metal mounting yoke is considered part of the effective ground-fault current path [250.2] by the use of one of the following means:

(1) Mounting Screw. The switch is mounted with metal screws to a metal box or a metal cover that's connected to an equipment grounding conductor of a type recognized in 250.118. **Figure 404–7**

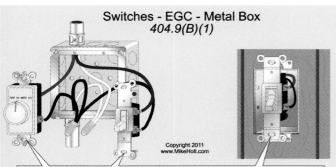

The switch is connected to an effective ground-fault current path when the yoke (strap) is mounted with metal screws to a metal box.

Snap switches, dimmers, and similar control switches must be connected to an equipment grounding conductor whether or not a metal faceplate is installed [404.9(B)].

Figure 404–7

Author's Comment: Direct metal-to-metal contact between the device yoke of a switch and the box isn't required.

(2) Equipment Grounding Conductor. An equipment grounding conductor or equipment bonding jumper is connected to the grounding terminal of the metal mounting yoke. **Figure 404–8**

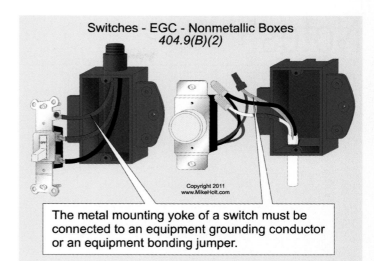

The metal mounting yoke of a switch must be connected to an equipment grounding conductor or an equipment bonding jumper.

Figure 404–8

Ex 1: The metal mounting yoke of a replacement switch isn't required to be connected to an equipment grounding conductor if the wiring at the existing switch doesn't contain an equipment grounding conductor, and the switch faceplate is nonmetallic with nonmetallic screws, or the replacement switch is GFCI protected.

Ex 2: Listed assemblies aren't required to be connected to an equipment grounding conductor if all of the following conditions are met:

(1) The device is provided with a nonmetallic faceplate that can't be installed on any other type of device,

(2) The device doesn't have mounting means to accept other configurations of faceplates,

(3) The device is equipped with a nonmetallic yoke, and

(4) All parts of the device that are accessible after installation of the faceplate are manufactured of nonmetallic material.

Ex 3: A snap switch with an integral nonmetallic enclosure complying with 300.15(E).

Notes

Receptacles, Cord Connectors, and Attachment Plugs (Caps)

ARTICLE 406

INTRODUCTION TO ARTICLE 406—RECEPTACLES, CORD CONNECTORS, AND ATTACHMENT PLUGS (CAPS)

This article covers the rating, type, and installation of receptacles, cord connectors, and attachment plugs (cord caps). It also addresses their grounding requirements. Some key points to remember include:

- Follow the grounding requirements of the specific type of device you're using.
- Provide GFCI protection where specified by 406.4(D)(3).
- Mount receptacles according to the requirements of 406.5, which are highly detailed.

Essential Rule 67   406.4

406.4 General Installation Requirements.

(A) Grounding Type. Receptacles installed on 15A and 20A branch circuits must be of the grounding type. Single receptacles must have an ampere rating not less than the rating of the branch circuit [210.21(B)(1)], and multioutlet receptacles (duplex receptacles) must have a rating in accordance with Table 210.21(B)(3). **Figures 406–1 and 406–2**

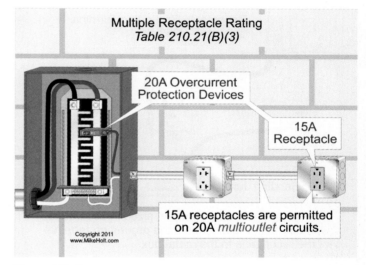

Figure 406–2

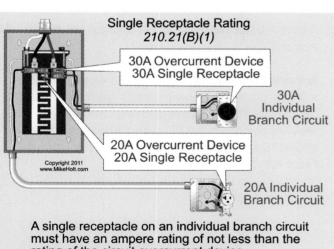

Figure 406–1

Table 210.21(B)(3) Receptacle Ratings	
Circuit Rating	**Receptacle Rating**
15A	15A
20A	15A or 20A
30A	30A
40A	40A or 50A
50A	50A

Ex: Nongrounding-type receptacles are permitted for replacement in an existing outlet box if no equipment grounding conductor exists in the outlet box, in accordance with 406.5(D).

(B) To be Grounded. Receptacles of the grounding type must have an equipment grounding conductor contact, and must have that contact connected to an equipment grounding conductor.

Ex 2: Replacement receptacles aren't required to have their grounding contacts connected to an equipment grounding conductor if the receptacles are GFCI protected and installed in accordance with 406.4(D).

(C) Methods of Equipment Grounding. The grounding terminals for receptacles must be connected to an equipment grounding conductor supplied with the branch-circuit wiring.

> Author's Comment: See 250.146 for the specific requirements on connecting the grounding terminals of receptacles to the circuit equipment grounding conductor. **Figure 406–3**

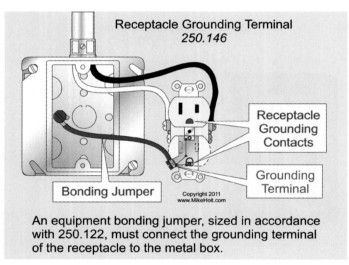

Receptacle Grounding Terminal
250.146

Receptacle Grounding Contacts

Grounding Terminal

Bonding Jumper

Copyright 2011
www.MikeHolt.com

An equipment bonding jumper, sized in accordance with 250.122, must connect the grounding terminal of the receptacle to the metal box.

Figure 406–3

(D) Receptacle Replacement.

(1) Grounding-Type Receptacles. If an equipment grounding conductor exists, grounding-type receptacles must replace nongrounding-type receptacles, and the receptacle's grounding terminal must be connected to an equipment grounding conductor in accordance with 406.4(C).

(2) Nongrounding-Type Receptacles. If no equipment grounding conductor exists in the outlet box for the receptacle, such as old 2-wire Type NM cable without an equipment grounding conductor, existing nongrounding-type receptacles can be replaced in accordance with (a), (b), or (c): **Figure 406–4**

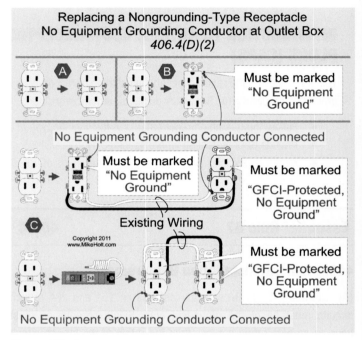

Replacing a Nongrounding-Type Receptacle
No Equipment Grounding Conductor at Outlet Box
406.4(D)(2)

A → B → Must be marked "No Equipment Ground"

No Equipment Grounding Conductor Connected

Must be marked "No Equipment Ground"

Must be marked "GFCI-Protected, No Equipment Ground"

C → Existing Wiring

Copyright 2011
www.MikeHolt.com

Must be marked "GFCI-Protected, No Equipment Ground"

No Equipment Grounding Conductor Connected

Figure 406–4

(a) Another nongrounding-type receptacle.

(b) A GFCI-type receptacle marked "No Equipment Ground."

(c) A grounding-type receptacle, if GFCI protected and marked "GFCI Protected" and "No Equipment Ground."

> **Author's Comment:** GFCI protection functions properly on a 2-wire circuit without an equipment grounding conductor because the circuit equipment grounding conductor serves no role in the operation of the GFCI-protection device. See the definition of "Ground-Fault Circuit Interrupter" for more information. **Figure 406–5**

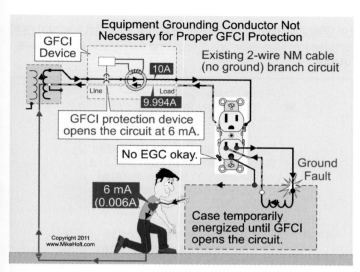

Figure 406–5

⚠ **CAUTION:** *The permission to replace nongrounding-type receptacles with GFCI-protected grounding-type receptacles doesn't apply to new receptacle outlets that extend from an existing outlet box that's not connected to an equipment grounding conductor. Once you add a receptacle outlet (branch-circuit extension), the receptacle must be of the grounding type and it must have its grounding terminal connected to an equipment grounding conductor of a type recognized in 250.118, in accordance with 250.130(C).*
Figure 406–6

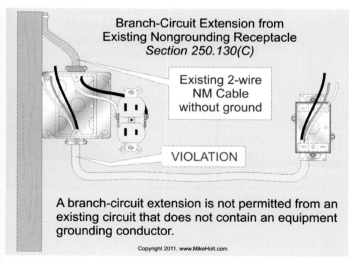

Figure 406–6

(3) GFCI Protection Required. When existing receptacles are replaced in locations where GFCI protection is currently required, the replacement receptacles must be GFCI protected. This includes the replacement of receptacles in dwelling unit bathrooms, garages, outdoors, crawl spaces, unfinished basements, kitchen countertops, rooftops, or within 6 ft of laundry, utility, and wet bar sinks.

> **Author's Comment:** See 210.8 in this textbook for specific GFCI-protection requirements.

(4) Arc-Fault Circuit Interrupters. Effective January 1, 2014, where a receptacle outlet is supplied by a branch circuit that requires arc-fault circuit-interrupter protection [210.12(A)], a replacement receptacle at this outlet must be one of the following:

(1) A listed (receptacle) outlet branch-circuit type arc-fault circuit-interrupter receptacle.

(2) A receptacle protected by a listed (receptacle) outlet branch-circuit type arc-fault circuit-interrupter type receptacle.

(3) A receptacle protected by a listed combination type arc-fault circuit interrupter type circuit breaker.

(5) Tamper-Resistant Receptacles. Listed tamper-resistant receptacles must be provided where replacements are made at receptacle outlets that are required to be tamper resistant in accordance with 406.12 for dwelling units, 406.13 for guest rooms and guest suites, and 406.14 for child care facilities.

(6) Weather-Resistant Receptacles. Weather-resistant receptacles must be provided where replacements are made at receptacle outlets that are required to be so protected in accordance with 406.9(A) and (B).

Essential Rule 68   **406.9**

406.9 Receptacles in Damp or Wet Locations.

(A) Damp Locations. Receptacles installed in a damp location must be installed in an enclosure that's weatherproof when an attachment plug cap isn't inserted, and the receptacle cover is closed, or an enclosure that's weatherproof when an attachment plug is inserted. All nonlocking 15A and 20A, 125V and 250V receptacles in a damp location must be listed as weather resistant. **Figure 406–7**

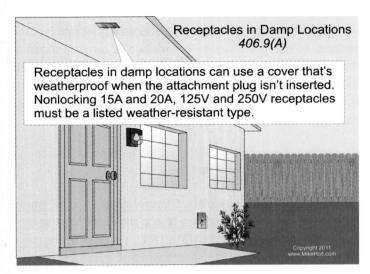

Figure 406–7

Author's Comment: Damp locations include locations protected from weather and not subject to saturation with water or other liquids, as well as locations partially protected under canopies, marquees, roofed open porches, and interior locations that are subject to moderate degrees of moisture, such as some basements, barns, and cold-storage warehouses [Article 100].

(B) Wet Locations.

(1) 15A and 20A Receptacles. All 15A and 20A receptacles installed in a wet location must be within an enclosure that's weatherproof when an attachment plug is inserted. **Figure 406–8**

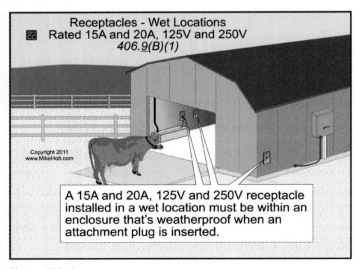

Figure 406–8

For other than one- or two-family dwellings, the outlet box hood must be listed for "extra-duty" use if supported from grade. **Figure 406–9**

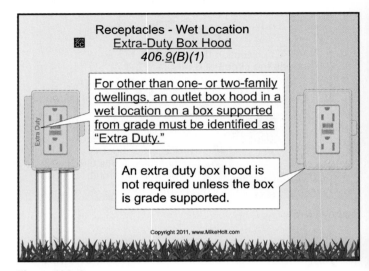

Figure 406–9

All nonlocking type 15A and 20A, 125V and 250V receptacles in a wet location must be listed as weather resistant. **Figure 406–10**

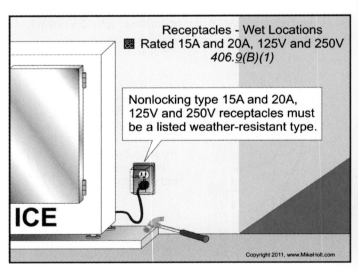

Figure 406–10

Author's Comment: Exposed plastic surface material of weather-resistant receptacles must have UV resistance to ensure that deterioration from sunlight doesn't take place, or that it's minimal. In testing, receptacles are subjected to temperature cycling from very cold to very warm conditions, and then subjected to additional dielectric testing. The rapid transition from the cold to warm temperatures will change the relative humidity and moisture content on the device, and the dielectric test ensures that this won't create a breakdown of the insulation properties.

Ex: Receptacles rated 15A and 20A that are subjected to routine high-pressure washing spray may have an enclosure that's weatherproof when the attachment plug is removed.

Author's Comment: A wet location is an area subject to saturation with water, as well as unprotected locations that are exposed to weather [Article 100].

(2) Other Receptacles. Receptacles rated 30A or more installed in a wet location must comply with (a) or (b).

(a) Wet Location Covers. A receptacle that's in a wet location, where the load isn't attended while in use, must be installed in an enclosure that's weatherproof when an attachment plug is inserted.

(b) Damp Location Covers. A receptacle installed in a wet location that will only be used while someone is in close proximity to it, such as one used with portable tools, can have an enclosure that's weatherproof when the attachment plug is removed and the cover is closed.

(C) Bathtub and Shower Space. Receptacles must not be installed within or directly over a bathtub or shower stall. **Figure 406–11**

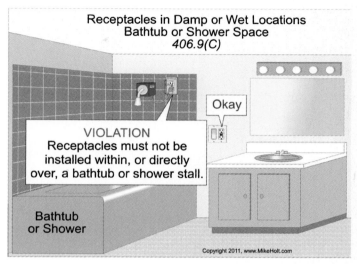

Figure 406–11

(E) Flush Mounting with Faceplate. The enclosure for a receptacle installed in an outlet box that's flush-mounted on a finished surface must be made weatherproof by a weatherproof faceplate that provides a watertight connection between the plate and the finished surface.

Notes

ARTICLE 408

Switchboards and Panelboards

INTRODUCTION TO ARTICLE 408—SWITCHBOARDS AND PANELBOARDS

Article 408 covers the specific requirements for switchboards and panelboards that control power and lighting circuits. Some key points to remember:

- One objective of Article 408 is that the installation prevents contact between current-carrying conductors and people or equipment.
- The circuit directory of a panelboard must clearly identify the purpose or use of each circuit that originates in the panelboard.
- You must understand the detailed grounding and overcurrent protection requirements for panelboards.

Essential Rule 69   **408.4**

PART I. GENERAL

408.4 Field Identification.

(A) Circuit Directory or Circuit Identification. All circuits, and circuit modifications, must be legibly identified as to their clear, evident, and specific purpose. Spare positions that contain unused overcurrent devices must also be identified. Identification must include sufficient detail to allow each circuit to be distinguished from all others, and the identification must be on a circuit directory located on the face or inside of the door of the panelboard. See 110.22. **Figure 408–1**

> **Author's Comment:** Circuit identification must not be based on transient conditions of occupancy, such as Steven's, or Brittney's bedroom. **Figure 408–2**

(B) Source of Supply. All switchboards and panelboards supplied by a feeder in other than one- or two-family dwellings must be marked as to the device or equipment where the power supply originates. **Figure 408–3**

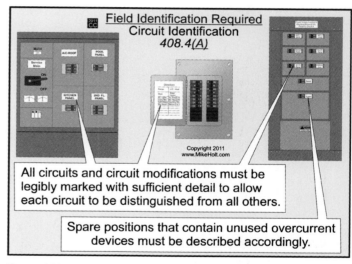

Field Identification Required
Circuit Identification
408.4(A)

Copyright 2011
www.MikeHolt.com

All circuits and circuit modifications must be legibly marked with sufficient detail to allow each circuit to be distinguished from all others.

Spare positions that contain unused overcurrent devices must be described accordingly.

Figure 408–1

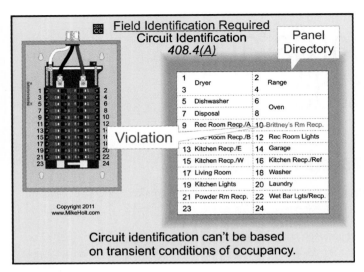

Field Identification Required
Circuit Identification
408.4(A)

Panel Directory

1	Dryer	2	Range
3		4	
5	Dishwasher	6	Oven
7	Disposal	8	
9	Rec Room Recp./A	10	Brittney's Rm Recp.
11	Rec Room Recp./B	12	Rec Room Lights
13	Kitchen Recp./E	14	Garage
15	Kitchen Recp./W	16	Kitchen Recp./Ref
17	Living Room	18	Washer
19	Kitchen Lights	20	Laundry
21	Powder Rm Recp.	22	Wet Bar Lgts/Recp.
23		24	

Violation

Copyright 2011
www.MikeHolt.com

Circuit identification can't be based
on transient conditions of occupancy.

Figure 408–2

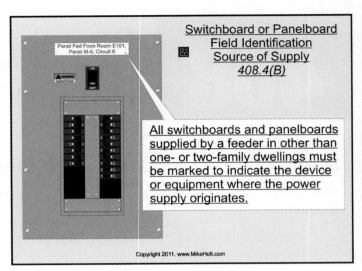

Panel Fed From Room E101,
Panel M-6, Circuit 6

Switchboard or Panelboard
Field Identification
Source of Supply
408.4(B)

All switchboards and panelboards
supplied by a feeder in other than
one- or two-family dwellings must
be marked to indicate the device
or equipment where the power
supply originates.

Copyright 2011, www.MikeHolt.com

Figure 408–3

ARTICLE 430

Motors, Motor Circuits, and Controllers

INTRODUCTION TO ARTICLE 430—MOTORS, MOTOR CIRCUITS, AND CONTROLLERS

Article 430 contains the specific rules for conductor sizing, overcurrent protection, control circuit conductors, controllers, and disconnecting means for electric motors. The installation requirements for motor control centers are covered in Part VIII, and air-conditioning and refrigeration equipment are covered in Article 440.

Article 430 is one of the longest articles in the *NEC*. It's also one of the most complex, but motors are also complex equipment. They're electrical and mechanical devices, but what makes motor applications complex is the fact that they're inductive loads with a high-current demand at start-up that's typically six, or more, times the running current. This makes overcurrent protection for motor applications necessarily different from the protection employed for other types of equipment. So don't confuse general overcurrent protection with motor protection—you must calculate and apply them differently using the rules in Article 430.

You might be uncomfortable with the allowances for overcurrent protection found in this article, such as protecting a 10 AWG conductor with a 60A overcurrent device, but as you learn to understand how motor protection works, you'll understand why these allowances aren't only safe, but necessary.

Essential Rule 70	430.6

PART I. GENERAL

430.6 Table FLC versus Motor Nameplate Current Rating.

(A) General Requirements. Figure 430–1

(1) Table Full-Load Current (FLC). The motor full-load current ratings listed in Tables 430.247, 430.248, and 430.250 are used to determine the conductor ampacity [430.22], the branch-circuit short-circuit and ground-fault overcurrent device size [430.52 and 430.62], and the ampere rating of disconnecting switches [430.110].

> **Author's Comment:** The actual current rating on the motor nameplate full-load amperes (FLA) [430.6(A)(2)] isn't permitted to be used to determine the conductor ampacity, the branch-circuit short-circuit and ground-fault overcurrent device size, nor the ampere rating of disconnecting switches.

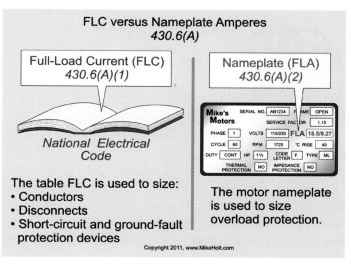

FLC versus Nameplate Amperes
430.6(A)

Full-Load Current (FLC)
430.6(A)(1)

Nameplate (FLA)
430.6(A)(2)

National Electrical Code

The table FLC is used to size:
• Conductors
• Disconnects
• Short-circuit and ground-fault protection devices

The motor nameplate is used to size overload protection.

Copyright 2011, www.MikeHolt.com

Figure 430–1

Motors built to operate at less than 1,200 RPM or that have high torques may have higher full-load currents, and multispeed motors have full-load current varying with speed, in which case the nameplate current ratings must be used.

Ex 3: For a listed motor-operated appliance, the actual current marked on the nameplate of the appliance must be used instead of the horsepower rating on the appliance nameplate to determine the ampacity or rating of the disconnecting means, the branch-circuit conductors, the controller, and the branch-circuit short-circuit and ground-fault protection.

(2) Motor Nameplate Current Rating (FLA). Overload devices must be sized based on the motor nameplate current rating in accordance with 430.31.

> **Author's Comment:** The motor nameplate full-load ampere rating is identified as full-load amperes (FLA). The FLA rating is the current in amperes the motor draws while producing its rated horsepower load at its rated voltage, based on its rated efficiency and power factor. **Figure 430–2**

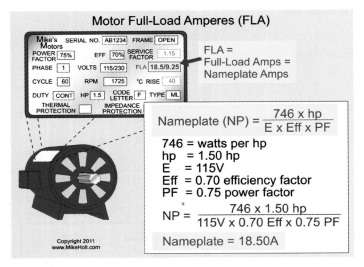

Figure 430–2

The actual current drawn by the motor depends upon the load on the motor and on the actual operating voltage at the motor terminals. That is, if the load increases, the current also increases, or if the motor operates at a voltage below its nameplate rating, the operating current will increase.

> ⚠ **CAUTION:** *To prevent damage to motor windings from excessive heat (caused by excessive current), never load a motor above its horsepower rating, and be sure the voltage source matches the motor's voltage rating.*

Essential Rule 71   430.22

PART II. CONDUCTOR SIZE

430.22 Single Motor Conductor Size. Conductors to a single motor must be sized not less than 125 percent of the motor FLC rating as listed in Table 430.247 Direct-Current Motors, Table 430.248 Single-Phase Motors, or Table 430.250 Three-Phase Motors. **Figure 430–3**

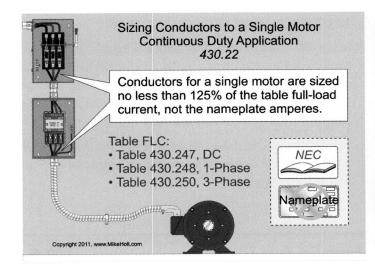

Figure 430–3

> *Question: What size branch-circuit conductor is required for a 7½ hp, 230V, three-phase motor?* **Figure 430–4**
>
> *(a) 14 AWG   (b) 12 AWG   (c) 10 AWG   (d) 8 AWG*
>
> ***Answer:*** *(c) 10 AWG*
>
> *Motor FLC = 22A [Table 430.250]*
>
> *Conductor's Size = 22A x 1.25*
>
> *Conductor's Size = 27.50A, 10 AWG, rated 30A at 75°C [Table 310.15(B)(16)]*
>
> *Note: The branch-circuit short-circuit and ground-fault protection device using an inverse time breaker is sized at 60A according to 430.52(C)(1) Ex 1:*
>
> *Circuit Protection = 22A x 2.50*
>
> *Circuit Protection = 55A, next size up 60A [240.6(A)]*

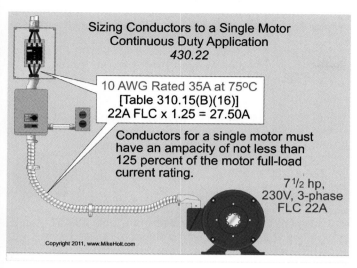

Sizing Conductors to a Single Motor Continuous Duty Application
430.22

10 AWG Rated 35A at 75ºC
[Table 310.15(B)(16)]
22A FLC x 1.25 = 27.50A

Conductors for a single motor must have an ampacity of not less than 125 percent of the motor full-load current rating.

7½ hp, 230V, 3-phase FLC 22A

Copyright 2011, www.MikeHolt.com

Figure 430–4

Essential Rule 72   430.52

PART IV. BRANCH-CIRCUIT SHORT-CIRCUIT AND GROUND-FAULT PROTECTION

430.52 Branch-Circuit Short-Circuit and Ground-Fault Protection.

(A) General. The motor branch-circuit short-circuit and ground-fault protective device must comply with 430.52(B) and 430.52(C).

(B) All Motors. A motor branch-circuit short-circuit and ground-fault protective device must be capable of carrying the motor's starting current.

(C) Rating or Setting.

(1) Table 430.52. Each motor branch circuit must be protected against short circuit and ground faults by a protective device sized no greater than the following percentages listed in Table 430.52.

Table 430.52			
Motor Type	Nontime Delay	Dual-Element Fuse	Inverse Time Breaker
Wound Rotor	150%	150%	150%
Direct Current	150%	150%	150%
All Other Motors	300%	175%	250%

Question: What size conductor and inverse time circuit breaker are required for a 2 hp, 230V, single-phase motor? **Figure 430–5**

(a) 14 AWG, 30A breaker   (b) 14 AWG, 35A breaker
(c) 14 AWG, 40A breaker   (d) 14 AWG, 45A breaker

Answer: (a) 14 AWG, 30A breaker

Step 1: Determine the branch-circuit conductor [Table 310.15(B)(16), 430.22, and Table 430.248]:

12A x 1.25 = 15A, 14 AWG, rated 20A at 75°C [Table 310.15(B)(16)]

Step 2: Determine the branch-circuit protection [240.6(A), 430.52(C)(1), and Table 430.248]:

12A x 2.50 = 30A

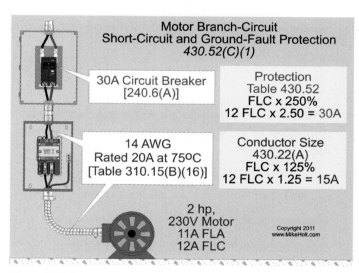

Motor Branch-Circuit Short-Circuit and Ground-Fault Protection
430.52(C)(1)

30A Circuit Breaker [240.6(A)]

Protection
Table 430.52
FLC x 250%
12 FLC x 2.50 = 30A

14 AWG
Rated 20A at 75ºC
[Table 310.15(B)(16)]

Conductor Size
430.22(A)
FLC x 125%
12 FLC x 1.25 = 15A

2 hp,
230V Motor
11A FLA
12A FLC

Copyright 2011
www.MikeHolt.com

Figure 430–5

Author's Comment: I know it bothers many in the electrical industry to see a 14 AWG conductor protected by a 30A circuit breaker, but branch-circuit conductors are protected against overloads by the overload device, which is sized between 115 and 125 percent of the motor nameplate current rating [430.32]. The small conductor rule contained in 240.4(D) which limits 15A protection for 14 AWG doesn't apply to motor circuit protection. See 240.4(D) and 240.4(G).

Ex 1: If the motor short-circuit and ground-fault protective device values derived from Table 430.52 don't correspond with the standard overcurrent device ratings listed in 240.6(A), the next higher overcurrent device rating can be used. **Figure 430–6**

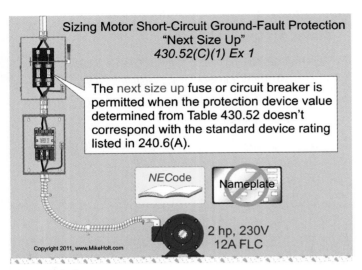

Figure 430–6

Question: *What size conductor and inverse time circuit breaker are required for a 7½ hp, 230V, three-phase motor?* **Figure 430–7**

(a) 10 AWG, 50A breaker   (b) 10 AWG, 60A breaker

(c) a or b   (d) none of these

Answer: *(b) 10 AWG, 60A breaker*

Step 1: Determine the branch-circuit conductor [Table 310.15(B)(16), 430.22, and Table 430.250]:

22A x 1.25 = 27.50A, 10 AWG, rated 30A at 75°C [Table 310.15(B)(16)]

Step 2: Determine the branch-circuit protection [240.6(A), 430.52(C)(1) Ex 1, and Table 430.250]:

22A x 2.50 = 55A, next size up = 60A

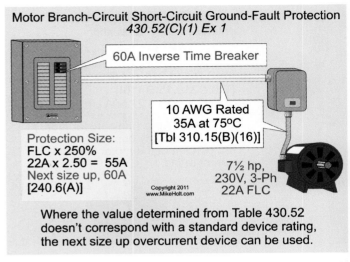

Figure 430–7

Essential Rule 73   **430.102**

PART IX. DISCONNECTING MEANS

430.102 Disconnect Requirement.

(A) Controller Disconnect. A disconnecting means is required for each motor controller, and it must be located within sight from the controller. **Figures 430–8 and 430–9**

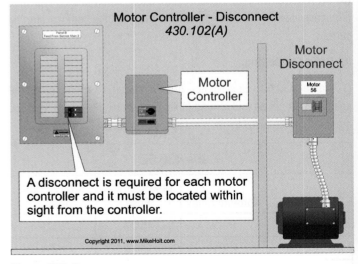

Figure 430–8

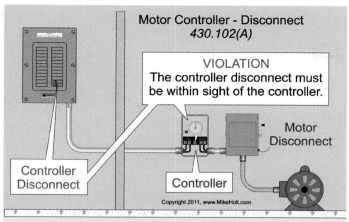

The controller disconnect must disconnect all circuit conductors of the controller simultaneously [430.103].

Figure 430–9

Author's Comment: According to Article 100, within sight means that it's visible and not more than 50 ft from one to the other.

(B) Motor Disconnect. A motor disconnect must be provided in accordance with (B)(1) or (B)(2). Figure 430–10

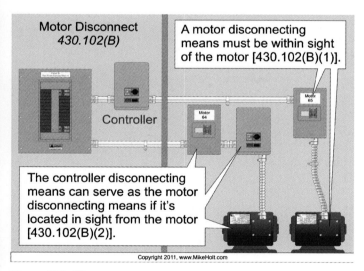

Figure 430–10

(1) Separate Motor Disconnect. A disconnecting means is required for each motor, and it must be located in sight from the motor location and the driven machinery location.

(2) Controller Disconnect. The controller disconnecting means [430.102(A)] can serve as the disconnecting means for the motor, if the disconnect is located in sight from the motor location.

Ex to (1) and (2): A motor disconnecting means isn't required under either condition (a) or (b), if the controller disconnecting means [430.102(A)] is capable of being locked in the open position. The provision for locking or adding a lock to the disconnecting means must be installed on or at the switch or circuit breaker, and it must remain in place with or without the lock installed. Figure 430–11

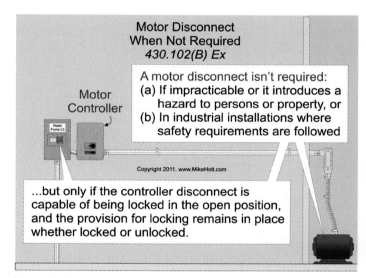

Figure 430–11

(a) If locating the disconnecting means is impracticable or introduces additional or increased hazards to persons or property.

(b) In industrial installations, with written safety procedures, where conditions of maintenance and supervision ensure only qualified persons will service the equipment.

Note 2: For information on lockout/tagout procedures, see NFPA 70E, *Standard for Electrical Safety in the Workplace.*

Notes

INTRODUCTION TO ARTICLE 450—TRANSFORMERS

Article 450 opens by saying, "This article covers the installation of all transformers." Then it lists eight exceptions. So what does Article 450 really cover? Essentially, it covers power transformers and most kinds of lighting transformers.

A major concern with transformers is preventing overheating. The *Code* doesn't completely address this issue. Article 90 explains that the *NEC* isn't a design manual, and it assumes that the person using the *Code* has a certain level of expertise. Proper transformer selection is an important part of preventing transformer overheating.

The *NEC* assumes you've already selected a transformer suitable to the load characteristics. For the *Code* to tell you how to do that would push it into the realm of a design manual. Article 450 then takes you to the next logical step—providing overcurrent protection and the proper connections. But this article doesn't stop there; 450.9 provides ventilation requirements, and 450.13 contains accessibility requirements.

Part I of Article 450 contains the general requirements such as guarding, marking, and accessibility, Part II contains the requirements for different types of transformers, and Part III covers transformer vaults.

Essential Rule 74	450.3

PART I. GENERAL

450.3 Overcurrent Protection.

Note 2: Nonlinear loads on 4-wire, wye-connected secondary wiring can increase heat in a transformer without operating the primary overcurrent device. **Figure 450–1**

(B) Overcurrent Protection for Transformers Not Over 600V. The primary winding of a transformer must be protected against overcurrent in accordance with the percentages listed in Table 450.3(B) and all applicable notes.

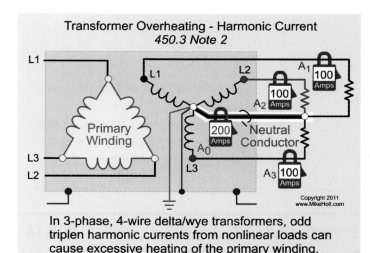

In 3-phase, 4-wire delta/wye transformers, odd triplen harmonic currents from nonlinear loads can cause excessive heating of the primary winding.

Figure 450–1

Table 450.3(B) Primary Protection Only	
Primary Current Rating	**Maximum Protection**
9A or More	125%, see Note 1
Less Than 9A	167%
Less Than 2A	300%

Note 1. If 125 percent of the primary current doesn't correspond to a standard rating of a fuse or nonadjustable circuit breaker, the next higher rating is permitted [240.6(A)].

Question: *What's the primary overcurrent device rating and conductor size required for a 45 kVA, three-phase, 480V transformer that's fully loaded? The terminals are rated 75°C.* **Figure 450–2**

(a) 8 AWG, 40A   (b) 6 AWG, 50A
(c) 6 AWG, 60A   (d) 4 AWG, 70A

Answer: *(d) 4 AWG, 70A*

Step 1: Determine the primary current:

$I = VA/(E \times 1.732)$

$I = 45,000\ VA/(480V \times 1.732)$

$I = 54A$

Step 2: Determine the primary overcurrent device rating [240.6(A)]:

54A x 1.25 = 68A, next size up 70A, Table 450.3(B), Note 1

Step 3: The primary conductor must be sized to carry 54A continuously (54A x 1.25 = 68A) [215.2(A)(1)] and be protected by a 70A overcurrent device [240.4(B)]. A 4 AWG conductor rated 85A at 75°C meets all of the requirements [110.14(C)(1) and 310.15(B)(16)].

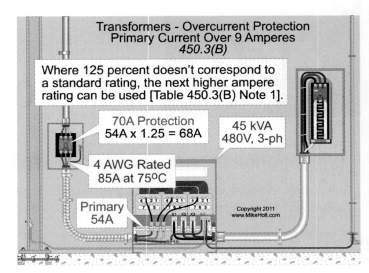

Figure 450–2

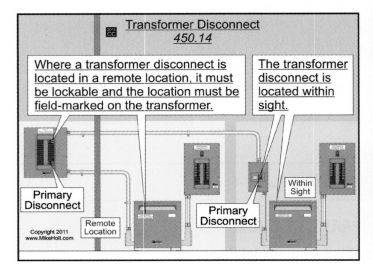

Figure 450–3

Author's Comment: Within sight means that it's visible and not more than 50 ft from one to the other [Article 100].

Essential Rule 75   450.14

PART I. GENERAL

450.14 Disconnecting Means. A disconnect is required to disconnect all transformer ungrounded primary conductors. The disconnect must be located within sight of the transformer, unless the location of the disconnect is field-marked on the transformer and the disconnect is lockable. **Figure 450–3**

Practice Questions

for the Essential Rules of the *National Electrical Code*

Based on the 2011 *NEC*

Article 90 — Practice Questions

 Please use the 2011 *Code* book to answer the following questions.

Article 90. Introduction

1. The *NEC* is _____.

   (a) intended to be a design manual
   (b) meant to be used as an instruction guide for untrained persons
   (c) for the practical safeguarding of persons and property
   (d) published by the Bureau of Standards

2. Compliance with the provisions of the *NEC* will result in _____.

   (a) good electrical service
   (b) an efficient electrical system
   (c) an electrical system essentially free from hazard
   (d) all of these

3. The *Code* contains provisions considered necessary for safety, which will not necessarily result in _____.

   (a) efficient use
   (b) convenience
   (c) good service or future expansion of electrical use
   (d) all of these

4. Hazards often occur because of _____.

   (a) overloading of wiring systems by methods or usage not in conformity with the *NEC*
   (b) initial wiring not providing for increases in the use of electricity
   (c) a and b
   (d) none of these

5. The *Code* isn't a design specification standard or instruction manual for the untrained and unqualified.

   (a) True
   (b) False

6. The following systems shall be installed in accordance with the *NEC* requirements:

   (a) signaling
   (b) communications
   (c) electrical conductors, equipment, and raceways
   (d) all of these

7. The *NEC* applies to the installation of _____.

   (a) electrical conductors and equipment within or on public and private buildings
   (b) outside conductors and equipment on the premises
   (c) optical fiber cables
   (d) all of these

8. This *Code* covers the installation of _____ for public and private premises, including buildings, structures, mobile homes, recreational vehicles, and floating buildings.

   (a) optical fiber cables
   (b) electrical equipment
   (c) raceways
   (d) all of these

9. The *NEC* does not cover electrical installations in ships, watercraft, railway rolling stock, aircraft, or automotive vehicles.

   (a) True
   (b) False

10. The *Code* covers underground mine installations and self-propelled mobile surface mining machinery and its attendant electrical trailing cable.

    (a) True
    (b) False

11. Installations of communications equipment that are under the exclusive control of communications utilities, and located outdoors or in building spaces used exclusively for such installations _____ covered by the *NEC*.

    (a) are
    (b) are sometimes
    (c) are not
    (d) may be

12. Electric utilities may include entities that install, operate, and maintain _____.

    (a) communications systems (telephone, CATV, Internet, satellite, or data services)
    (b) electric supply systems (generation, transmission, or distribution systems)
    (c) local area network wiring on the premises
    (d) a or b

13. Utilities may be subject to compliance with codes and standards covering their regulated activities as adopted under governmental law or regulation.

    (a) True
    (b) False

14. Utilities may include entities that are designated or recognized by governmental law or regulation by public service/utility commissions.

    (a) True
    (b) False

15. The *NEC* does not apply to electric utility-owned wiring and equipment _____.

    (a) installed by an electrical contractor
    (b) installed on public property
    (c) consisting of service drops or service laterals
    (d) in a utility office building

16. Chapters 1 through 4 of the *NEC* apply _____.

    (a) generally to all electrical installations
    (b) only to special occupancies and conditions
    (c) only to special equipment and material
    (d) all of these

17. Communications wiring such as telephone, antenna, and CATV wiring within a building shall not be required to comply with the installation requirements of Chapters 1 through 7, except where specifically referenced in Chapter 8.

    (a) True
    (b) False

18. The material located in the *NEC* Annexes are part of the requirements of the *Code* and shall be complied with.

    (a) True
    (b) False

19. The authority having jurisdiction shall not be allowed to enforce any requirements of Chapter 7 (Special Conditions) or Chapter 8 (Communications Systems).

    (a) True
    (b) False

20. The _____ has the responsibility for deciding on the approval of equipment and materials.

    (a) manufacturer
    (b) authority having jurisdiction
    (c) testing agency
    (d) none of these

21. By special permission, the authority having jurisdiction may waive specific requirements in this *Code* where it is assured that equivalent objectives can be achieved by establishing and maintaining effective safety.

    (a) True
    (b) False

22. The authority having jurisdiction has the responsibility for _____.

    (a) making interpretations of rules
    (b) deciding upon the approval of equipment and materials
    (c) waiving specific requirements in the *Code* and permitting alternate methods and material if safety is maintained
    (d) all of these

23. If the *NEC* requires new products that are not yet available at the time a new edition is adopted, the _____ may permit the use of the products that comply with the previous edition of the *Code* adopted by that jurisdiction.

    (a) electrical engineer
    (b) master electrician
    (c) authority having jurisdiction
    (d) permit holder

24. In the *NEC*, the words "_____" indicate a mandatory requirement.

    (a) shall
    (b) shall not
    (c) shall be permitted
    (d) a or b

25. When the *Code* uses "_____," it means the identified actions are allowed but not required, and they may be options or alternative methods.

    (a) shall
    (b) shall not
    (c) shall be permitted
    (d) a or b

26. Explanatory material, such as references to other standards, references to related sections of the *NEC*, or information related to a *Code* rule, are included in the form of Informational Notes.

    (a) True
    (b) False

27. Nonmandatory Informative Annexes contained in the back of the *Code* book _____.

    (a) are for information only
    (b) aren't enforceable as a requirement of the *Code*
    (c) are enforceable as a requirement of the *Code*
    (d) a and b

Practice Questions

 Please use the 2011 *Code* book to answer the following questions.

Article 110. Requirements for Electrical Installations

1. In judging equipment for approval, considerations such as the following shall be evaluated:

   (a) mechanical strength
   (b) wire-bending space
   (c) arcing effects
   (d) all of these

2. Listed or labeled equipment shall be installed and used in accordance with any instructions included in the listing or labeling.

   (a) True
   (b) False

3. Conductor terminal and splicing devices must be _____ for the conductor material and they must be properly installed and used.

   (a) listed
   (b) approved
   (c) identified
   (d) all of these

4. Connectors and terminals for conductors more finely stranded than Class B and Class C, as shown in Table 10 of Chapter 9, must be _____ for the specific conductor class or classes.

   (a) listed
   (b) approved
   (c) identified
   (d) all of these

5. Many terminations and equipment are marked with _____.

   (a) an etching tool
   (b) a removable label
   (c) a tightening torque
   (d) the manufacturer's initials

6. Connection of conductors to terminal parts shall ensure a thoroughly good connection without damaging the conductors and shall be made by means of _____.

   (a) solder lugs
   (b) pressure connectors
   (c) splices to flexible leads
   (d) any of these

7. Connection by means of wire-binding screws, studs, or nuts having upturned lugs or the equivalent shall be permitted for _____ or smaller conductors.

   (a) 12 AWG
   (b) 10 AWG
   (c) 8 AWG
   (d) 6 AWG

8. Soldered splices shall first be spliced or joined so as to be mechanically and electrically secure without solder and then be soldered.

   (a) True
   (b) False

9. The temperature rating associated with the ampacity of a _____ shall be so selected and coordinated so as not to exceed the lowest temperature rating of any connected termination, conductor, or device.

   (a) terminal
   (b) conductor
   (c) device
   (d) all of these

10. Conductor ampacity shall be determined using the _____ column of Table 310.15(B)(16) for circuits rated 100A or less or marked for 14 AWG through 1 AWG conductors, unless the equipment terminals are listed for use with conductors that have higher temperature ratings.

    (a) 30°C
    (b) 60°C
    (c) 75°C
    (d) 90°C

11. For circuits rated 100A or less, when the equipment terminals are listed for use with 75°C conductors, the _____ column of Table 310.15(B)(16) shall be used to determine the ampacity of THHN conductors.

    (a) 30°C
    (b) 60°C
    (c) 75°C
    (d) 90°C

12. Conductors shall have their ampacity determined using the _____ column of Table 310.15(B)(16) for circuits rated over 100A, or marked for conductors larger than 1 AWG, unless the equipment terminals are listed for use with higher temperature-rated conductors.

    (a) 30°C
    (b) 60°C
    (c) 75°C
    (d) 90°C

13. Separately installed pressure connectors shall be used with conductors at the _____ not exceeding the ampacity at the listed and identified temperature rating of the connector.

    (a) voltages
    (b) temperatures
    (c) listings
    (d) ampacities

14. Electrical equipment such as switchboards, panelboards, industrial control panels, meter socket enclosures, and motor control centers that are in other than dwelling units, and are likely to require _____ while energized shall be field-marked to warn qualified persons of potential electric arc flash hazards.

    (a) examination
    (b) adjustment
    (c) servicing or maintenance
    (d) any of these

15. _____ in other than dwelling units must be legibly field marked with the maximum available fault current, including the date the fault current calculation was performed and be of sufficient durability to withstand the environment involved.

    (a) Service equipment
    (b) Subpanels
    (c) Motor control centers
    (d) all of these

16. When modifications to the electrical installation affect the maximum available fault current at the service, the maximum available fault current shall be verified or _____ to ensure the service equipment ratings are sufficient for the maximum available fault current at the line terminals of the equipment.

    (a) recalculated
    (b) increased
    (c) decreased
    (d) adjusted

17. Field markings of maximum available fault current at a service are not required for industrial installations where conditions of maintenance and supervision ensure that only qualified persons service the equipment.

    (a) True
    (b) False

18. Access and _____ shall be provided and maintained about all electrical equipment to permit ready and safe operation and maintenance of such equipment.

    (a) ventilation
    (b) cleanliness
    (c) circulation
    (d) working space

19. A minimum working space depth of _____ to live parts operating at 277 volts-to-ground is required where there are exposed live parts on one side and no live or grounded parts on the other side.

    (a) 2 ft
    (b) 3 ft
    (c) 4 ft
    (d) 6 ft

20. The minimum working space on a circuit that is 120 volts-to-ground, with exposed live parts on one side and no live or grounded parts on the other side of the working space, is

    _____.

    (a) 1 ft
    (b) 3 ft
    (c) 4 ft
    (d) 6 ft

21. Concrete, brick, or tile walls are considered _____, as applied to working space requirements.

    (a) inconsequential
    (b) in the way
    (c) grounded
    (d) none of these

22. The required working space for access to live parts operating at 300 volts-to-ground, where there are exposed live parts on one side and grounded parts on the other side, is _____.

    (a) 3 ft
    (b) 3½ ft
    (c) 4 ft
    (d) 4½ ft

23. The required working space for access to live parts operating at 300 volts-to-ground, where there are exposed live parts on both sides of the workspace is _____.

    (a) 3 ft
    (b) 3½ ft
    (c) 4 ft
    (d) 4½ ft

24. Working space distances for enclosed live parts shall be measured from the _____ of equipment or apparatus, if the live parts are enclosed.

    (a) enclosure
    (b) opening
    (c) a or b
    (d) none of these

25. The working space in front of the electric equipment shall not be less than _____ wide, or the width of the equipment, whichever is greater.

    (a) 15 in.
    (b) 30 in.
    (c) 40 in.
    (d) 60 in.

26. Equipment associated with the electrical installation can be located above or below other electrical equipment within their working space when the associated equipment does not extend more than _____ from the front of the electrical equipment.

    (a) 3 in.
    (b) 6 in.
    (c) 12 in.
    (d) 30 in.

27. The minimum height of working spaces about electrical equipment, switchboards, panelboards, or motor control centers operating at 600V, nominal, or less and likely to require examination, adjustment, servicing, or maintenance while energized shall be 6½ ft or the height of the equipment, whichever is greater, except for service equipment or panelboards in existing dwelling units that do not exceed 200A.

    (a) True
    (b) False

28. Working space shall not be used for _____.

    (a) storage
    (b) raceways
    (c) lighting
    (d) accessibility

29. When normally enclosed live parts are exposed for inspection or servicing, the working space, if in a passageway or general open space, shall be suitably _____.

    (a) accessible
    (b) guarded
    (c) open
    (d) enclosed

30. For equipment rated 1,200A or more and over 6 ft wide that contains overcurrent devices, switching devices, or control devices, there shall be one entrance to and egress from the required working space not less than 24 in. wide and _____ high at each end of the working space.

    (a) 5½ ft
    (b) 6 ft
    (c) 6½ ft
    (d) any of these

31. For equipment rated 1,200A or more that contains overcurrent devices, switching devices, or control devices; and where the entrance to the working space has a personnel door less than 25 ft from the working space, the door shall _____.

    (a) open either in or out with simple pressure and shall not have any lock
    (b) open in the direction of egress and be equipped with panic hardware or other devices so the door can open under simple pressure
    (c) be equipped with a locking means
    (d) be equipped with an electronic opener

32. Illumination shall be provided for all working spaces about service equipment, switchboards, panelboards, and motor control centers _____.

    (a) over 600V
    (b) located indoors
    (c) rated 1,200A or more
    (d) using automatic means of control

33. All switchboards, panelboards, and motor control centers shall be _____.

    (a) located in dedicated spaces
    (b) protected from damage
    (c) in weatherproof enclosures
    (d) a and b

34. The minimum height of dedicated equipment space for motor control centers installed indoors is _____ above the enclosure, or to the structural ceiling, whichever is lower.

    (a) 3 ft
    (b) 5 ft
    (c) 6 ft
    (d) 6½ ft

35. For indoor installations, heating, cooling, or ventilating equipment shall not be installed in the dedicated space above a panelboard or switchboard.

    (a) True
    (b) False

36. The dedicated equipment space for electrical equipment that is required for panelboards installed indoors is measured from the floor to a height of _____ above the equipment, or to the structural ceiling, whichever is lower.

    (a) 3 ft
    (b) 6 ft
    (c) 12 ft
    (d) 30 ft

37. The dedicated space above a panelboard extends to a dropped or suspended ceiling, which is considered a structural ceiling.

    (a) True
    (b) False

38. Electrical equipment rooms or enclosures housing electrical apparatus that are controlled by a lock(s) shall be considered _____ to qualified persons.

    (a) readily accessible
    (b) accessible
    (c) available
    (d) none of these

Practice Questions

 Please use the 2011 *Code* book to answer the following questions.

Article 200. Use and Identification of Grounded Conductors

1. An insulated grounded conductor of _____ or smaller shall be identified by a continuous white or gray outer finish, or by three continuous white stripes on other than green insulation along its entire length.

   (a) 8 AWG
   (b) 6 AWG
   (c) 4 AWG
   (d) 3 AWG

2. Grounded conductors _____ and larger can be identified by distinctive white or gray markings at their terminations.

   (a) 10 AWG
   (b) 8 AWG
   (c) 6 AWG
   (d) 4 AWG

3. If grounded conductors of different voltage systems are installed in the same raceway, cable, or enclosure, each neutral conductor must be identified to distinguish the systems by _____.

   (a) a continuous white or gray outer finish for one system
   (b) a neutral conductor with a different continuous white or gray outer finish or white or gray with a stripe for one system
   (c) other identification allowed by 200.6(a) or (b) that distinguishes each system from other systems.
   (d) a, b, or c

4. If neutral conductors of different voltage systems are installed in the same raceway, cable, or enclosure, the means of identification of the different neutrals shall be documented in a manner that's _____ or be permanently posted where the conductors of different systems originate.

   (a) available to the AHJ
   (b) available through the engineer
   (c) readily available
   (d) included in the as-built drawings

Please use the 2011 *Code* book to answer the following questions.

Article 210. Branch Circuits

1. A three-phase, 4-wire, _____ power system used to supply power to nonlinear loads may necessitate that the power system design allow for the possibility of high harmonic current on the neutral conductor.

   (a) wye-connected
   (b) delta-connected
   (c) wye/delta-connected
   (d) none of these

2. Each multiwire branch circuit shall be provided with a means that will simultaneously disconnect all _____ conductors at the point where the branch circuit originates.

   (a) circuit
   (b) grounded
   (c) grounding
   (d) ungrounded

3. Multiwire branch circuits shall _____.

   (a) supply only line-to-neutral loads
   (b) not be permitted in dwelling units
   (c) have their conductors originate from different panelboards
   (d) none of these

4. The ungrounded and grounded conductors of each _____ shall be grouped by wire ties or similar means at the panelboard or other point of origination.

   (a) branch circuit
   (b) multiwire branch circuit
   (c) feeder circuit
   (d) service-entrance conductor

5. Where more than one nominal voltage system supplies branch circuits in a building, each _____ conductor of a branch circuit shall be identified by phase and system at all termination, connection, and splice points.

   (a) grounded
   (b) ungrounded
   (c) grounding
   (d) all of these

6. The GFCI protection required by 210.8(A), (b) and (c) must be _____.

   (a) the circuit breaker type only
   (b) accessible
   (c) readily accessible
   (d) concealed

7. All 15A and 20A, 125V receptacles installed in bathrooms of _____ shall have ground-fault circuit-interrupter (GFCI) protection for personnel.

   (a) guest rooms in hotels/motels
   (b) dwelling units
   (c) office buildings
   (d) all of these

8. GFCI protection shall be provided for all 15A and 20A, 125V receptacles installed in a dwelling unit _____.

   (a) attic
   (b) garage
   (c) laundry room
   (d) all of these

9. GFCI protection shall be provided for all 15A and 20A, 125V receptacles in dwelling unit accessory buildings that have a floor located at or below grade level not intended as _____ and limited to storage areas, work areas, or similar use.

(a) habitable rooms
(b) finished space
(c) a or b
(d) none of these

10. All 15A and 20A, 125V receptacles located outdoors of dwelling units, including receptacles installed under the eaves of roofs, must be GFCI protected except for a receptacle that's supplied by a branch circuit dedicated to _____ if the receptacle isn't readily accessible and the equipment or receptacle has ground-fault protection of equipment (GFPE) [426.28 or 427.22].

(a) fixed electric snow-melting or deicing equipment
(b) pipeline and vessel heating equipment
(c) holiday decorative lighting
(d) a or b

11. All 15A and 20A, 125V receptacles installed in crawl spaces at or below grade level of dwelling units shall have GFCI protection.

(a) True
(b) False

12. All 15A and 20A, 125V receptacles installed in _____ of dwelling units shall have GFCI protection.

(a) unfinished attics
(b) finished attics
(c) unfinished basements and crawl spaces
(d) finished basements

13. GFCI protection shall be provided for all 15A and 20A, 125V receptacles _____ in dwelling unit kitchens.

(a) installed to serve the countertop surfaces
(b) within 6 ft of the sink
(c) for all receptacles
(d) that are readily accessible

14. GFCI protection shall be provided for all 15A and 20A, 125V receptacles installed within 6 ft of all dwelling unit sinks located in areas other than the _____.

(a) laundry room
(b) bathroom
(c) den
(d) kitchen

15. All 15A and 20A, 125V receptacles installed in dwelling unit boathouses shall have GFCI protection.

(a) True
(b) False

16. All 15A and 20A, 125V receptacles _____ of commercial occupancies shall have GFCI protection.

(a) in bathrooms
(b) on rooftops
(c) in kitchens
(d) all of these

17. In other than dwelling units, GFCI protection shall be provided for all outdoor 15A and 20A, 125V receptacles.

(a) True
(b) False

18. All 15A and 20A, 125V receptacles located outdoors or on rooftops in locations other than dwelling units must be GFCI protected except for a receptacle that's supplied by a branch circuit dedicated to _____ if the receptacle isn't readily accessible and the equipment or receptacle has ground-fault protection of equipment (GFPE) [426.28 and 427.22].

(a) fixed electric snow-melting or deicing equipment
(b) pipeline and vessel heating equipment
(c) holiday decorative lighting
(d) a or b

19. In other than dwelling locations, GFCI protection is required in _____.

    (a) indoor wet locations
    (b) locker rooms adjacent to showering facilities
    (c) garages, service bays, and similar areas
    (d) all of these

20. All 15A and 20A, 125V receptacles installed within 6 ft of the outside edge of a sink in locations other than dwelling units must be _____ .

    (a) AFCI protected
    (b) GFCI protected
    (c) tamperproof
    (d) a and b

21. In industrial laboratories, 15A and 20A, 125V receptacles used to supply equipment where removal of power would introduce a greater hazard aren't required to be GFCI protected.

    (a) True
    (b) False

22. 15A and 20A, 125V receptacles located in patient bed locations of general care or critical care areas of health care facilities aren't required to be GFCI protected.

    (a) True
    (b) False

23. All 15A and 20A, 125V receptacles installed indoors in wet locations must be GFCI protected.

    (a) True
    (b) False

24. All 15A and 20A, 125V receptacles installed in locker rooms with associated showering facilities must be GFCI protected.

    (a) True
    (b) False

25. All 15A and 20A, 125V receptacles installed in garages, service bays, and similar areas where _____ are to be used must be GFCI protected.

    (a) electrical diagnostic equipment
    (b) electrical hand tools
    (c) portable lighting equipment
    (d) all of these

26. Ground-fault circuit-interrupter protection shall be provided for outlets not exceeding 240V that supply boat hoists installed in dwelling unit locations.

    (a) True
    (b) False

27. All 15A or 20A, 120V branch circuits that supply outlets in dwelling unit family rooms, dining rooms, living rooms, parlors, libraries, dens, bedrooms, sunrooms, recreation rooms, closets, hallways, or similar rooms or areas shall be AFCI protected by a listed arc-fault circuit interrupter of the combination type.

    (a) True
    (b) False

28. An arc-fault circuit interrupter can be located at the first outlet to provide protection for the remaining portion of the branch circuit if _____.

    (a) the arc-fault circuit interrupter is installed within 8 ft of the branch-circuit overcurrent device
    (b) the circuit conductors up to the arc-fault circuit interrupter are in a metal raceway or steel armored Type AC or Type MC cable with metal outlet and junction boxes
    (c) a and b
    (d) the branch circuit serves only lighting loads

29. Where a listed metal or nonmetallic conduit or tubing is encased in not less than _____ of concrete for the portion of the branch circuit between the branch-circuit overcurrent device and the first outlet, an outlet branch circuit AFCI at the first outlet is permitted to provide protection for the remaining portion of the branch circuit.

(a) 2 in.
(b) 4 in.
(c) 6 in.
(d) 8 in.

30. AFCI protection can be omitted for an individual branch-circuit to a _____ in accordance with 760.41(b) and 760.121(B), if the circuit conductors are installed in RMC, IMC, EMT, or steel sheath Type AC or MC cable that qualifies as an equipment grounding conductor in accordance with 250.118, with metal outlet and junction boxes.

(a) smoke alarm
(b) communication system
(c) fire alarm system
(d) sump pump

31. Where branch-circuit wiring in a dwelling unit is modified, replaced or extended in any of the areas specified in 210.12(A), the branch circuit must be protected by _____.

(a) a listed combination AFCI located at the origin of the branch circuit
(b) a listed outlet branch circuit AFCI located at the first receptacle outlet of the existing branch circuit
(c) a GFCI circuit breaker or receptacle
(d) a or b

32. The recommended maximum total voltage drop on branch-circuit conductors is _____ percent.

(a) 2
(b) 3
(c) 4
(d) 6

33. Where a branch circuit supplies continuous loads, or any combination of continuous and noncontinuous loads, the rating of the overcurrent device shall not be less than the noncontinuous load plus 125 percent of the continuous load.

(a) True
(b) False

ARTICLE 225 — Practice Questions

 Please use the 2011 *Code* book to answer the following questions.

Article 225. Outside Wiring

1. The disconnecting means for a building supplied by a feeder shall be installed at a(n) _____ location.

   (a) accessible
   (b) readily accessible
   (c) outdoor
   (d) indoor

2. Where documented safe switching procedures are established and maintained and monitored by _____ individuals, the disconnecting means for a building supplied by a feeder can be located elsewhere on the premises.

   (a) maintenance
   (b) management
   (c) service
   (d) qualified

3. There shall be no more than _____ switches or circuit breakers to serve as the disconnecting means for a building supplied by a feeder .

   (a) two
   (b) four
   (c) six
   (d) eight

4. The two to six disconnects for a disconnecting means for a building supplied by a feeder shall be _____. .

   (a) the same size
   (b) grouped
   (c) in the same enclosure
   (d) none of these

Please use the 2011 *Code* book to answer the following questions.

Article 230. Services

1. There shall be no more than _____ disconnects installed for each service or for each set of service-entrance conductors as permitted in 230.2 and 230.40.

   (a) two
   (b) four
   (c) six
   (d) eight

2. When the service contains two to six service disconnecting means, they shall be _____.

   (a) the same size
   (b) grouped
   (c) in the same enclosure
   (d) none of these

3. The additional service disconnecting means for fire pumps, emergency systems, legally required standby, or optional standby services, shall be installed remote from the one to six service disconnecting means for normal service to minimize the possibility of _____ interruption of supply.

   (a) intentional
   (b) accidental
   (c) simultaneous
   (d) prolonged

4. In a multiple-occupancy building, each occupant shall have access to the occupant's _____.

   (a) service disconnecting means
   (b) service drops
   (c) distribution transformer
   (d) lateral conductors

5. In a multiple-occupancy building where electric service and electrical maintenance are provided by the building management under continuous building management supervision, the service disconnecting means can be accessible to authorized _____ only.

   (a) inspectors
   (b) tenants
   (c) management personnel
   (d) qualified persons

Please use the 2011 *Code* book to answer the following questions.

Article 240. Overcurrent Protection

1. Conductor overload protection shall not be required where the interruption of the _____ would create a hazard, such as in a material-handling magnet circuit or fire pump circuit. However, short-circuit protection is required.

   (a) circuit
   (b) line
   (c) phase
   (d) system

2. The next higher standard rating overcurrent device above the ampacity of the ungrounded conductors being protected shall be permitted to be used, provided all of the following conditions are met:

   (a) The conductors are not part of a branch circuit supplying more than one receptacle for cord-and-plug-connected portable loads.
   (b) The ampacity of the conductors doesn't correspond with the standard ampere rating of a fuse or circuit breaker.
   (c) The next higher standard rating selected doesn't exceed 800A.
   (d) all of these

3. If the circuit's overcurrent device exceeds _____, the conductor ampacity must have a rating not less than the rating of the overcurrent device.

   (a) 800A
   (b) 1,000A
   (c) 1,200A
   (d) 2,000A

4. Overcurrent protection shall not exceed _____.

   (a) 15A for 14 AWG copper
   (b) 20A for 12 AWG copper
   (c) 30A for 10 AWG copper
   (d) all of these

5. Conductors supplied under the tap rules are allowed to supply another conductor using the tap rules.

   (a) True
   (b) False

6. Tap conductors not over 25 ft shall be permitted, providing the _____.

   (a) ampacity of the tap conductors is not less than one-third the rating of the overcurrent device protecting the feeder conductors being tapped
   (b) tap conductors terminate in a single circuit breaker or set of fuses that limit the load to the ampacity of the tap conductors
   (c) tap conductors are suitably protected from physical damage
   (d) all of these

7. The maximum length of a feeder tap conductor in a high-bay manufacturing building over 35 ft high shall be _____.

   (a) 15 ft
   (b) 20 ft
   (c) 50 ft
   (d) 100 ft

8. Outside feeder tap conductors can be of unlimited length without overcurrent protection at the point they receive their supply if:

(a) The tap conductors are suitably protected from physical damage.

(b) The tap conductors terminate at a single circuit breaker or a single set of fuses that limits the load to the ampacity of the conductors.

(c) a and b

(d) none of these

9. Outside secondary conductors can be of unlimited length without overcurrent protection at the point they receive their supply if:

(a) The conductors are suitably protected from physical damage.

(b) The conductors terminate at a single circuit breaker or a single set of fuses that limits the load to the ampacity of the conductors.

(c) a and b

(d) none of these

Please use the 2011 *Code* book to answer the following questions.

Article 250. Grounding and Bonding

1. A conductor on the supply side of a service or within a service equipment enclosure or separately derived system to ensure the electrical conductivity between metal parts required to be electrically connected is know as the _____.

   (a) supply-side bonding jumper
   (b) ungrounded conductor
   (c) the electrical supply source
   (d) grounding electrode conductor

2. An effective ground-fault current path is an intentionally constructed, permanent, low-impedance path designed and intended to carry fault current from the point of a ground fault on a wiring system to _____.

   (a) ground
   (b) earth
   (c) the electrical supply source
   (d) none of these

3. A ground-fault current path is an electrically conductive path from the point of a ground fault through normally noncurrent-carrying conductors, equipment, or the earth to the _____.

   (a) ground
   (b) earth
   (c) electrical supply source
   (d) none of these

4. Examples of ground-fault current paths include any combination of conductive materials including _____.

   (a) equipment grounding conductors
   (b) metallic raceways
   (c) metal water and gas piping
   (d) all of these

5. Grounded electrical systems shall be connected to earth in a manner that will _____.

   (a) limit voltages due to lightning, line surges, or unintentional contact with higher-voltage lines
   (b) stabilize the voltage-to-ground during normal operation
   (c) facilitate overcurrent device operation in case of ground faults
   (d) a and b

6. An important consideration for limiting imposed voltage on electrical systems is to remember that bonding and grounding electrode conductors shouldn't be any longer than necessary and unnecessary bends and loops should be avoided.

   (a) True
   (b) False

7. For grounded systems, normally noncurrent-carrying conductive materials enclosing electrical conductors or equipment shall be connected to earth so as to limit the voltage-to-ground on these materials.

   (a) True
   (b) False

8. For grounded systems, noncurrent-carrying conductive materials enclosing electrical conductors or equipment, or forming part of such equipment, shall be connected together and to the _____ to establish an effective ground-fault current path.

   (a) ground
   (b) earth
   (c) electrical supply source
   (d) none of these

9. In grounded systems, normally noncurrent-carrying electrically conductive materials that are likely to become energized shall be _____ in a manner that establishes an effective ground-fault current path.

(a) connected together
(b) connected to the electrical supply source
(c) connected to the closest grounded conductor
(d) a and b

10. For grounded systems, electrical equipment and conductive material likely to become energized, shall be installed in a manner that creates a _____ from any point on the wiring system where a ground fault may occur to the electrical supply source.

(a) circuit facilitating the operation of the overcurrent device
(b) low-impedance path
(c) path capable of safely carrying the ground-fault current likely to be imposed on it
(d) all of these

11. For grounded systems, electrical equipment and electrically conductive material likely to become energized, shall be installed in a manner that creates a low-impedance circuit capable of safely carrying the maximum ground-fault current likely to be imposed on it from where a ground fault may occur to the _____.

(a) ground
(b) earth
(c) electrical supply source
(d) none of these

12. For grounded systems, the earth is considered an effective ground-fault current path.

(a) True
(b) False

13. For ungrounded systems, noncurrent-carrying conductive materials enclosing electrical conductors or equipment shall be connected to the _____ in a manner that will limit the voltage imposed by lightning or unintentional contact with higher-voltage lines.

(a) ground
(b) earth
(c) electrical supply source
(d) none of these

14. For ungrounded systems, noncurrent-carrying conductive materials enclosing electrical conductors or equipment, or forming part of such equipment, shall be connected together and to the supply system equipment in a manner that creates a low-impedance path for ground-fault current that is capable of carrying _____.

(a) the maximum branch-circuit current
(b) at least twice the maximum ground-fault current
(c) the maximum fault current likely to be imposed on it
(d) the equivalent to the main service rating

15. Electrically conductive materials that are likely to _____ in ungrounded systems shall be connected together and to the supply system grounded equipment in a manner that creates a low-impedance path for ground-fault current that is capable of carrying the maximum fault current likely to be imposed on it.

(a) become energized
(b) require service
(c) be removed
(d) be coated with paint or nonconductive materials

16. In ungrounded systems, electrical equipment, wiring, and other electrically conductive material likely to become energized shall be installed in a manner that creates a low-impedance circuit from any point on the wiring system to the electrical supply source to facilitate the operation of overcurrent devices should a(n) _____ fault from a different phase occur on the wiring system.

(a) isolated ground
(b) second ground
(c) arc
(d) high impedance

17. The grounding of electrical systems, circuit conductors, surge arresters, surge protective devices, and conductive normally noncurrent-carrying metal parts of equipment shall be installed and arranged in a manner that will prevent objectionable current.

    (a) True
    (b) False

18. Temporary currents resulting from abnormal conditions, such as ground faults, are not considered to be objectionable currents.

    (a) True
    (b) False

19. Currents that introduce noise or data errors in electronic equipment are considered objectionable currents in the context of 250.6(d) of the *NEC*.

    (a) True
    (b) False

20. The grounding electrode conductor shall be connected to the grounded service conductor at the _____.

    (a) load end of the service drop
    (b) load end of the service lateral
    (c) service disconnecting means
    (d) any of these

21. Where the main bonding jumper is installed from the grounded conductor terminal bar to the equipment grounding terminal bar in service equipment, the _____ conductor is permitted to be connected to the equipment grounding terminal bar.

    (a) grounding
    (b) grounded
    (c) grounding electrode
    (d) none of these

22. For a grounded system, an unspliced _____ shall be used to connect the equipment grounding conductor(s) and the service disconnecting means to the grounded conductor of the system within the enclosure for each service disconnect.

    (a) grounding electrode
    (b) main bonding jumper
    (c) busbar
    (d) insulated copper conductor

23. Where an alternating-current system operating at less than 1,000V is grounded at any point, the _____ conductor(s) shall be routed with the ungrounded conductors to each service disconnecting means and shall be connected to each disconnecting means grounded conductor(s) terminal or bus.

    (a) ungrounded
    (b) grounded
    (c) grounding
    (d) none of these

24. The grounded conductor of an alternating-current system operating at less than 1,000V shall be routed with the ungrounded conductors and connected to each disconnecting means grounded conductor terminal or bus, which is then connected to the service disconnecting means enclosure via a(n) _____ that's installed between the service neutral conductor and the service disconnecting means enclosure.

    (a) equipment bonding conductor
    (b) main bonding jumper
    (c) grounding electrode
    (d) intersystem bonding terminal

25. The grounded conductor brought to service equipment shall be routed with the phase conductors and shall not be smaller than specified in Table _____ when the service-entrance conductors are 1,100 kcmil copper and smaller.

    (a) 250.66
    (b) 250.122
    (c) 310.16
    (d) 430.52

26. When service-entrance conductors exceed 1,100 kcmil for copper, the required grounded conductor for the service shall be sized not less than _____ percent of the circular mil area of the largest set of ungrounded service-entrance conductor(s).

(a) 9
(b) 11
(c) 12½
(d) 15

27. Where service-entrance phase conductors are installed in parallel in two or more raceways, the size of the grounded conductor in each raceway shall be based on the total circular mil area of the parallel ungrounded service-entrance conductor in the raceway, sized per 250.24(C)(1), but not smaller than _____.

(a) 1/0 AWG
(b) 2/0 AWG
(c) 3/0 AWG
(d) 4/0 AWG

28. A grounding electrode conductor, sized in accordance with 250.66, shall be used to connect the equipment grounding conductors, the service-equipment enclosures, and, where the system is grounded, the grounded service conductor to the grounding electrode(s).

(a) True
(b) False

29. A grounded conductor shall not be connected to normally noncurrent-carrying metal parts of equipment on the _____ side of the system bonding jumper of a separately derived system except as otherwise permitted in Article 250.

(a) supply
(b) grounded
(c) high-voltage
(d) load

30. An unspliced _____ that is sized based on the derived phase conductors shall be used to connect the grounded conductor and the supply-side bonding jumper, or the equipment grounding conductor, or both, at a separately derived system.

(a) system bonding jumper
(b) equipment grounding conductor
(c) grounded conductor
(d) grounding electrode conductor

31. The connection of the system bonding jumper for a separately derived system shall be made _____ on the separately derived system from the source to the first system disconnecting means or overcurrent device.

(a) in at least two locations
(b) in every location that the grounded conductor is present
(c) at any single point
(d) none of these

32. Where a supply-side bonding jumper of the wire type is run with the derived phase conductors from the source of a separately derived system to the first disconnecting means, it shall be sized in accordance with 250.102(C), based on _____.

(a) the size of the primary conductors
(b) the size of the secondary overcurrent protection
(c) the size of the derived phase conductors
(d) one third the size of the primary grounded conductor

33. The grounding electrode for a separately derived system shall be as near as practicable to, and preferably in the same area as, the grounding electrode conductor connection to the system.

(a) True
(b) False

34. For a single separately derived system, the grounding electrode conductor connects the grounded conductor of the derived system to the grounding electrode at the same point on the separately derived system where the _____ is connected.

    (a) metering equipment
    (b) transfer switch
    (c) system bonding jumper
    (d) largest circuit breaker

35. The grounding electrode conductor for a single separately derived system is used to connect the grounded conductor of the derived system to the grounding electrode.

    (a) True
    (b) False

36. Grounding electrode conductor taps from a separately derived system to a common grounding electrode conductor are permitted when a building or structure has multiple separately derived systems, provided that the taps terminate at the same point as the system bonding jumper.

    (a) True
    (b) False

37. The common grounding electrode conductor installed for multiple separately derived systems shall not be smaller than _____ copper when using a wire-type conductor.

    (a) 1/0 AWG
    (b) 2/0 AWG
    (c) 3/0 AWG
    (d) 4/0 AWG

38. Each tap conductor to a common grounding electrode conductor for multiple separately derived systems shall be sized in accordance with _____, based on the derived phase conductors of the separately derived system it serves.

    (a) 250.66
    (b) 250.118
    (c) 250.122
    (d) 310.15

39. Tap connections to a common grounding electrode conductor for multiple separately derived systems shall be made at an accessible location by _____.

    (a) a connector listed as grounding and bonding equipment
    (b) listed connections to aluminum or copper busbars
    (c) by the exothermic welding process
    (d) any of these

40. Tap connections to a common grounding electrode conductor for multiple separately derived systems may be made to a copper or aluminum busbar that is _____.

    (a) not over ½ in. x 4 in.
    (b) not over ¼ in. x 2 in.
    (c) at least ¼ in. x 2 in.
    (d) a and c

41. In an area served by a separately derived system, the _____ shall be connected to the grounded conductor of the separately derived system.

    (a) structural steel
    (b) metal piping
    (c) metal building skin
    (d) a and b

42. A grounding electrode shall be required if a building or structure is supplied by a feeder.

    (a) True
    (b) False

43. A grounding electrode at a separate building or structure shall be required where one multiwire branch circuit serves the building or structure.

    (a) True
    (b) False

44. When supplying a grounded system at a separate building or structure, an equipment grounding conductor shall be run with the supply conductors and connected to the building or structure disconnecting means.

    (a) True
    (b) False

45. For a separate building or structure supplied by a feeder or branch circuit, the neutral conductor can serve as the ground-fault return path for the building/structure disconnecting means for existing installations made in compliance with previous editions of the *Code* as long as the installation continues to meet the condition(s) that _____.

    (a) there are no continuous metallic paths between buildings and structures
    (b) ground-fault protection of equipment isn't installed on the supply side of the feeder
    (c) the neutral conductor is sized no smaller than the larger required by 220.61 or 250.122
    (d) all of these

46. For a separate building or structure supplied by a separately derived system when overcurrent protection is provided where the conductors originate, the supply conductors must contain a(n) _____.

    (a) equipment grounding conductor
    (b) copper conductors only
    (c) GFCI protection for the feeder
    (d) all of these

47. For a separate building or structure supplied by a separately derived system when overcurrent protection isn't provided for the supply conductors to the building/structure as permitted by 240.21(C)(4), the installation must be _____ in accordance with 250.30(A).

    (a) AFCI protected
    (b) grounded and bonded
    (c) isolated
    (d) all of these

48. The size of the grounding electrode conductor for a building or structure supplied by a feeder shall not be smaller than that identified in _____, based on the largest ungrounded supply conductor.

    (a) 250.66
    (b) 250.122
    (c) Table 310.15(B)(16)
    (d) none of these

49. The frame of a portable generator shall not be required to be connected to a(n) _____ if the generator only supplies equipment mounted on the generator or cord-and-plug connected equipment using receptacles mounted on the generator.

    (a) grounding electrode
    (b) grounded conductor
    (c) ungrounded conductor
    (d) equipment grounding conductor

50. The frame of a vehicle-mounted generator shall not be required to be connected to a(n) _____ if the generator only supplies equipment mounted on the vehicle or cord-and-plug connected equipment, using receptacles mounted on the vehicle.

    (a) grounding electrode
    (b) grounded conductor
    (c) ungrounded conductor
    (d) equipment grounding conductor

51. Concrete-encased electrodes of _____ shall not be required to be part of the grounding electrode system where the steel reinforcing bars or rods aren't accessible for use without disturbing the concrete.

    (a) hazardous (classified) locations
    (b) health care facilities
    (c) existing buildings or structures
    (d) agricultural buildings with equipotential planes

52. In order for a metal underground water pipe to be used as a grounding electrode, it shall be in direct contact with the earth for _____ .

    (a) 5 ft
    (b) 10 ft or more
    (c) less than 10 ft
    (d) 20 ft or more

53. The metal frame of a building shall be considered a grounding electrode where one of the *NEC*-prescribed methods for connection of the metal frame to earth has been met:

    (a) True
    (b) False

54. A bare 4 AWG copper conductor installed horizontally near the bottom or vertically, and within that portion of a concrete foundation or footing that is in direct contact with the earth can be used as a grounding electrode when the conductor is at least _____ in length.

    (a) 10 ft
    (b) 15 ft
    (c) 20 ft
    (d) 25 ft

55. An electrode encased by at least 2 in. of concrete, located horizontally near the bottom or vertically and within that portion of a concrete foundation or footing that is in direct contact with the earth, shall be permitted as a grounding electrode when it consists of _____ .

    (a) at least 20 ft of ½ in. or larger steel reinforcing bars or rods
    (b) at least 20 ft of bare copper conductor of 4 AWG or larger
    (c) a or b
    (d) none of these

56. Reinforcing bars for use as a concrete-encased electrode can be bonded together by the usual steel tie wires or other effective means.

    (a) True
    (b) False

57. Where more than one concrete-encased electrode is present at a building or structure, it shall be permitted to connect to only one of them.

    (a) True
    (b) False

58. A ground ring encircling the building or structure can be used as a grounding electrode when _____ .

    (a) the ring is in direct contact with the earth
    (b) the ring consists of at least 20 ft of bare conductor
    (c) the bare copper conductor is not smaller than 2 AWG
    (d) all of these

59. Grounding electrodes that are driven rods require a minimum of _____ in contact with the soil.

    (a) 6 ft
    (b) 8 ft
    (c) 10 ft
    (d) 12 ft

60. Grounding electrodes of the rod type less than _____ in. in diameter shall be listed.

    (a) ½ in.
    (b) 5/8 in.
    (c) ¾ in.
    (d) none of these

61. A buried iron or steel plate used as a grounding electrode shall expose not less than _____ of surface area to exterior soil.

    (a) 2 sq ft
    (b) 4 sq ft
    (c) 9 sq ft
    (d) 10 sq ft

62. Local metal underground systems or structures such as _____ are permitted to serve as grounding electrodes.

    (a) piping systems
    (b) underground tanks
    (c) underground metal well casings
    (d) all of these

63. _____ shall not be used as grounding electrodes.

    (a) Underground gas piping systems
    (b) Aluminum
    (c) Metal well casings
    (d) a and b

64. Where practicable, rod, pipe, and plate electrodes shall be installed _____.

    (a) directly below the electrical meter
    (b) on the north side of the building
    (c) below permanent moisture level
    (d) all of these

65. Where the resistance-to-ground of 25 ohms or less is not achieved for a single rod electrode, _____.

    (a) other means besides electrodes shall be used in order to provide grounding
    (b) the single rod electrode shall be supplemented by one additional electrode
    (c) no additional electrodes are required
    (d) none of these

66. Two or more grounding electrodes bonded together are considered a single grounding electrode system.

    (a) True
    (b) False

67. Where a metal underground water pipe is used as a grounding electrode, the continuity of the grounding path or the bonding connection to interior piping shall not rely on _____ and similar equipment.

    (a) bonding jumpers
    (b) water meters or filtering devices
    (c) grounding clamps
    (d) all of these

68. Where the supplemental electrode is a rod, that portion of the bonding jumper that is the sole connection to the supplemental grounding electrode shall not be required to be larger than _____ AWG copper.

    (a) 8
    (b) 6
    (c) 4
    (d) 1

69. When a ground ring is used as a grounding electrode, it shall be buried at a depth below the earth's surface of not less than _____.

    (a) 18 in.
    (b) 24 in.
    (c) 30 in.
    (d) 8 ft

70. Ground rod electrodes shall be installed so that at least _____ of the length is in contact with the soil.

    (a) 5 ft
    (b) 8 ft
    (c) one-half
    (d) 80 percent

71. The upper end of a ground rod electrode shall be _____ ground level unless the aboveground end and the grounding electrode conductor attachment are protected against physical damage.

    (a) above
    (b) flush with
    (c) below
    (d) b or c

72. Where rock bottom is encountered when driving a ground rod at an angle up to 45 degrees, the electrode can be buried in a trench that is at least _____ deep.

    (a) 18 in.
    (b) 30 in.
    (c) 4 ft
    (d) 8 ft

73. Where used outside, aluminum or copper-clad aluminum grounding electrode conductors shall not be terminated within _____ of the earth.

    (a) 6 in.
    (b) 12 in.
    (c) 15 in.
    (d) 18 in.

74. Bare aluminum or copper-clad aluminum grounding electrode conductors shall not be used where in direct contact with _____ or where subject to corrosive conditions.

    (a) masonry or the earth
    (b) bare copper conductors
    (c) wooden framing members
    (d) all of these

75. Grounding electrode conductors _____ and larger that are not subject to physical damage can be run exposed along the surface of the building construction if it is securely fastened to the construction.

    (a) 10 AWG
    (b) 8 AWG
    (c) 6 AWG
    (d) 4 AWG

76. Grounding electrode conductors smaller than _____ shall be in rigid metal conduit, IMC, PVC conduit, electrical metallic tubing, or cable armor.

    (a) 10 AWG
    (b) 8 AWG
    (c) 6 AWG
    (d) 4 AWG

77. Grounding electrode conductors shall be installed in one continuous length without a splice or joint, unless spliced _____.

    (a) by connecting together sections of a busbar
    (b) by irreversible compression-type connectors listed as grounding and bonding equipment
    (c) by the exothermic welding process
    (d) any of these

78. Where service equipment consists of more than one enclosure, grounding electrode connections shall be permitted to be _____.

    (a) multiple individual grounding electrode conductors
    (b) one grounding electrode conductor at a common location
    (c) common grounding electrode conductor and taps.
    (d) any of these

79. Ferrous metal enclosures for grounding electrode conductors shall be electrically continuous, from the point of attachment to cabinets or equipment, to the grounding electrode.

    (a) True
    (b) False

80. A grounding electrode conductor shall be permitted to be run to any convenient grounding electrode available in the grounding electrode system where the other electrodes, if any, are connected by bonding jumpers per 250.53(C).

    (a) True
    (b) False

81. A service consisting of 12 AWG service-entrance conductors requires a grounding electrode conductor sized no less than _____.

    (a) 10 AWG
    (b) 8 AWG
    (c) 6 AWG
    (d) 4 AWG

82. The largest size grounding electrode conductor required is _____ copper.

(a) 6 AWG
(b) 1/0 AWG
(c) 3/0 AWG
(d) 250 kcmil

83. What size copper grounding electrode conductor is required for a service that has three sets of 600 kcmil copper conductors per phase?

(a) 1 AWG
(b) 1/0 AWG
(c) 2/0 AWG
(d) 3/0 AWG

84. In an ac system, the size of the grounding electrode conductor to a concrete-encased electrode shall not be required to be larger than a(n) _____ copper conductor.

(a) 10 AWG
(b) 8 AWG
(c) 6 AWG
(d) 4 AWG

85. The noncurrent-carrying metal parts of service equipment, such as _____, shall be bonded together.

(a) service raceways or service cable armor
(b) service equipment enclosures containing service conductors, including meter fittings, boxes, or the like, interposed in the service raceway or armor
(c) service cable trays
(d) all of these

86. Bonding jumpers for service raceways shall be used around impaired connections such as _____ .

(a) concentric knockouts
(b) eccentric knockouts
(c) reducing washers
(d) any of these

87. Electrical continuity at service equipment, service raceways, and service conductor enclosures shall be ensured by _____.

(a) bonding equipment to the grounded service conductor
(b) connections utilizing threaded couplings on enclosures, if made up wrenchtight
(c) by listed bonding devices, such as bonding-type locknuts, bushings, or bushings with bonding jumpers
(d) any of these

88. Service raceways threaded into metal service equipment such as bosses (hubs) are considered to be effectively _____ to the service metal enclosure.

(a) attached
(b) bonded
(c) grounded
(d) none of these

89. Service metal raceways and metal-clad cables are considered effectively bonded when using threadless couplings and connectors that are _____.

(a) nonmetallic
(b) made up tight
(c) sealed
(d) classified

90. A means external to enclosures for connecting intersystem _____ conductors shall be provided at service equipment or metering equipment enclosure and disconnecting means of buildings or structures supplied by a feeder.

(a) bonding
(b) ungrounded
(c) secondary
(d) a and b

91. The intersystem bonding termination shall _____.

    (a) be accessible for connection and inspection
    (b) consist of a set of terminals with the capacity for connection of not less than three intersystem bonding conductors
    (c) not interfere with opening the enclosure for a service, building/structure disconnecting means, or metering equipment
    (d) all of these

92. The intersystem bonding termination shall _____.

    (a) be securely mounted and electrically connected to service equipment, the meter enclosure, or exposed nonflexible metallic service raceway, or be mounted at one of these enclosures and be connected to the enclosure or grounding electrode conductor with a minimum 6 AWG copper conductor
    (b) be securely mounted to the building/structure disconnecting means, or be mounted at the disconnecting means and be connected to the metallic enclosure or grounding electrode conductor with a minimum 6 AWG copper conductor
    (c) have terminals that are listed as grounding and bonding equipment
    (d) all of these

93. At existing buildings or structures, an intersystem bonding termination is not required if other acceptable means of bonding exits. An external accessible means for bonding communications systems together can be by the use of _____.

    (a) nonflexible metallic raceway
    (b) an exposed grounding electrode conductor
    (c) a connection to grounded raceway or equipment approved by the authority having jurisdiction
    (d) any of these

94. For circuits over 250 volts-to-ground, electrical continuity can be maintained between a box or enclosure where no over-sized, concentric or eccentric knockouts are encountered, and a metal conduit by _____.

    (a) threadless fittings for cables with metal sheath
    (b) double locknuts on threaded conduit (one inside and one outside the box or enclosure)
    (c) fittings that have shoulders that seat firmly against the box with a locknut on the inside or listed fittings
    (d) all of these

95. Equipment bonding jumpers shall be of copper or other corrosion-resistant material.

    (a) True
    (b) False

96. Equipment bonding jumpers on the supply side of the service shall be no smaller than the sizes shown in _____.

    (a) Table 250.66
    (b) Table 250.122
    (c) Table 310.15(B)(16)
    (d) Table 310.15(B)(6)

97. The supply-side bonding jumper on the supply side of services shall be sized according to the _____.

    (a) overcurrent device rating
    (b) ungrounded supply conductor size
    (c) service-drop size
    (d) load to be served

98. What is the minimum size copper supply-side bonding jumper for a service raceway containing 4/0 THHN aluminum conductors?

    (a) 6 AWG aluminum
    (b) 4 AWG aluminum
    (c) 4 AWG copper
    (d) 3 AWG copper

99. Where ungrounded supply conductors are paralleled in two or more raceways or cables, the bonding jumper for each raceway or cable shall be based on the size of the _____ in each raceway or cable.

    (a) overcurrent protection for conductors
    (b) grounded conductors
    (c) ungrounded supply conductors
    (d) sum of all conductors

100. A service is supplied by three metal raceways, each containing 600 kcmil ungrounded conductors. Determine the copper supply side bonding jumper size for each service raceway.

    (a) 1/0 AWG
    (b) 3/0 AWG
    (c) 250 kcmil
    (d) 500 kcmil

101. What is the minimum size copper equipment bonding jumper for a 40A rated circuit?

    (a) 14 AWG
    (b) 12 AWG
    (c) 10 AWG
    (d) 8 AWG

102. An equipment bonding jumper can be installed on the outside of a raceway, providing the length of the equipment bonding jumper is not more than _____ and the equipment bonding jumper is routed with the raceway.

    (a) 12 in.
    (b) 24 in.
    (c) 36 in.
    (d) 72 in.

103. Metal water piping system(s) shall be bonded to the _____.

    (a) grounded conductor at the service
    (b) service equipment enclosure
    (c) equipment grounding bar or bus at any panelboard within a single occupancy building
    (d) a or b

104. The bonding jumper used to bond the metal water piping system shall be sized in accordance with _____.

    (a) Table 250.66
    (b) Table 250.122
    (c) Table 310.15(B)(16)
    (d) Table 310.15(B)(6)

105. Where isolated metal water piping systems are installed in a multiple-occupancy building, the water pipes can be bonded with bonding jumpers sized according to Table 250.122, based on the size of the _____.

    (a) service-entrance conductors
    (b) feeder conductors
    (c) rating of the service equipment overcurrent device
    (d) rating of the overcurrent device supplying the occupancy

106. A building or structure that is supplied by a feeder shall have the interior metal water piping system bonded with a conductor sized in accordance with _____.

    (a) Table 250.66
    (b) Table 250.122
    (c) Table 310.15(B)(16)
    (d) none of these

107. Metal gas piping shall be considered bonded by the equipment grounding conductor of the circuit that is likely to energize the piping.

    (a) True
    (b) False

108. Exposed structural metal interconnected to form a metal building frame that is not intentionally grounded and is likely to become energized, shall be bonded to the _____.

    (a) service equipment enclosure or building disconnecting means
    (b) grounded conductor at the service
    (c) grounding electrode conductor where of sufficient size
    (d) any of these

109. Lightning protection system ground terminals _____ be bonded to the building grounding electrode system.

    (a) shall
    (b) shall not
    (c) shall be permitted to
    (d) none of these

110. Listed FMC can be used as the equipment grounding conductor if the length in any ground return path does not exceed 6 ft and the circuit conductors contained in the conduit are protected by overcurrent devices rated at _____ or less.

    (a) 15A
    (b) 20A
    (c) 30A
    (d) 60A

111. Listed FMC and LFMC shall contain an equipment grounding conductor if the raceway is installed for the reason of _____.

    (a) physical protection
    (b) flexibility after installation
    (c) minimizing transmission of vibration from equipment
    (d) b or c

112. The *Code* requires the installation of an equipment grounding conductor of the wire type in _____.

    (a) Rigid metal conduit (RMC).
    (b) Intermediate metal conduit (IMC).
    (c) Electrical metallic tubing (EMT).
    (d) Listed flexible metal conduit over 6 ft in length

113. Listed liquidtight flexible metal conduit (LFMC) is acceptable as an equipment grounding conductor when it terminates in listed fittings and is protected by an overcurrent device rated 60A or less for sizes 3/8 in. through ½ in.

    (a) True
    (b) False

114. The armor of Type AC cable containing an aluminum bonding strip is recognized by the *NEC* as an equipment grounding conductor.

    (a) True
    (b) False

115. Type MC cable provides an effective ground-fault current path and is recognized by the *NEC* as an equipment grounding conductor when _____.

    (a) it contains an insulated or uninsulated equipment grounding conductor in compliance with 250.118(1).
    (b) the combined metallic sheath and uninsulated equipment grounding/bonding conductor of interlocked metal tape–type MC cable is listed and identified as an equipment grounding conductor.
    (c) a or b
    (d) only when it is hospital grade Type MC cable

116. The equipment grounding conductor shall not be required to be larger than the circuit conductors.

    (a) True
    (b) False

117. When ungrounded circuit conductors are increased in size, the equipment grounding conductor must be proportionately increased in size according to the _____ of the ungrounded conductors.

    (a) ampacity
    (b) circular mil area
    (c) diameter
    (d) none of these

118. When a single equipment grounding conductor is used for multiple circuits in the same raceway, cable or cable tray, the single equipment grounding conductor shall be sized according to _____.

    (a) the combined rating of all the overcurrent devices
    (b) the largest overcurrent device of the multiple circuits
    (c) the combined rating of all the loads
    (d) any of these

119. Equipment grounding conductors for motor branch circuits shall be sized in accordance with Table 250.122, based on the rating of the _____ device.

    (a) motor overload
    (b) motor over-temperature
    (c) branch-circuit short-circuit and ground-fault protective
    (d) feeder overcurrent protection

120. Where conductors are run in parallel in multiple raceways or cables and include an EGC of the wire type, the equipment grounding conductor must be installed in parallel in each raceway or cable, sized in compliance with 250.122.

    (a) True
    (b) False

121. Equipment grounding conductors for feeder taps are not required to be larger than the tap conductors.

    (a) True
    (b) False

122. A grounded circuit conductor is permitted to ground noncur-rent-carrying metal parts of equipment, raceways, and other enclosures on the supply side or within the enclosure of the ac service-disconnecting means.

    (a) True
    (b) False

123. It shall be permissible to ground meter enclosures located near the service disconnecting means to the _____ circuit conductor on the load side of the service disconnect, if service ground-fault protection is not provided.

    (a) grounding
    (b) bonding
    (c) grounded
    (d) phase

124. A(n) _____ shall be used to connect the grounding terminal of a grounding-type receptacle to a grounded box.

    (a) equipment bonding jumper
    (b) grounded conductor jumper
    (c) a or b
    (d) a and b

125. Where the box is mounted on the surface, direct metal-to-metal contact between the device yoke and the box shall be permitted to ground the receptacle to the box if at least _____ of the insulating washers of the receptacle is(are) removed.

    (a) one
    (b) two
    (c) three
    (d) none of these

126. A listed exposed work cover can be the grounding and bonding means when the device is attached to the cover with at least _____ permanent fastener(s) and the cover mounting holes are located on a non-raised portion of the cover.

    (a) one
    (b) two
    (c) three
    (d) none of these

127. Receptacle yokes designed and _____ as self-grounding can establish the grounding circuit between the device yoke and a grounded outlet box.

    (a) approved
    (b) advertised
    (c) listed
    (d) installed

128. The receptacle grounding terminal of an isolated ground recep-tacle shall be connected to a(n) _____ equipment grounding conductor run with the circuit conductors.

    (a) insulated
    (b) covered
    (c) bare
    (d) solid

129. Where circuit conductors are spliced or terminated on equipment within a box, any equipment grounding conductors associated with those circuit conductors shall be connected to the box with devices suitable for the use.

(a) True
(b) False

130. The arrangement of grounding connections shall be such that the disconnection or the removal of a receptacle, luminaire, or other device does not interrupt the grounding continuity.

(a) True
(b) False

131. A connection between equipment grounding conductors and a metal box shall be by _____.

(a) a grounding screw used for no other purpose
(b) equipment listed for grounding
(c) a listed grounding device
(d) any of these

 Please use the 2011 *Code* book to answer the following questions.

Article 300. Wiring Methods

1. Conductors shall be installed within a raceway, cable, or enclosure.

   (a) True
   (b) False

2. All conductors of a circuit, including the grounded and equipment grounding conductors, shall be contained within the same _____, unless otherwise permitted elsewhere in the *Code*.

   (a) raceway
   (b) cable
   (c) trench
   (d) all of these

3. Conductors of ac and dc circuits, rated 600V or less, shall be permitted to occupy the same _____ provided that all conductors have an insulation rating equal to the maximum voltage applied to any conductor.

   (a) enclosure
   (b) cable
   (c) raceway
   (d) all of these

4. Where cables or nonmetallic raceways are installed through bored holes in joists, rafters, or wood members, holes shall be bored so that the edge of the hole is _____ the nearest edge of the wood member.

   (a) not less than 1¼ in. from
   (b) immediately adjacent to
   (c) not less than 1/16 in. from
   (d) 90° away from

5. Cables laid in wood notches require protection against nails or screws by using a steel plate at least _____ thick, installed before the building finish is applied.

   (a) 1/16 in.
   (b) 1/8 in.
   (c) ¼ in.
   (d) ½ in.

6. Where Type NM cable passes through factory or field openings in metal members, it shall be protected by _____ bushings or _____ grommets that cover metal edges.

   (a) approved
   (b) identified
   (c) listed
   (d) none of these

7. Where Type NM cables pass through cut or drilled slots or holes in metal members, the cable shall be protected by _____ which are installed in the opening prior to the installation of the cable and which securely cover all metal edges.

   (a) listed bushings
   (b) listed grommets
   (c) plates
   (d) a or b

8. Where nails or screws are likely to penetrate nonmetallic-sheathed cable or ENT installed through metal framing members, a steel sleeve, steel plate, or steel clip not less than _____ in thickness shall be used to protect the cable or tubing.

   (a) 1/16 in.
   (b) 1/8 in.
   (c) ½ in.
   (d) ¾ in.

9. Wiring methods installed behind panels that allow access shall be _____ according to their applicable articles.

    (a) supported
    (b) painted
    (c) in a metal raceway
    (d) all of these

10. Where cables and nonmetallic raceways are installed parallel to framing members, the nearest outside surface of the cable or raceway shall be _____ the nearest edge of the framing member where nails or screws are likely to penetrate.

    (a) not less than 1¼ in. from
    (b) immediately adjacent to
    (c) not less than 1/16 in. from
    (d) 90°away from

11. A cable, raceway, or box installed under metal-corrugated sheet roof decking shall be supported so the top of the cable, raceway, or box is not less than _____ from the lowest surface of the roof decking to the top of the cable, raceway, or box.

    (a) ½ in.
    (b) 1 in.
    (c) 1½ in.
    (d) 2 in.

12. When installed under metal-corrugated sheet roof decking, cables, raceways, and enclosures are permitted in concealed locations of metal-corrugated sheet decking type roofing if they are at least 2 in. away from a structural support member.

    (a) True
    (b) False

13. When installed under metal-corrugated sheet roof decking, the rules for spacing from roof decking apply equally to rigid metal conduit and intermediate metal conduit.

    (a) True
    (b) False

14. Where raceways contain insulated circuit conductors _____ AWG and larger, the conductors shall be protected from abrasion during and after installation by a fitting that provides a smooth, rounded insulating surface.

    (a) 8
    (b) 6
    (c) 4
    (d) 2

15. A listed expansion/deflection fitting or other approved means must be used where a raceway crosses a _____ intended for expansion, contraction or deflection used in buildings, bridges, parking garages, or other structures.

    (a) junction box
    (b) structural joint
    (c) cable tray
    (d) unistrut hanger

16. What is the minimum cover requirement for direct burial Type UF cable installed outdoors that supplies a 120V, 30A circuit?

    (a) 6 in.
    (b) 12 in.
    (c) 18 in.
    (d) 24 in.

17. Rigid metal conduit that is directly buried outdoors shall have at least _____ of cover.

    (a) 6 in.
    (b) 12 in.
    (c) 18 in.
    (d) 24 in.

18. When installing PVC conduit underground without concrete cover, there shall be a minimum of _____ of cover.

    (a) 6 in.
    (b) 12 in.
    (c) 18 in.
    (d) 22 in.

19. What is the minimum cover requirement for Type UF cable supplying power to a 120V, 15A GFCI-protected circuit outdoors under a driveway of a one-family dwelling?

(a) 6 in.
(b) 12 in.
(c) 16 in.
(d) 24 in.

20. Type UF cable used with a 24V landscape lighting system can have a minimum cover of _____.

(a) 6 in.
(b) 12 in.
(c) 18 in.
(d) 24 in.

21. _____ is defined as the area between the top of direct-burial cable and the top surface of the finished grade.

(a) Notch
(b) Cover
(c) Gap
(d) none of these

22. The interior of underground raceways shall be considered a _____ location.

(a) wet
(b) dry
(c) damp
(d) corrosive

23. Type MC Cable listed for _____ is permitted to be installed underground under a building without installation in a raceway.

(a) direct burial
(b) damp and wet locations
(c) rough service
(d) b and c

24. Where direct-buried conductors and cables emerge from grade, they shall be protected by enclosures or raceways to a point at least _____ above finished grade.

(a) 3 ft
(b) 6 ft
(c) 8 ft
(d) 10 ft

25. Direct-buried service conductors that are not encased in concrete and that are buried 18 in. or more below grade shall have their location identified by a warning ribbon placed in the trench at least _____ above the underground installation.

(a) 6 in.
(b) 10 in.
(c) 12 in.
(d) 18 in.

26. Direct-buried conductors or cables can be spliced or tapped without the use of splice boxes when the splice or tap is made in accordance with 110.14(B).

(a) True
(b) False

27. Backfill used for underground wiring shall not _____.

(a) damage the wiring method
(b) prevent compaction of the fill
(c) contribute to the corrosion of the raceway
(d) all of these

28. Conduits or raceways through which moisture may contact live parts shall be _____ at either or both ends.

(a) sealed
(b) plugged
(c) bushed
(d) a or b

29. When installing direct-buried cables, a _____ shall be used at the end of a conduit that terminates underground.

    (a) splice kit
    (b) terminal fitting
    (c) bushing
    (d) b or c

30. All conductors of the same circuit shall be _____, unless otherwise specifically permitted in the *Code*.

    (a) in the same raceway or cable
    (b) in close proximity in the same trench
    (c) the same size
    (d) a or b

31. Each direct-buried single conductor cable must be located _____ in the trench to the other single conductor cables in the same parallel set of conductors, including equipment grounding conductors.

    (a) perpendicular
    (b) bundled together
    (c) in close proximity
    (d) spaced apart

32. Direct-buried conductors, cables, or raceways, which are subject to movement by settlement or frost, shall be arranged to prevent damage to the _____ or to equipment connected to the raceways.

    (a) siding of the building mounted on
    (b) landscaping around the cable or raceway
    (c) the enclosed conductors
    (d) expansion fitting

33. Cables or raceways installed using directional boring equipment shall be _____ for this purpose.

    (a) marked
    (b) listed
    (c) labeled
    (d) approved

34. Metal raceways, cable armors, and other metal enclosures shall be _____ joined together into a continuous electric conductor so as to provide effective electrical continuity.

    (a) electrically
    (b) permanently
    (c) metallically
    (d) none of these

35. Raceways, cable assemblies, boxes, cabinets, and fittings shall be securely fastened in place.

    (a) True
    (b) False

36. Where independent support wires of a ceiling assembly are used to support raceways, cable assemblies, or boxes above a ceiling, they shall be secured at _____ ends.

    (a) one
    (b) both
    (c) a or b
    (d) none of these

37. Electrical wiring within the cavity of a fire-rated floor-ceiling or roof-ceiling assembly shall not be supported by the ceiling assembly or ceiling support wires.

    (a) True
    (b) False

38. The independent support wires for supporting electrical wiring methods in a fire-rated ceiling assembly shall be distinguishable from fire-rated suspended-ceiling framing support wires by _____.

    (a) color
    (b) tagging
    (c) other effective means
    (d) any of these

39. Ceiling-support wires used for the support of electrical race-ways and cables within nonfire-rated assemblies shall be distinguishable from the suspended-ceiling framing support wires.

(a) True
(b) False

40. Raceways can be used as a means of support of Class 2 circuit conductors or cables that connect to the same equipment.

(a) True
(b) False

41. Cable wiring methods shall not be used as a means of support for _____.

(a) other cables
(b) raceways
(c) nonelectrical equipment
(d) all of these

42. Metal or nonmetallic raceways, cable armors, and cable sheaths _____ between cabinets, boxes, fittings or other enclosures or outlets.

(a) can be attached with electrical tape
(b) are allowed gaps for expansion
(c) shall be continuous
(d) none of these

43. Raceways and cables installed into the _____ of open-bottom equipment shall not be required to be mechanically secured to the equipment.

(a) bottom
(b) sides
(c) top
(d) any of these

44. Fittings and connectors shall be used only with the specific wiring methods for which they are designed and listed.

(a) True
(b) False

45. A box or conduit body shall not be required where cables enter or exit from conduit or tubing that is used to provide cable support or protection against physical damage.

(a) True
(b) False

46. A box or conduit body shall not be required for splices and taps in direct-buried conductors and cables as long as the splice is made with a splicing device that is identified for the purpose.

(a) True
(b) False

47. A box or conduit body shall not be required for conductors in handhole enclosures, except where connected to electrical equipment.

(a) True
(b) False

48. A bushing shall be permitted in lieu of a box or terminal where the conductors emerge from a raceway and enter or terminate at equipment such as open switchboards, unenclosed control equipment, or similar equipment.

(a) True
(b) False

49. Electrical installations in hollow spaces, vertical shafts, and ventilation or air-handling ducts shall be made so that the possible spread of fire or products of combustion is not _____.

(a) substantially increased
(b) allowed
(c) inherent
(d) possible

50. Openings around electrical penetrations into or through fire-resistant-rated walls, partitions, floors, or ceilings shall _____ to maintain the fire-resistance rating.

(a) be documented
(b) not be permitted
(c) be firestopped using approved methods
(d) be enlarged

51. No wiring of any type shall be installed in ducts used to transport _____.

    (a) dust
    (b) flammable vapors
    (c) loose stock
    (d) all of these

52. Equipment and devices shall only be permitted within ducts or plenum chambers specifically fabricated to transport environmental air if necessary for their direct action upon, or sensing of, the _____.

    (a) contained air
    (b) air quality
    (c) air temperature
    (d) none of these

53. The space above a hung ceiling used for environmental air-handling purposes is an example of _____, and the wiring limitations of _____ apply.

    (a) a specifically fabricated duct used for environmental air
    (b) other space used for environmental air (plenum)
    (c) a supply duct used for environmental air
    (d) none of these

54. Wiring methods permitted in the ceiling areas used for environmental air include _____.

    (a) electrical metallic tubing
    (b) FMC of any length
    (c) RMC without an overall nonmetallic covering
    (d) all of these

55. _____ shall be permitted to support the wiring methods and equipment permitted to be used in other spaces used for environmental air (plenum).

    (a) Metal cable tray system
    (b) Nonmetallic wireways
    (c) PVC conduit
    (d) Surface nonmetallic raceways

56. Electrical equipment with _____ and having adequate fire-resistant and low-smoke-producing characteristics can be installed within an air-handling space (plenum).

    (a) a metal enclosure
    (b) a nonmetallic enclosure listed for use within an air-handling (plenum) space
    (c) any type of enclosure
    (d) a or b

Please use the 2011 *Code* book to answer the following questions.

Article 310. Conductors for General Wiring

1. No conductor shall be used where its operating temperature exceeds that designated for the type of insulated conductor involved.

   (a) True
   (b) False

2. The _____ rating of a conductor is the maximum temperature, at any location along its length, which the conductor can withstand over a prolonged period of time without serious degradation.

   (a) ambient
   (b) temperature
   (c) maximum withstand
   (d) short-circuit

3. There are four principal determinants of conductor operating temperature, one of which is _____ generated internally in the conductor as the result of load current flow, including fundamental and harmonic currents.

   (a) friction
   (b) magnetism
   (c) heat
   (d) none of these

4. The ampacities listed in the Tables of Article 310.15(B)(6) do not take _____ into consideration.

   (a) continuous loads
   (b) voltage drop
   (c) insulation
   (d) wet locations

5. The ampacity of a conductor can be different along the length of the conductor. The higher ampacity can be used beyond the point of transition for a distance of no more than _____ ft, or no more than _____ percent of the circuit length figured at the higher ampacity, whichever is less.

   (a) 10, 10
   (b) 10, 20
   (c) 15, 15
   (d) 20, 10

6. Each current-carrying conductor of a paralleled set of conductors shall be counted as a current-carrying conductor for the purpose of applying the adjustment factors of 310.15(B)(3)(a).

   (a) True
   (b) False

7. Where six current-carrying conductors are run in the same conduit or cable, the ampacity of each conductor shall be adjusted by a factor of _____ percent.

   (a) 40
   (b) 60
   (c) 80
   (d) 90

8. Conductor adjustment factors shall not apply to conductors in raceways having a length not exceeding _____

   (a) 12 in.
   (b) 24 in.
   (c) 36 in.
   (d) 48 in.

9. The ampacity adjustment factors of Table 310.15(B)(3)(a) does not apply to Type AC or Type MC cable without an overall outer jacket, if which of the following conditions are met?

   (a) Each cable has not more than three current-carrying conductors.
   (b) The conductors are 12 AWG copper.
   (c) No more than 20 current-carrying conductors are installed without maintaining spacing.
   (d) all of these

10. Where conductors or cables are installed in circular conduits exposed to direct sunlight on or above rooftops, the ambient temperature shall be increased by _____ where the conduits are less than ½ in. from the rooftop.

    (a) 30°F
    (b) 40°F
    (c) 50°F
    (d) 60°F

11. When bare conductors are installed with insulated conductors, their ampacities shall be limited to _____.

    (a) 60°C
    (b) 75°C
    (c) 90°C
    (d) the lowest temperature rating for any of the insulated conductors

12. A _____ conductor that carries only the unbalanced current from other conductors of the same circuit shall not be required to be counted when applying the provisions of 310.15(B)(3)(a).

    (a) neutral
    (b) ungrounded
    (c) grounding
    (d) none of these

13. On a three-phase, 4-wire, wye circuit, where the major portion of the load consists of nonlinear loads, the neutral conductor shall be counted when applying 310.15(B)(3)(a) adjustment factors.

    (a) True
    (b) False

14. When determining the number of current-carrying conductors, a grounding or bonding conductor shall not be counted when applying the provisions of 310.15(B)(3)(a) _____.

    (a) True
    (b) False

15. For individual dwelling units of _____ dwellings, Table 310.15(B)(7) can be used to size 3-wire, single-phase, 120/240V service or feeder conductors that serve as the main power feeder.

    (a) one-family
    (b) two-family
    (c) multifamily
    (d) any of these

Please use the 2011 *Code* book to answer the following questions.

Article 312. Cabinets, Cutout Boxes, and Meter Socket Enclosures

1. Enclosures for switches or overcurrent devices are allowed to have conductors feeding through where the wiring space at any cross section is not filled to more than _____ percent of the cross-sectional area of the space.

    (a) 20
    (b) 30
    (c) 40
    (d) 60

2. Cabinets, cutout boxes, and meter socket enclosures can be used for conductors feeding through, spliced, or tapping off to other enclosures, switches, or overcurrent devices where _____.

    (a) the total area of the conductors at any cross section doesn't exceed 40 percent of the cross-sectional area of the space
    (b) the total area of conductors, splices, and taps installed at any cross section doesn't exceed 75 percent of the cross-sectional area of that space
    (c) a warning label on the enclosure identifies the disconnecting means for feed-through conductors
    (d) all of these

Please use the 2011 *Code* book to answer the following questions.

Article 314. Outlet, Device, Pull and Junction Boxes; Conduit Bodies; Fittings; and Handhole Enclosures

1. The total volume occupied by two internal cable clamps, six 12 AWG conductors, and a single-pole switch is _____.

   (a) 2.00 cu in.
   (b) 4.50 cu in.
   (c) 14.50 cu in.
   (d) 20.25 cu in.

2. According to the *NEC*, the volume of a 3 x 2 x 2 in. device box is _____

   (a) 8 cu in.
   (b) 10 cu in.
   (c) 12 cu in.
   (d) 14 cu in.

3. When counting the number of conductors in a box, a conductor running through the box with an unbroken loop or coil not less than twice the minimum length required for free conductors shall be counted as _____ conductor(s).

   (a) one
   (b) two
   (c) three
   (d) four

4. Equipment grounding conductor(s), and not more than _____ fixture wires smaller than 14 AWG can be omitted from the calculations where they enter the box from a domed luminaire or similar canopy and terminate within that box.

   (a) one
   (b) two
   (c) three
   (d) four

5. Where one or more internal cable clamps are present in the box, a single volume allowance in accordance with Table 314.16(b) shall be made, based on the largest conductor present in the box.

   (a) True
   (b) False

6. Where a luminaire stud or hickey is present in the box, a _____ volume allowance in accordance with Table 314.16(b) shall be made for each type of fitting, based on the largest conductor present in the box.

   (a) single
   (b) double
   (c) single allowance for each gang
   (d) none of these

7. For the purposes of determining box fill, each device or utilization equipment in the box which is wider than a single device box counts as two conductors for each _____ required for the mounting.

   (a) inch
   (b) kilometer
   (c) gang
   (d) box

8. Each strap containing one or more devices shall count as a _____ volume allowance in accordance with Table 314.16(B), based on the largest conductor connected to a device(s) or equipment supported by the strap.

   (a) single
   (b) double
   (c) triple
   (d) none of these

9. A device or utilization equipment wider than a single 2 in. device box shall have _____ volume allowances provided for each gang required for mounting.

   (a) single
   (b) double
   (c) triple
   (d) none of these

10. Where one or more equipment grounding conductors enter a box, a _____ volume allowance in accordance with Table 314.16(b) shall be made, based on the largest equipment grounding conductor.

   (a) single
   (b) double
   (c) triple
   (d) none of these

11. Conduit bodies containing conductors larger than 6 AWG shall have a cross-sectional area at least twice that of the largest conduit to which they can be attached.

   (a) True
   (b) False

12. Conduit bodies that are durably and legibly marked by the manufacturer with their volume can contain splices, taps, or devices

   (a) True
   (b) False

13. Short-radius conduit bodies such as capped elbows, and service-entrance elbows that enclose conductors 6 AWG and smaller shall not contain _____.

   (a) splices
   (b) taps
   (c) devices
   (d) any of these

14. Surface-mounted outlet boxes shall be _____.

   (a) rigidly and securely fastened in place
   (b) supported by cables that protrude from the box
   (c) supported by cable entries from the top and permitted to rest against the supporting surface
   (d) none of these

15. _____ can be used to fasten boxes to structural members of a building using brackets on the outside of the enclosure.

   (a) Nails
   (b) Screws
   (c) Bolts
   (d) a and b

16. A wood brace used for supporting a box for structural mounting shall have a cross-section not less than nominal _____.

   (a) 1 in. x 2 in.
   (b) 2 in. x 2 in.
   (c) 2 in. x 3 in.
   (d) 2 in. x 4 in.

17. When mounting an enclosure in a finished surface, the enclosure shall be _____ secured to the surface by clamps, anchors, or fittings identified for the application.

   (a) temporarily
   (b) partially
   (c) never
   (d) rigidly

18. Outlet boxes can be secured to suspended-ceiling framing members by mechanical means such as _____, or by other means identified for the suspended-ceiling framing member(s).

    (a) bolts
    (b) screws
    (c) rivets
    (d) all of these

19. Enclosures not over 100 cu in. having threaded entries and not containing a device shall be considered to be adequately supported where _____ or more conduits are threaded wrenchtight into the enclosure and each conduit is secured within 3 ft of the enclosure.

    (a) one
    (b) two
    (c) three
    (d) none of these

20. Two intermediate metal or rigid metal conduits threaded wrenchtight into the enclosure can be used to support an outlet box containing devices or luminaires, if each raceway is supported within _____ of the box.

    (a) 12 in.
    (b) 18 in.
    (c) 24 in.
    (d) 36 in.

21. In straight pulls, the length of the box or conduit body shall not be less than _____ times the trade size of the largest raceway.

    (a) six
    (b) eight
    (c) twelve
    (d) none of these

22. Where angle or U pulls are made, the distance between each raceway entry inside the box or conduit body and the opposite wall of the box or conduit body shall not be less than _____ times the trade size of the largest raceway in a row plus the sum of the trade sizes of the remaining raceways in the same wall and row .

    (a) six
    (b) eight
    (c) twelve
    (d) none of these

23. Pull boxes or junction boxes with any dimension over _____ shall have all conductors cabled or racked in an approved manner.

    (a) 3 ft
    (b) 6 ft
    (c) 9 ft
    (d) 12 ft

24. Power distribution blocks shall be permitted in pull and junction boxes over 100 cubic inches when they comply with the provisions of 314.28(E).

    (a) True
    (b) False

25. Power distribution blocks shall be permitted in pull and junction boxes over 100 cubic inches when _____.

    (a) they are listed as a power distribution block.
    (b) they are installed in a box not smaller than required by the installation instructions of the power distribution block.
    (c) the junction box is sized so that the wire-bending space requirements of 312.6 can be met.
    (d) all of these

26. Exposed live parts on the power distribution block are allowed when the junction box cover is removed.

    (a) True
    (b) False

27. Where the junction box contains a power distribution block, and it has conductors that don't terminate on the power distribution block(s), the through conductors must be arranged so the power distribution block terminals are _____ following installation.

(a) unobstructed
(b) above the through conductors
(c) visible
(d) labeled

28. _____ shall be installed so that the wiring contained can be rendered accessible without removing any part of the building or, in underground circuits, without excavating sidewalks, paving, or earth.

(a) Boxes
(b) Conduit bodies
(c) Handhole enclosures
(d) all of these

29. Listed boxes and handhole enclosures designed for underground installation can be directly buried when covered by _____, if their location is effectively identified and accessible.

(a) concrete
(b) gravel
(c) noncohesive granulated soil
(d) b or c

ARTICLE 404 Practice Questions

Please use the 2011 *Code* book to answer the following questions.

Article 404. Switches

1. Three-way and four-way switches shall be wired so that all switching is done only in the _____ circuit conductor.

   (a) ungrounded
   (b) grounded
   (c) equipment ground
   (d) neutral

2. When grouping conductors of switch loops in the same raceway, it is not required to include a grounded conductor in every switch loop.

   (a) True
   (b) False

3. Switches or circuit breakers shall not disconnect the grounded conductor of a circuit unless the switch or circuit breaker _____.

   (a) can be opened and closed by hand levers only
   (b) simultaneously disconnects all conductors of the circuit
   (c) opens the grounded conductor before it disconnects the ungrounded conductors
   (d) none of these

4. As a general rule, switches controlling line-to-neutral lighting loads must have a neutral provided at the switch location.

   (a) True
   (b) False

5. Switches controlling line-to-neutral lighting loads must have a neutral provided at the switch location unless _____.

   (a) the conductors for switches enter the device box through a raceway that has sufficient cross-sectional area to accommodate a neutral conductor
   (b) cable assemblies for switches enter the box through a framing cavity that's open at the top or bottom on the same floor level, or through a wall, floor, or ceiling that's unfinished on one side
   (c) the lighting consists of all fluorescent fixtures with integral disconnects for the ballasts
   (d) a or b

6. Snap switches, including dimmer and similar control switches, shall be connected to an equipment grounding conductor and shall provide a means to connect metal faceplates to the equipment grounding conductor, whether or not a metal faceplate is installed.

   (a) True
   (b) False

7. Snap switches are considered to be part of the effective ground-fault current path when _____.

   (a) the switch is connected to the intersystem bonding termination
   (b) the switch is mounted with metal screws to a metal box or a metal cover that's connected to an equipment grounding conductor of a type recognized in 250.118
   (c) an equipment grounding conductor or equipment bonding jumper is connected to the grounding terminal of the metal mounting yoke
   (d) b or c

8. A snap switch that does not have means for connection to an equipment grounding conductor shall be permitted for replacement purposes only where the wiring method does not include an equipment grounding conductor and the switch is _____.

   (a) provided with a faceplate of nonconducting, noncombustible material with nonmetallic screws
   (b) GFCI protected
   (c) a or b
   (d) none of these

9. The metal mounting yoke of a replacement switch isn't required to be connected to an equipment grounding conductor if the wiring at the existing switch doesn't contain an equipment grounding conductor, and _____

   (a) the switch faceplate is nonmetallic with nonmetallic screws
   (b) the replacement switch is GFCI protected.
   (c) a or b
   (d) the circuit is AFCI protected

10. Snap switches in listed assemblies aren't required to be connected to an equipment grounding conductor if _____.

    (a) the device is provided with a nonmetallic faceplate that cannot be installed on any other type of device and the device does not have mounting means to accept other configurations of faceplates
    (b) the device is equipped with a nonmetallic yoke
    (c) all parts of the device that are accessible after installation of the faceplate are manufactured of nonmetallic material
    (d) all of these

11. A snap switch with integral nonmetallic enclosure complying with 300.15(E) is required to be connected to an equipment grounding conductor.

    (a) True
    (b) False

 Please use the 2011 *Code* book to answer the following questions.

Article 406. Receptacles, Cord Connectors, and Attachment Plugs (Caps)

1. Receptacles and cord connectors having equipment grounding conductor contacts shall have those contacts connected to a(n) _____ conductor.

   (a) grounded
   (b) ungrounded
   (c) equipment grounding
   (d) neutral

2. Where a grounding means exists in the receptacle enclosure a(n) _____-type receptacle shall be used.

   (a) isolated ground
   (b) grounding
   (c) GFCI
   (d) dedicated

3. When replacing a nongrounding-type receptacle where attachment to an equipment grounding conductor does not exist in the receptacle enclosure, the receptacle can use a _____.

   (a) nongrounding-type receptacle
   (b) grounding receptacle
   (c) GFCI-type receptacle
   (d) a or c

4. When replacing receptacles in locations that would require GFCI protection under the current *NEC*, _____ receptacles shall be installed.

   (a) dedicated
   (b) isolated ground
   (c) GFCI-protected
   (d) grounding

5. Effective January 1, 2014, where a receptacle outlet is supplied by a branch circuit that requires arc-fault circuit interrupter protection [210.12(A)], a replacement receptacle at this outlet shall be _____.

   (a) a listed (receptacle) outlet branch circuit type arc-fault circuit interrupter receptacle
   (b) a receptacle protected by a listed (receptacle) outlet branch circuit type arc-fault circuit interrupter type receptacle
   (c) a receptacle protected by a listed combination type arc-fault circuit interrupter type circuit breaker
   (d) all of these

6. Listed tamper-resistant receptacles shall be provided where replacements are made at receptacle outlets that are required to be tamper resistant elsewhere in this *Code*.

   (a) True
   (b) False

7. Weather-resistant receptacles _____ where replacements are made at receptacle outlets that are required to be so protected elsewhere in the *Code*.

   (a) shall be provided
   (b) are not required
   (c) are optional
   (d) are not allowed

8. Receptacles, cord connectors, and attachment plugs shall be constructed so that the receptacles or cord connectors do not accept an attachment plug with a different _____ or current rating than that for which the device is intended.

   (a) voltage rating
   (b) ampere interrupting capacity (AIC)
   (c) temperature rating
   (d) all of these

Practice Questions

 Please use the 2011 *Code* book to answer the following questions.

Article 408. Switchboards and Panelboards

1. Circuit directories can include labels that depend on transient conditions of occupancy.

   (a) True
   (b) False

2. The purpose or use of panelboard circuits and circuit _____, including spare positions, shall be legibly identified on a circuit directory located on the face or inside of the door of a panelboard, and at each switch or circuit breaker on a switchboard.

   (a) manufacturers
   (b) conductors
   (c) feeders
   (d) modifications

3. All switchboards and panelboards supplied by a feeder in _____ shall be marked as to the device or equipment where the power supply originates.

   (a) other than one- or two-family dwellings
   (b) all dwelling units
   (c) all non dwelling units
   (d) b and c

ARTICLE 430 Practice Questions

Please use the 2011 *Code* book to answer the following questions.

Article 430. Motors, Motor Circuits and Controllers

1. For general motor applications, the motor branch-circuit short-circuit and ground-fault protection device shall be sized based on the _____ values.

   (a) motor nameplate
   (b) NEMA standard
   (c) *NEC* Table
   (d) Factory Mutual

2. The motor _____ currents listed in Tables 430.247 through 430.250 shall be used to determine the ampacity of motor circuit conductors and short-circuit and ground-fault protection devices.

   (a) nameplate
   (b) full-load
   (c) power factor
   (d) service factor

3. Branch-circuit conductors supplying a single continuous-duty motor shall have an ampacity not less than _____ rating.

   (a) 125 percent of the motor's nameplate current
   (b) 125 percent of the motor's full-load current as determined by 430.6(A)(1)
   (c) 125 percent of the motor's full locked-rotor
   (d) 80 percent of the motor's full-load current

4. The maximum rating or setting of an inverse time breaker used as the motor branch-circuit short-circuit and ground-fault protective device for a single-phase motor is _____ percent of the full-load current given in Table 430.248.

   (a) 125
   (b) 175
   (c) 250
   (d) 300

5. The motor branch-circuit short-circuit and ground-fault protective device shall be capable of carrying the _____ current of the motor.

   (a) varying
   (b) starting
   (c) running
   (d) continuous

6. Where the motor short-circuit and ground-fault protection devices determined by Table 430.52 do not correspond to the standard sizes or ratings, a higher rating that does not exceed the next higher standard ampere rating shall be permitted.

   (a) True
   (b) False

7. A _____ shall be located in sight from the motor location and the driven machinery location.

   (a) controller
   (b) protection device
   (c) disconnecting means
   (d) all of these

8. The motor disconnecting means shall not be required to be in sight from the motor and the driven machinery location, provided _____.

   (a) the controller disconnecting means is capable of being individually locked in the open position
   (b) the provisions for locking are permanently installed on, or at, the switch or circuit breaker used as the controller disconnecting means
   (c) locating the motor disconnecting means within sight of the motor is impractical or introduces additional or increased hazards to people or property
   (d) all of these

Article 450. Transformers and Transformer Vaults

 Please use the 2011 *Code* book to answer the following questions.

1. The primary overcurrent protection for a transformer rated 600V, nominal, or less, with no secondary protection and having a primary current rating of over 9A must be set at not more than _____ percent.

   (a) 125
   (b) 167
   (c) 200
   (d) 300

2. For transformers, other than Class 2 and Class 3, a means is required to disconnect all transformer ungrounded primary conductors. The disconnecting means must be located within sight of the transformer unless the _____.

   (a) disconnect location is field-marked on the transformer
   (b) disconnect is lockable
   (c) disconnect is nonfusible
   (d) a and b

Notes

Mike Holt's Illustrated Guide to Essential Rules of the National Electrical Code, Based on the 2011 NEC